WHO ON EARTH IS TOM BAKER?

WHO ON EARTH IS
TOM BAKER?

———◆———

AN AUTOBIOGRAPHY

HarperCollins*Publishers*

HarperCollins*Publishers*
77–85 Fulham Palace Road,
Hammersmith, London W6 8JB

Published by HarperCollins *Publishers* 1997
Copyright © Tom Baker 1997

A catalogue record for this book
is available from the British Library

ISBN 0 00 255834 3

Set in Fairfield Light by
Rowland Phototypesetting Ltd, Bury St Edmunds, Suffolk

Printed and bound in Great Britain by
The Bath Press,
Bath

For my wife, Sue Jerrard

ACKNOWLEDGEMENTS

This book, such as it is, describes the influences on me over the last sixty years. The following people helped to make me what I am, and to them I wish to express my gratitude as I remember: my beloved mother Mary Jane Baker, who in the way of loving mothers, never doubted that I was worth something; her sister Louisa O'Boyle and her family who were so very kind to me at a critical moment in my life. I remember my Uncle Willie and Auntie Annie Fleming and their family, and my wonderful brother, John, whom I nursed as a baby and my sister Lulu, too. And then: Hannah Egan, Eileen Reynolds, Mary Murphy, Chrissie Aspey, Marge Edwards, Jane Williams, who gave me the kiss of life, Joan Shultz and her mother, Beth; Annie Smith and Barney, Maggie Rowlands, Fred and Barney Roberts; and Molly Weston who taught me the Latin responses of the Mass; and Richard and Rowena Ainley who took me in when I was homeless and helpless. I cannot omit to mention what I owe to Professor Laurie Taylor who wrote *Late Night Lowther* all those years ago, giving me the chance to play a dog called Clint. That dog led me to the National Theatre and a horse called Rosinante. I remember an act of kindness when Sir Laurence Olivier used his great power to take me into the National Theatre simply because he had kept me waiting. His wife Joan Plowright was good to me in those days and invited me to more than my share of parties at Stagg Place. Diana Boddington nearly always gave me the benefit of the doubt and, once, in a big emergency, gave the use of her car and Lionel Guyett to drive it as I rushed towards Park Lane and what I thought was to be stardom. To Jonathan Miller I owe my only success at the National Theatre. I have mentioned the kindness of Edward Petherbridge elsewhere in my book. It was in those days that I met and was overpowered by John Dexter, a director of genius and mood swings who switched from soppy encouragement to vicious cruelty. He was very hard on me on many occasions. But still, I owe him a dept and I gladly say so here. Another stupendous ego I must acknowledge is Sam Spiegel who tried to make me into a film star. And then there is Michael Jayston who treated me like a brother when he had lots of other things to do including loving Heather Sneddon, who also tolerated me in the days of their ecstasy. Robert and Suzanne Massie encouraged me in my dreams; and Ray Harryhousen did the same in *The Golden Voyage of Sinbad*. When I worked for Paolo Pasolini I thought things were looking up. They did look up but led nowhere and that surely was not the fault of Paolo or of Laura Betti either, who also was very helpful. And when the flirtation with movies was over Paul Angelis and his then love, Rosa, saved me from disaster by taking me in and watching over me.

And Paul introduced me to the Fox and Hounds in Passmore Street, Pimilico, where Diane Samuels led the company. Beryl Cawthra also fed me and was very nice to David Cawthra, too, who used to tease Fred Fellowes, who teased him right back when he married Beryl and lived happily every after. There was a girl called Sally Everest who was adored by everyone and somehow settled for a chap called Edwin. Sheila Allen gave a great Lady Macbeth while I was making the audience screech with derision, especially after the murder scene. And Ted and Gwenda Whitehead, too, always encouraged me. Bill Slater introduced me to Barry Letts, who in turn introduced me to Shaun Sutton, which led to me being the fourth Doctor Who. Then there is Elisabeth Sladen, 'my first companion' who laughed at my jokes; Philip Hinchcliffe, Jim Acheson and Roger Murrary Leach; Christopher Barry who directed me as the new Doctor and David Maloney who found me funny; June Hudson who took the designs of my costume to operatic extremes which I tried to match in my performance. I owe a special thanks to Maurice Leonard who found me Vivien Green. And I remember Tom Bell and Ralph Bates who were on my side when I was in *Hedda Gabler* and, God knows, I needed some help in that production. And at Harper Collins I must thank Michael Fishwick who responded so quickly to my early manuscript and then introduced me to Rebecca Lloyd, and thereby hangs the tale. To Richard O'Callaghan and his wife Elizabeth Quinn I own thanks. There are people who are close to me whom I never meet though I talk to them most days. Jackie Lane and Susan Barrit at Ad Voice know how much I love them. And Annette Stone and Edward Hill must have a good idea of my sentiments for them, too. And if there is any merit in this book I hope it pleases my sons, Daniel Baker and his brother Piers who made me so happy just now in New Zealand. And then there is my wife, Sue Jerrard, to whom I owe so much for her devotion to me in dark moments. She has never wavered even when I was afraid. And, in return, I hope I shall never waver in my affection for her. She and my sons will drink champagne.

ILLUSTRATIONS

All photographs are supplied courtesy of the author unless otherwise stated.
Photographs supplied courtesy of Adrian Rigglesford are indicated as AR.

My parents' wedding picture, 1932.

Mother, Auntie Louie, Uncle Billy O'Boyle, Ninny Fleming, Joan O'Boyle.

My father at fourteen as a boy-waiter.

Me, aged twenty-two.

A publicity still from *Nicholas and Alexandra*.

As Rosinante in *The Travails of Sancho Panza* © Zoë Dominic.

Joan Plowright, Anthony Hopkins and myself in John Dexter's National
Theatre production of *A Woman Killed with Kindness* © Zoë Dominic.

As the Prince of Morocco in *The Merchant of Venice*, photograph by
Anthony Crickmay © Board of Trustees of Victoria and Albert Museum.

Derek Jacobi and myself in *A Woman Killed with Kindness*
© Zoë Dominic.

A still from *The Author of Beltraffio*. Photograph by Mike Wells.

With Kate Fitzgerald in *Educating Rita*.

From *She Stoops to Conquer* with Julia Watson © Catherine Ashmore.

With Julie T. Wallace in *The Life and Loves of a She-Devil*.

In Liverpool, 1992 © Sue Baker.

Auckland, New Zealand, 1997, with my son Piers © Sue Baker.

Planting a tree at Dickens's house, Gadshill Place, Kent © Reg Jerrard.

Off duty from Sherlock Holmes in Dublin © Sue Baker.

As Sherlock Holmes in *The Mask of Moriarty* by Hugh Leonard with Alan
Stanford as Watson.

ix

As Holmes with Ingrid Craigie as the villain.

With my wife, Sue, who encouraged me by laughing a lot.

Among my beloved neighbours in 1986 © Sue Baker.

Chez nous.

INTRODUCTION

'WOULD YOU LIKE TO GO to New Zealand to do a commercial?'
That's the sort of question an actor likes to hear from his agent in
freezing mid-January.

'Certainly,' I replied. 'What's it about?'

'Oh, pensions, I think,' replied Annette, who is the second
most beautiful agent in Europe. 'Does that bother you? The dosh
would not be light, and you could take your wife as well, first
class.'

Suddenly I was desperate to go to New Zealand. But two
weeks passed and I began to forget the offer. I had also been
interviewed twice for the part of an irascible Raj man in a piece
about the Indian Mutiny. Funny how all the old Raj chaps are
seen as irascible. It wasn't a very good part and I was not keen to
go all the way to India just to be irascible. Fortunately the director,
looking again at his video, realized I would be no good and I was
dropped.

So to pass the time I went down to the village and had my hair
cut short. Life can be dull in the country and a haircut can sometimes
be high drama. I gave the girl cutter a good tip for laughing at my
jokes and went back home. My wife was looking out of the window
as I drove in.

'New Zealand is on,' she said. 'They want you to leave in eight
days' time and to do the job as an old Doctor Who. Oh, you've had
your hair cut.'

I spoke to Annette and she confirmed the job and the dosh.
June Hudson, one of my favourite designers from the BBC days,

agreed to get the costumes ready with the help of Angells* and I took my trousers to the cleaners.

It was a wild few days. The alterations to the old costumes were done with great tact. June even managed to locate an original scarf from Madame Tussaud's waxworks where I am still unmelted after all these years. The scarf, being twenty-five feet long was, along with the boots, the only part of my old costume to fit me.

So eight days later on a Thursday morning after a nice ride in a limousine, my wife Sue and I arrived at Heathrow's Terminal 3 and checked in. I cannot tell you how much I was looking forward to going Air New Zealand. Haymaking in January! Everybody had assured me it was a very special experience. Everybody was right.

'I'm afraid one of your tickets has been cancelled, sir,' said a charming contralto at the check-in desk.

'Why has one of my tickets been cancelled?' I asked. 'I don't want to pry, you understand, but I had planned on sitting next to my wife all the way to New Zealand and back on your airline.'

'Would you come with me, madam?' said the contralto, and my dear wife meekly followed her out of my sight.

Meantime, to avoid falling into a berserk attack, I struck up a conversation with the rather fraught-looking parents of a fourteen-year-old boy. Their problem dwarfed mine. As my wife would not be allowed to sit on my knee all the way across the world all I needed was another seat. These anxious parents had ordered ten bottles of oxygen for their frail child.

'But surely nothing has gone wrong?' I murmured in bedside tones.

'I'm afraid it has,' said the father sorrowfully. 'There is no oxygen and the plane leaves in about forty minutes.'

Just then my wife returned with her helper and told me that a solution could not be found. The impulse for a berserk attack came rushing back, swept to my head in a few pints of blood by the feel of it.

* The costumiers, Cambridge Circus.

The contralto looked at me anxiously. My wife looked at me anxiously. I looked at them both anxiously and wondered how long it had been since an old man went berserk at their check-in desk. My meditation was interrupted by the arrival of one of the airline's male Samaritans clutching a mobile phone. There was a good deal of movement under his clean white shirt in the area of his sternum, as if his heart was trying to break out. His Adam's apple was jumping, too. In fact as he gasped 'Hello' to me I caught a clear view of his uvula; it was fluttering audibly.

'We may have found a solution, sir,' he panted. I smiled encouragingly at him. 'Yes, sir, we've found two seats for you, sir.'

I clapped my hands gently together in the manner of a sophisticated Jap and said: 'Why that's wonderful.'

'The only thing is, sir,' added the Samaritan, 'they're broken.'

'What are broken?' I asked.

'The seats, sir,' smiled the saint from customer services.

I matched his smile to the millimetre as I enquired, 'What do you mean by broken?'

'I mean the electronics are not working, sir. I mean you would not be able to listen to the stereo or hear the sound track on the films.'

It occurred to me that these seats might be just the ticket. No sound? Great. No music or commercials from the airline. Great. The sacred sickness that a moment before might have endangered the man's life receded miraculously and I nodded my agreement.

I wished the anxious parents good luck and said I was sure that Air New Zealand were bound to solve their problem: I mean look at how quickly they had sorted mine. As I followed the miracle worker through secret passages which led us aboard in about five minutes and twenty seconds, I thought I heard the price of £800 a bottle being discussed with British Airways. They're in a good bargaining position, I thought. We were ushered on to the plane and to our new-found silent seats. To a layman like me they seemed to be handsome seats. I longed to give myself up to them. As I approached them, my New Zealand guide was called aside for a moment by some other poor pilgrim seeking a miracle. Instantly, the cabin steward appeared at my side.

'Do you realize what you are letting yourself in for, sir, with these seats?' and he looked at them with cruel contempt.

'Oh, yes,' I answered, 'we won't be able to hear the sound tracks, that's all. We don't mind at all. In fact,' and here I leaned towards him, 'in fact, we are quite glad not to be able to hear.' My wife nodded in agreement and my relief was profound. It was also brief.

'But sir,' urged the steward, 'nothing works in these seats. The lights don't work and the backs won't recline.'

Swiftly I tried a seat. The steward disappeared instantly in the ensuing darkness. The reclining button was pressed and, as a doctor, I could easily and swiftly diagnose the seat as dead.

The original fixer now materialized at our elbows and then knelt down! He too had received the latest news, that the seats were dead. The steward passed my wife and me a glass each of champagne. It was quite good champagne.

'My latest information, sir, is that these seats are very severely handicapped, sir,' whispered the fixer who couldn't mend the seats. I swigged down my drink.

'But,' pressed the would-be miracle worker, 'but, there is one seat right up front and if either, you, [a little bow] or your wife, sir, got a bit fed up you could always do turn and turn about with the good seat up front.'

My wife was splendid. She just smiled, shook her head and said 'I think not', and we left the plane.

Sixteen hours after our early morning wakening at home we left Heathrow on Singapore Airlines and thirteen hours after that we arrived in Singapore. We had been awake for twenty-nine hours. A quick hour and a half in Singapore, where chewing gum is forbidden by law, and we were on our way again towards Auckland. Thirty hours and a half. This next bit was also twelve or so hours. The service was very stylish with a great deal of bowing and smiling. Continuous smiling can get to you after thirty odd hours. Sometimes you have the impression that they are smiling because they know something that you don't. And they probably do. With a smile (what else?) a girl delivered a seafood omelette to my wife. But such is the charm of their style nobody seems to look at the food with anything other than gratitude.

The long hours drag by and we are a bit discouraged. Fortunately my wife is brave and knows something about Buddhism so she does not despair. I know nothing of such philosophy so my suffering is meaningless.

At last, forty or so hours after getting out of our beds, we arrive. And the seafood omelette begins to do its work. My poor wife looks grey in the face and at times is unsteady on her legs.

'Christ,' I thought, 'I've come all this way to be a widower.'

This thought turned out to be alarmist, but she was very sick indeed.

Fortunately we were in a wonderful hotel in the best seats and there were taps which delivered luxury in torrents. My colleagues were tactful enough not to meet us off the plane, so we were able to crawl discreetly to the beds we had feared we might never see again.

And after a good long sleep I met my new employers and we got ready to shoot some commercials. While I was busy at this my wife was taken around the sights by wonderfully kind and amusing friends.

One evening my wife and I went to a harbourside restaurant for dinner and we had a very good time. It was a perfect summer's evening, the food and wine were excellent and the view over the harbour was quite delightful. The service, too, was perfect. The waiter could not have been more attentive without being importunate. G. K. Chesterton once said that all dining out begins with fear of the waiter. Not in New Zealand it doesn't. In London, yes. There dining out begins with fear of the waiter and ends with the same feeling. And as I looked up at our perfect waiter I nearly passed out. I was looking into the mysterious liquid eyes of Sir Anthony Hopkins. I was stupefied. Why didn't he notice that I was close to fainting? I watched him working his table magic all over the place.

A deep melancholy came over me. Melancholy tinged with affection. What? Yes, sadness and love, old love to be more exact. In a driven whisper I remarked on this discovery to my wife. 'Yes,' she said, 'It is Anthony Hopkins. But what would Sir Anthony be doing as a waiter in New Zealand?'

In London one would not be surprised to be waited on by say Michael Caine or Jeremy Irons; though, of course, Irons only waits on insomniacs who are very grateful and make up the majority of his fans. But Anthony Hopkins? As a waiter? A butler, yes, we've all seen *The Remains of the Day*, but a waiter? At the Ferry House in Auckland, New Zealand? Is it possible?

As he brought my main dish and placed it in front of me with perfect grace and tact I allowed my hand to touch his. Not in a marked manner, but accidentally, as it were. The effect on me was electric, just like the old days. The effect on Sir Anthony was imperceptible. Perhaps he's forgotten me I thought and my heart dropped like a stone. I saw the wonderful liquid eyes work their magic on all around me. I saw and remembered that marvellous enigmatic smile of so long ago. He seemed to be paying an awful lot of attention to a rather dreary-looking man with a very high forehead and his blonde female companion who only had one leg. They also felt that they were being served by a knight that evening and both seemed to be shaking uncontrollably. Looking closer at the blonde I realized that she did have two legs but that in the manner so typical of certain blondes she was sitting on the invisible one. Soon the whole area realized who the waiter was and the place simply bristled with static.

'Why doesn't he recognize me?' I asked my wife, sadly.

'Perhaps it isn't really Tony Hopkins,' she suggested. 'Perhaps he's just a look alike?'

'Perhaps he is,' I muttered, and I called for the bill.

Sir Anthony materialized at my elbow and said: 'Your bill is taken care of, sir,' and he smiled strangely and away he went. Isn't life cruel?

As I gaped in astonishment at my wife another waiter came up and asked me if everything was all right. All right? How could everything be all right? Why didn't I just nod and say: 'Fine, fine, thank you?' But no, I said that I understood my bill had been paid and that I was surprised. The waiter knew all about it. He said: 'The gentleman who paid your bill is in the bar, sir. He says he's an admirer of yours and knows you, sir, and would like to say hello.'

The romance dropped out of the evening. An admirer? I looked to my wife and sighed. 'A fan,' I whispered. We both guessed that this acceptance of a dinner might lead to two hours of talk on the history of *Doctor Who*. The waiter offered to lead us and we got up from our table. I nearly fell into the harbour as I had one last look around for Sir Anthony.

We entered the bar and the waiter signalled towards a tall figure standing in strong light. He was smiling quizzically at me. I looked at him carefully and was about to say that there was no need for him to pay my bill when a tiny feeling of unease hit me. His steady smile unsettled me for a moment. Then, ever the master of the meaningless and bullshitting enquiry, I said: 'Is your name Morgan by any chance?'

The man shook his head, though now his smile seemed ironical.

'No,' he said, 'my name is Baker, Piers Baker, I'm your son.'

I could taste again the garlic in the lamb I had just eaten.

'Piers?' I whispered.

He nodded and glanced from me to my wife; and still he smiled. I looked towards my wife, too, and saw that she was smiling, and with real delight. 'Piers,' I thought to myself. 'It's Piers, my son, Piers.' I put out my hand to him and he took it firmly, holding on to it.

I remembered him being born. I remembered wanting to call him Solomon and allowing myself to be bullied out of it by Constance the Fury.

I said, 'This is Sue, my wife.' And the memories would not stop as I saw him as a baby. I could not have known of the grief to come. My suicide. My attempted murder of Constance. All the losses. Of course I couldn't have known. And now here he was. Piers. He ordered drinks with great confidence. I looked at him and suddenly I thought, perhaps all may yet be well. Perhaps this is a new beginning. And still he smiled and it was fine to see him. Oh, Piers.

Auckland, New Zealand. January 1997

ONE

MY FIRST AMBITION was to be an orphan. During the war of 1939–45, Liverpool was a good place to be. All routine was broken by the fear of death from the Germans' bombs. The pleasure of being a child at that time is not easy to describe without seeming flippant. But it was drama, high drama: fires at night, the fires that burned people's houses away; bombs fell and left exotically shaped fragments in the form of shrapnel. And we collected it and traded it. As long as we were not hurt – and I wasn't – life seemed wonderful. At the gasworks one night a landmine, which was a bomb on a parachute, had descended gently and was hanging from one of the arms of the gasometer. Hundreds of people gathered and stood around, conjecturing about the size of the bomb. Bets were placed. The police and the fire brigade tried to get the people clear of the scene and, with difficulty, did so. Grumbling and arguing people were forced away from the danger area bitterly resenting the bossiness of the authorities.

Policemen and air-raid wardens and fire watchers loved the power they had to shout at their neighbours and tell them what to do, and they exercised it. In the shelters we sat all night or until the 'All Clear'. And people talked and talked and prayed and prayed that God would spare us. We were convinced, like all good Christians, that God was on *our* side.

Later, when prisoners of war began to be seen in the district we found them interesting and often very nice. My mother encouraged us to be kind to the Italian prisoners who reminded her that the Pope was Italian. The tall and ascetic Pius XII, Eugene Pacelli

I think he was called in civvy street, had a big influence on us even then. That the Pope could be on the side of the enemy was easily explained away by the teachers and priests. The Italians were not really the enemy, it was all a misunderstanding. How could they possibly be the enemy when the Pope himself was Italian? But it was admitted that the Germans were the enemy even if they did go to Mass, carry rosary beads and have mothers. So there was no punishment if you threw stones at Germans, oh no. Italians innocent, Germans guilty; unless of course they could play the piano or keep goal like Bert Trautmann of Manchester City. Prayer became dramatic, as it always does in times of danger. Like exercise to a heart patient, it takes on an importance that makes us love it. And God, in His omnipresence was said to be everywhere, even in the hearts of the bombs. I worried about Him so much. I didn't want Him to get hurt, and I prayed that He wouldn't get hurt, and He always answered my prayers. He never did catch it.

The advantage of being an orphan sprang from the generosity of the American people. If your Dad or Mam were blown up then you really got some attention. Presents would arrive from America with a nice card from the President himself: funny hats and jackets that were considered very smart. At that time, the *Superman* comics were widely read and there were American soldiers all over the place. As American accents only reached us through the films, it was like being in a movie to meet them or to wear clothes that came from their country. We adored everything about America. We just could not get enough of it, from gum to caps to shirts with funny figures printed on them. We even copied the way the Americans walked, though Father Leonard didn't like that bit of admiration. He disapproved of rolling buttocks.

The only drawback was that to qualify for the goodies your Mam had to be in Heaven. So I prayed hard that a bomb would drop on mine as she trudged home from the Sefton Arms.

It was common in those days for adults to ask quite small children what they wanted to be when they grew up. What a question in the middle of a world war! You can't ask that question now because it would be tactless as so many children are not going to become anything at all. But then everybody seemed to be asking children what their future would be. As if a child might know. These days when I see a child in Waitrose and smile and say, 'Hello, are you going to visit your Mum in her sheltered accommodation when you grow up?' it provokes glistening eyes and hollow laughter. And if you pursue it with, 'Or are you going to be a drugs dealer?' it may result in a snub. But in the days I'm talking about such enquiries were quite commonplace. Of course there was also a repertoire of stock answers from the child. One might answer: the Merchant Navy, the foreign missionaries, the Adelphi Hotel, Tate and Lyle's sugar factory or, best of all, 'I'm going to stay at home with me Mam and look after her.' I don't know which precocious little sod first said that but the phrase passed into the language and made hard, sceptical men nod and bow their heads and strong, good-living women weep. It often led to a hug of such intensity that your nose would be broken. There were several broken-nosed five-year-olds in my school. 'And what are you going to be when you grow up?' a neighbour would caw. And to prompt a dumbstruck infant (they were not all glib), an adult witness, usually the mother, would stand on the child's foot. The rising anguish would jolt the memory and the poor little sod would gasp: 'I'm going to be a Foreign Missionary.' That was a safe answer and always provoked a smile and a roll of the eyes. 'Perhaps you'll be a bishop too?' would be the likely riposte to this agony-induced lie. And so in school, between singing 'Faith of Our Fathers' and 'We're Going to Hang out the Washing on the Siegfried Line', Miss Egan, our pious headmistress might easily change the subject and ask us what we wanted to be when we grew up.

So when she asked us one day, after a roaring chorus of 'She'll be Coming Round the Mountain When She Comes', what we wanted to be, Tommy Ryan produced sighs of admiration with 'I should like to be a priest, Miss Egan, God willing,' and Len McAndrews made us laugh for wanting to be a tram driver. Then Miss Egan turned to me and said, 'And what about you, Tommy Baker, what do you

3

want to be?'. I answered like a shot, 'An orphan, please, Miss.' The class roared with laughter until they saw the expression of horror on Miss's face and then they copied her expression. 'So, you want to be rid of your mother and father?' she asked me.

'Yes, Miss,' I answered, 'both of them.'

'Jesus, Mary and Joseph, but why?' choked Miss Egan.

'So that I can get presents from America,' I told her.

Miss Egan looked at Miss Lynch who made a clenched-fist gesture and looked on to Miss O'Leary who in turn looked towards Miss McCabe. There was an amazed silence which I smiled through. Miss Egan pointed a finger at me and the venom in her voice made me shiver as she said: 'Go to Father Barry and tell him I sent you.'

'What shall I tell him, Miss?' I asked her. And the finger began to quiver.

'Tell him you want to be a murderer and ask him to forgive you.' And I did go to to Father Barry and he forgave me.

TWO

MY SCAVENGING INSTINCT was developed during the war by the need for salvage. It was a way for everyone to feel involved in the war effort. Every cardboard box or roll of newspaper might swing the war our way. Even the Italian prisoners of war would help us to save rubbish. It was partly for that reason we were encouraged to be nice to them. We were to be nice to the 'Eyeties' but urged to throw stones at the German prisoners. I never did, though not out of piety. The chaos of our lives suited me; I don't think I wanted it to end. In a way, I suppose, I was a traitor.

Anyway, the shrapnel we all loved to collect was from German bombs. My companion in scavenging was Leslie Hampson, a boy with nearly white blond hair and a very tricky bowling action at cricket. We worked every afternoon. Nothing was safe from us; if it looked as it could be turned into a weapon we snaffled it. Of course we had no idea how a cardboard box could possibly damage the Germans. We were just obeying orders. Perhaps we thought the English bombers were actually dropping cardboard boxes on the Nazis.

Most of all, the collecting gave us a sense of purpose. And we won the Oscar for rubbish collection in our district. Miss Egan took Leslie and me to the town hall in Dale Street to meet the Lord Mayor, Lord Sefton. He gave us a certificate and to Miss Egan a pound note. After the ceremony we went to Cooper's Café for a lunch – my first taste of eating out. Then we went off to the Hippodrome cinema and saw a film called *Laughing Irish Eyes*. It felt so strange to be with our headmistress all day. After the film we were taken to the Kardomah for tea in silver pots. My thirst for salvage had made me very shifty by now; no matter what Miss was saying I was always on the look-out for cardboard. 'Forget salvage for a minute,' Miss hissed. But I've never been able to forget it. Today I'm just as keen as ever to find it and bag it up.

After tea we arrived home with ten pence each out of Lord Sefton's pound. So for less than a quid we'd had a great day out for three people and some change left over. It is the only award I have ever won.

I just remarked that looking for salvage had made me shifty. That is not quite true. Most well-brought-up Roman Catholics are very self-conscious. Mine was expressed by shiftiness and furtiveness. This condition was only exacerbated by the salvage bug. The true cause of my slyness was rooted in the doctrine of God's *omnipresence*. The notion that God was everywhere put paid to any possible peace of mind by the time I was six. Not only was He everywhere and watching but so was my Guardian Angel. I was quite an imaginative child so going to the lavatory was torture. It still is. I still cannot do a big job if my wife is in the house, or if the light is on. I can't even evacuate if the telly is on, though the wireless doesn't cause any commotion in that area. It may be that having God and the Guardian Angel present all the time is what makes Catholics fast shaggers. One tortured soul I know who suffers from amazingly premature ejaculation – I mean so premature that he hasn't got any children after eleven years of marriage – was told by the priest that it was probably a blessing in disguise. What a piece of advice to give to a poor sod who comes off at the sound of his wife's car in the drive.

Nowadays, when I think about dying it makes me clear my throat uneasily. It didn't always have that effect on me. When I was a child I longed to die: I was baptised, we were poor, the house was dirty, my feet smelled and I was no good at school. What was the point in hanging about waiting for things to get better? To have a bath meant the murder of six thousand cockroaches. After that you had to go out and find maybe twenty pairs of old shoes for the fire. So really it was quite hard to get clean. Anyway everybody else stank and to be too scrubbed might lead to charges of getting above one's station, or worse. It was much easier in the circumstances to launch into a novena of prayer and hope that over the ensuing nine days we'd somehow be snatched up by God. And we could have a quick bath up there, and as school would no longer be of importance it would be just heaven. The crucifix was always held up to us for kissing. We even had a relic of the True Cross that got kissed by the whole school on Wednesday afternoons. There was a *pietà* just inside the doorway of the church, a ghastly figure of the dead Christ lying across His mother's knee. The wounds were very clearly and scarily painted in: a strong visual aid to post-crucifixion. The Sacred Heart of Jesus stood nearby, a romantic figure with his heart on the outside of his chest and his right forefinger pointing towards the bleeding heart in case we hadn't noticed it. And on both sides of the church, seven along each aisle, were the fourteen Stations of the Cross. This depiction of Christ's journey to Calvary was very clear and frightening; not like today's, abstract, in the style of charcuterie in Soho butchers' shops. They were full of blood and tears. And that was good. We prayed for the gift of tears, and drank blood every day; we heard every day how unworthy we were and thumped our breasts and said that we were not worthy, in Latin. Ashes to ashes, dust to dust and cries of 'Tommy Baker's a piss the bed', confirmed me in my belief that I would be better off elsewhere. That was fifty-three years ago and He still hasn't returned the call. But it can't be long now and so I clear my throat. Maybe it's nerves?

I remember we used to be interrupted in our doings when I was a boy. You'd be in the middle of some little lie you were pitching to your pal when he would go rigid and roll his eye towards the source of his sudden paralysis. It was often Fr. McHale on his bike, riding one-handed with the other one tucked into his coat like Napoleon. This posture meant he had God in his inside pocket and was on his way to a dying parishioner. We swivelled as He went by, bowed our heads and thought of our last ends. Not a word could be spoken; and it wasn't, until Fr. McHale and his Maker were out of sight. And just as you tried to pick up the thread of your fib wouldn't a funeral follow. Another silence and a bow and more thoughts of last ends. Even now after more than fifty years I don't like to be interrupted in a tale, especially if it's not true.

And in school we stood for Miss Lynch and then sat down again only to leap to our feet at the entrance of Miss Egan, the head-mistress. Once she was leading an infant by the name of Moira Kelly who had just that morning waggled one of her teeth out and then casually pushed it up her nose. For some reason Miss Egan was slapping her on the back. Moira Kelly was led away to be shown to some other group and I never saw her again, or if I did I didn't recognize her. This rising and bowing went on everywhere: 'Stand up when you're spoken to'; 'Tell the Doctor your name's Tommy.' I wonder we had time to grow normally with all the nodding and squirming towards our betters.

My mother was a pick-up point for my aunt who was a street book-maker, an illegal activity in those days. She and I would stand near the gates of West Derby cemetery and 'act natural' very badly. After a while another terrible actor, my dear Uncle Barney, would come along and, sauntering by, whistling the while, he'd drop a leather bag into Mam's shopper. As I reached out in welcome to Barney my mother would knuckle me savagely, causing me to forget who he was for the sudden pain that enveloped me.

As I grew older I learned to spot strangers who might be policemen in the street and pass the word to another lad who would do the same, so the man taking the bets would easily evade the law. We also had God on our side, for many of the best punters were the local priests who were gambling the money they had stolen from poor unemployed men they'd caught playing pitch and toss in some alley way. The poor are marvellous, aren't they? They hardly ever complained. Mind you the first Beatitude kept us going: 'Blessed are the poor, for theirs is the Kingdom of Heaven.' So you see it wasn't too bad.

Because the process of taking bets, or making a book, was illegal, the system of identifying betting slips was important. How to identify the winner of a bet? The punter couldn't put his real name on the slip for fear the police might raid the premises, find the slips and identify the gambler. This risk was avoided by a system of *noms de plumes*. Once chosen the name was better kept to so that the bookie's clerk didn't get confused. There was often surprising ingenuity shown in the choice of name. 'Valentine Dyall' was a popular one, or simply 'The Man in Black'. One disgraced classicist used Thucydides which caused pronunciation problems back at base. The accepted explanation was that Thucydides was Turkish for nancy boy. The excitement of this watching for 'The Law' was intense. We were brought up to hate the police only slightly less than the Billy Boys from Salisbury Road. 'Once a policeman, never a man' went the saying, and nobody denied it. We could not name a single saint who had been a policeman, nor did they have a patron saint. It was always said that policemen got a half day off on the feast of the Slaughter of the Holy Innocents because Herod was their sort. And so with my Guardian Angel on my shoulder, detesting the Orange Lodgers and the Jews for killing Our Lord, and believing that monkeys could talk and that the letters INRI scrolled above the crucified Christ stood for 'Iron Nails Ran In', I pursued the next bit of my childhood.

Desperate for comfort and distraction I became more and more involved in the church services. This parted me from my fellows in the district who were not nearly so impressed by God being every-where nor by Guardian Angels sitting on their shoulders; they were more preoccupied by their dicks.

For a little while I attended Wanking School in the house of one of the lads called Rex Barrow. We would gather in a circle and extract our organs. Barrow himself had a prodigious cock and was very proud of it. We would all watch nervously while he got going. Even at the slack his member was daunting. But as he began to recite

9

the names of local girls and rock back and forth to our accompanying groans, the miracle took place before our eyes.

'Rosie Ball, Rosie Ball,' Rex would mutter hoarsely, for libido and hoarseness always go together. 'Rosie Ball,' and as we groaned his snake flickered into life. 'Evelyn Coffee,' said somebody else to a new groan of approval and Rex's prick filled out further, mesmerizing those of us whose tackle remained inert.

'Bertha Moonan?' I suggested, desperate to kindle the flames further. There was a howl of anger as Rex's dick died.

'You daft bugger, now look at what you've done,' snarled Derek Houghton, 'you've killed his dick.'

This extravagant statement produced a mournful silence that would have fetched down all the dicks in Liverpool. But at 'Beatty Holmes' hissed suggestively by George Beswick, Barrow's member began to recover consciousness and its head would sway from side to side. Then the names came thick and fast as we were all seized with lust and grasped the alchemy of girls' names and realized what a name could do for a flabby dick. 'Mildred Barton'(groan of agreement), 'Doreen Manning' (more groans), 'Moira Lynch' (that was inspirational), and Barrow's nob rose and looked him straight in the eye – eye to eye you could say – 'Mary Barlowe' (ooh, ah).

'Say it again,' grunted Barrow, and Wilfred Usher obliged in just the right way and Barrow shot his lot to cries of admiration from the whole circle. And so it went on as we all helped each other from slackness to stiffness to joy. Reckless and Godless as we felt ourselves to be, I do remember one session being ruined completely when the litany ran from Mildred to Moira to Mary Barlowe and so on, when just as several were at spilling point, someone cried out 'Blessed Maria Goretti'. Christ, that did it. All dicks were struck down dead by this blasphemy and we went home ashamed.

I wasn't too immense at this activity, though I could call a name with the best of them; and so after a particularly satisfying confession which allowed me to walk upright again, I broke with the Wankers and settled for sniffing incense and God.

*   *   *

Mr Harte, our headmaster, was always banging on about how short life was, 'For now thou canst be steward no longer.' It was very difficult for fourteen-year-olds to swallow this line of thought. He meant well, of course, but it carried no real weight. But the organization of the school gave strength to Paddy Harte. The sexes were strictly segregated both in classroom and playground. I was only there for one year and I can't say if the teaching was any good as I was classified as dull. That was the euphemism for thick in those days. One day Mr Fred Roberts, my favourite teacher watched me trying to work out some problem in long division or something.

'You know, Baker, I was talking to my wife about you last night,' he said. This caused sixty eyes to swivel my way and sixty ears to cock. Teachers just did not say things like that. 'Yes,' resumed my hero, 'I said to her, you know, "I've got this lad in my class, Baker he's called. Thick? He's as thick as the Pier Head. Not a brain in his head. A good-living lad, goes to Mass every day, fast bowler and all, but thick." Poor old Baker,' he said, patting me on the shoulder. 'Still you can always drive a tram.'

The concentration among the boys raised the temperature, as the casual harshness of Mr Roberts' judgement fascinated them. I was too upset to try to argue the point of my thickness with the teacher I liked most in the school and the boys were watching to see if I would crack under the mockery. I didn't show the pain I felt, at least I don't remember saying anything back. I wanted to, of course. I wanted to tell him that I wasn't thick but I didn't know how to set about it. In many ways, I am thick. There is so much I don't understand. A woman I was working with recently was staggered at my inability to grasp the slow foxtrot. I'm not too immense at being able to make a telephone call come to think of it. It's to do with fear, I suppose. I can't swim or dance, nor do I know whether a London bus has been to the place listed on the front or whether it's going there; which means I've never been on a bus by myself. Or perhaps it's to do with being tall. I remember being at six feet one, the tallest nine-year-old in Liverpool.

THREE

AND NOW I CAST my mind back to the ones who loved me.

My Auntie Louie was good to me. Because my father was away so much and my Mam was working at scrubbing floors and being a barmaid at the Sefton Arms, we were a bit undisciplined my sister and me. If there was jam in the house we had it today. Never mind tomorrow or any other day, we had everything now. I still like it now and I still love jam. I wonder if children still have jam as often as we did? 'You jammy bugger,' was sweet to hear. 'He's dead jammy,' said people with envy of anyone who was touched with luck. Though the meaning was often wrenched in the sardonic way of frightened people trying to be brave.

'Did you hear about Alfie Richards's Dad?'

'No. Why, what happened?'

'He fell off a crane at Albert Dock, eighty feet he fell, on to a an empty cage.'

'Oh aye, what happened then?'

'Well, there were twelve bars in the cage, so he was cut into twelve pieces.'

There would be a pause, then:

'I always thought that Alfie Richards was a jammy sod.'

When my brother was being born in the winter of 1942, Mam was too ill to look after us so Auntie Louie O'Boyle took us on. She had three of her own, Michael, Joan and Billy. And it makes me cry to think of the kindness of them all. I always thought of my cousin Joan as very beautiful; I still do.

Even at the age of eight I was an embarrassment to everyone because of my preoccupation with God.

'Do you realize that God is everywhere?' I'd ask, echoing Miss Egan from school.

'Yes, we know He's everywhere, we know the catechism too, you know.'

'No, I mean *everywhere*,' I'd insist, ignoring the tone of voice from my uncle Bill, who didn't seem to be impressed by God's omnipresence.

'Yes, God is all over the place, there isn't anywhere that God is not in. Or up.' I had to have the last word even if it meant hell. 'He's even up the leg of Mrs Pierrepoint's drawers.'

Auntie Louie would look at me warningly and I'd take the hint from her and her alone. I was spoiled by the comments of neighbours on my appearance. I was tall for my age. In fact, I haven't actually grown since then – not in the tallness, I mean. I was very blond and curly and a prodigious bedwetter. Piss-the-bed Baker they called me at school for they had sharp tongues as well as sharp noses. One bath a week could not conceal my incontinence. There's a statue of some famous little pisser in Holland, I think, or is it Belgium? Anyway this little statue pisses away in the street every day bold as brass and everybody takes photographs of him. He's famous and if he stopped piddling then he'd probably get the push. I did it every night and not a single admirer to hand. 'I'll cure him,' said Louie, 'if it's the last thing I do and as God is my judge.'

In our house we drank tea all the time. The kettle was on all day. My mother was a thirty-cup-a-day supper and we easily burned the arse out of three kettles a year. Today I can easily drink nine cups a day and probably, if I wasn't married, I could emulate me Mam and approach the magic thirty mark. There was only one woman in the street who could out-drink our Mam and that was Mrs Goodstone who had a son with a club foot. On a bad day, we'd hear that Brenda, that was her name, had reached thirty-three cups. This news would be received in tight-lipped silence and me Mam would lower her head. Thirty-three was Mam's ideal number. She was proud to be in the thirty group as that was the age of Our Blessed Lord when he did His first miracle at the marriage feast at Canaan, the changing of the water into wine. What a beautiful miracle that was, just as impressive though less showy than the feeding of the five thousand, though both were prodigious feats of catering that have never been surpassed as far as I know – and I have kept my ear to the ground these last sixty odd years, I can assure you, oh, yes. 'The first miracle,' Mam would mutter in a whisper. To be fair I think my mother would have been more impressed if Jesus had turned the water into tea. Especially if He'd managed to make it sweet as well. But to sup thirty-three cups of tea was considered a great achievement that compelled our admiration for Mrs Goodstone, and her with a boy with a club foot.

Thirty-three was a sacred number as it was the age of Our Blessed Lord at the time of His last miracle, the sticking back of the ear*. It was said that a woman who could drink thirty-three cups down to the lees would receive a message from Pope Pius the XII, Eugene Pacelli that was. But I can't be certain of this for great piss-the-beds often have very selective memories.

The cure for my affliction was very simple in Louie's mind. As piddle was simply recycled tea all we had to do was reduce the intake of the Typhoo. And so my last cup of tea was to be at four o'clock. We went to bed at about seven forty-three. Before that I would be marched to the lav by Louie and emptied. At nine o'clock I would be roused and squeezed again. To no avail, in the morning I would be found steaming. The morning discovery of my incontinence would lower the spirits of all of us, for Louie was above all fair and didn't want to be too harsh.

'Fetch the time forward,' suggested Bill, a methodical sort of man who in another country, and given the opportunity, might have been a great watchmaker. So his suggestion was acted upon and two was the new deadline. I was watched at school for the slightest sign of liquid. Moisture on the lip would have caused uproar. I was

* See Luke, Chapter 22, 50–51.

surrounded by informers who took a keen interest in my cure. They were only amateur informers for there was no reward except the sadistic pleasure of the pious doing a good deed.

Later I grew quite fond of the informers and joined their ranks as we spied on the police who sought to steal the dreams of poor gamblers in the alleyways of Liverpool 22. In that way the police were nearly as bad as the priests. And so I was supervised by gleeful little sods who climbed the door of the lavvy while I was at my grunting. And parched as I don't know what, but parched as one of them, I would go home to Auntie Louie who loved me but was strict.

With so little liquid in me I must have been near danger point. I was fed, then bed and roused again to see if that would do the trick and keep me dry. And it began to work and Louie was pleased with me. The pleasure of waking up in the morning nice and dry was wonderful. I still think of it as a great pleasure.

My Auntie Louie who was strict but fair was, as a young woman, extremely pretty. I remember when she brought the food to the table she expected only one reaction, head down, your irons in hand and get to it. Anything less than this made her very impatient. If for instance you looked at the food as though assessing it shooooooo . . . gone! Nothing said. No need to say anything. Nobody else at table seemed to see what had happened and there you were, ravenous. You sat through the meal, ignored by Louie and the rest of the company and that was that. By the next meal you had grasped the rule and when the plate arrived you troughed it joyously and Louie would nod. No need to talk about it; the signal had been received. My Auntie Louie was simply wonderful to us.

She would often be in the company at our house to visit Ninny, my grandmother. But if, for reasons of extra work – for Louie was also a barmaid – she wasn't there, then the story of Pat Heinz might be told. You couldn't be certain because like all good storytellers Ninny Fleming could be quite capricious. Sometimes her tales would make my mother sigh with resentment though she never dared to express open disapproval of any of them. So, after enough of the

Guinness, when bits of cheese and pickle had been downed and various little tales of, say, The High Rip Gang* had been turned over yet again, there would be a pause. Ninny had a way of getting comfortable with a little growl and a sigh that suggested that she might suddenly say, 'I wonder what happened to our Pat?'

So, adjusted to her liking, and lips and throat moistened, and apparently not seeing the nudging going on among the visitors or the mouthing of 'I wonder what happened to our Pat?' she'd say: 'I wonder what happened to our Pat?' Corsets would creak everywhere as all got comfortable. There would be a general murmur of approval from the assembly and the tale would unfold. Willie, Tom, Jane, Maggie, Chrissie, Annie and Louie Fleming all lived at 27 Lemon Street, Liverpool, under the small mottled iron hand of their mother, Christina Fleming, a widow whose husband had been found dead in a tram shelter on the old Dock Road. Like many married women, once widowed the partner in former happiness was never mentioned again. Fierce Catholics all, who toed the Church's line on everything, they'd hit anything they disagreed with and not let it get in the way of supper. They had no doubts at all about anything. They were marvellous examples of total bigotry, like all good Catholics at that time. They were what is known as 'good living'. That meant they were priest-ridden and jealous of their reputation, and hated Protestants or any other race of pagans.

Tom Fleming, the eldest, was said to look like King George V, and indeed, was often mistaken for His Majesty when in the vicinity of Scotland Road, Anfield Road or Lime Street. Why people would suspect that the King might be working in Tate and Lyle's sugar factory is beyond me, but there you are. He was a devoted son and brother and would always meet his sisters from school or work or a parish dance. The girls were all members of the Children of Mary, a society dedicated to the preservation of chastity among young Catholic girls, and so were objects of lust to passing heathens or even passing true believers. Willie also prized his sisters' virtue and

* Well-known gang of Liverpool street hooligans in my grandmother's youth.

would beat any man who showed lack of respect. But they were all quick with their fists and with their wits, too; you had to be to preserve identity and self respect.

Well, it so happened that Willie had a friend at St John's School by the name of Pat Heinz. This boy was an orphan and Willie, being a good talker, warmed the whole family towards his pal Pat. Ma said one day, 'Why don't you bring him home to us, one more won't make any difference.' Things were not so complicated then in the matter of disposing of children or snaffling the buggers, if that's what you fancied. And so after quick consultations with the teachers and a woman from the orphanage, Pat Heinz was transferred to the Flemings at no fee and to everybody's satisfaction. So the story went. And Pat was happy and Willie was happy and the rest of them soon became fond of the lad and referred to him as 'our Pat'. Being surrounded by lovely kind girls who sometimes spoiled him made Pat feel he was in heaven. He copied Willie and Tom and met whichever of the girls was out of the house. But Louie was his favourite. He adored her and would do anything for her. If he got on Louie's nerves a bit, she hid it pretty well and was genuinely fond of Pat. At Mass Pat would try to sit next to Louie. He'd walk her to Benediction, too, and come home with her, both reeking of incense. And so the time passed and Pat's adoration increased, and everybody was charmed by his devotion to Louie. The others teased him but Louie defended him. While spoiling and defending the poor lovesick orphan, Louie never ever gave the impression to Pat or anyone else that her fondness for the boy was anything more than sisterly affection. And so the years went by and Bill O'Boyle came along, a handsome, Liverpool–Irish factory worker who thought he was a born watchmaker. And Louie fell in love with Bill. Pat went a bit quiet. Jane and Annie and Maggie and Chrissie tried to make it up to him; but they were falling in love, too. Anyway, to get on with this tale, Louie and Bill got married and a right old celebration took place. And Pat was there and Louie was very, very nice to him.

Ten weeks later Pat Heinz announced he was marrying a girl from off Great Mersey Street, not far from Lemon Street, and quite near Fountains Road where I was to be born in January 1934. The banns were read out over the usual number of Sundays with the happy couple present. And so Pat and his girl, Dorothy, I think her name was, got married. And Louie met Pat at the church door and embraced him and cried and wished him well and Pat just smiled.

Now in those days wedding celebrations were broken into two parts. Immediately after the ceremony, everybody went to the church hall or function room above a pub for a few drinks and to see the bits and pieces of presents and show off their gear. This would last a couple of hours and then there would be a short interlude of another couple of hours. People would nip off home and get into something comfortable. The groom would just have time to knock up the bride and then the real drinking would begin.

Now Pat and Dorothy were married at eleven fifteen. The service was over by ten past twelve. Right on twelve fifteen at the church door Louie kissed Pat, as I mentioned, and I suppose pictures were taken. I never saw any photographs but we were not too good at preserving souvenirs in our family. At twelve thirty the happy couple and their guests had arrived at St John's Parish Hall and were having a drink. At twelve forty-five Willie, Tom and Barney their brother-in-law got to the hall having stopped off at some pub. They got themselves some Bass Blue Label and surveyed the scene. It was now ten to one. The boys, as they were called, suddenly wanted to drink to Pat, to be with him and tease him, too, I suppose, but they couldn't see him. One of them went to the back of the hall where the catering preparations were taking place – but no Pat. Willie then went to the gents to see if the happy man might be throwing up his regrets. No Pat. It was not a very big hall. Dorothy's family were gathered at one side in the time-honoured fashion of wedding parties in those days. The boys nipped outside and walked around the perimeter of the hall – but no Pat. They became uneasy when Dorothy's mother asked about her new son-in-law. It was now one twenty and no Pat. The wedding had only started two hours and five minutes ago. Pat had been kissed by Louie at the door of the church at twelve fifteen. He'd been seen to arrive at the hall at twelve thirty with his brand new wife, Dorothy. Where was he? As discreetly as possible, Tom Fleming, his brother Willie, and their brothers-in-law, Bill O'Boyle and Ernie Rowlands circled the church hall inside and out. There was no sign of Pat Heinz. By one thirty everyone knew Pat was missing. Dorothy the bride just kept on smiling and smiling and saying, 'I don't know what all the fuss is about.' And indeed she didn't. Poor Dorothy didn't know what anything was about that day and neither did anyone else either, because Pat Heinz had disappeared. And he was never seen again by anyone who was at that wedding.

Through the Merchant Navy there was an immense network of contacts in all the English-speaking ports of the world. It was not unusual for a man to jump ship in Canada or New York or Fremantle say, but sooner or later he'd be seen in a bar by someone from the Pool. But Pat wasn't even in the Merchant Navy, so where did he go? And while Louie was pulling pints at the Legs O'Man, Ninny would sigh, sip her stout, and wiping her mouth would sigh again and say,'I wonder what happened to our Pat?' And we wondered with her, but we never did find out.

FOUR

DURING THE 1940s every boy I knew read the comics. Our whole week was dominated by the arrival of these tales of propaganda and stories of public school life. There was nothing published on a Monday as I remember, but the week went like this: Tuesday, the *Adventure* and the *Wizard*; Thursday came the *Rover* and the *Hotspur*; and Friday brought the *Champion*. There were stories about young footballers of prodigious strength, Cannonball Kid, who played for Burhill United and once scored for England with a stupendous shot from the halfway line. The manager's name was Baldy Hogan, and he'd once been a canny player himself whose career was tragically ended through injury and the loss of his hair. In the *Wizard* there was a character called Wilson. We didn't know his first name. He lived on the moors, communed with nature, and wore black tights. He was ahead of his time and of his opponents and nearly always won his races. Thursday was a great day for us with the *Hotspur*. The most popular stories in that comic were about public schools. Boys were inundated with tales of how our betters behaved at schools where there was tradition, fags, prep and detention. Places where chaps called each other by their second names. As far as I knew, only the Irish could effortlessly call each other by their surnames without causing offence. I knew some Irish women who called their husbands by their surnames. They would come to the pub and enquire with glittering eye: 'Is Boyce there?'

Only teachers called us by our second names. In the *Hotspur* there was a long-running story about a school called Red Circle. The headmaster was called Dixie Dale, ever such a fair chap, and most of the adventures were written around a character called Rob Roy MacGregor. In another story in the *Rover* we followed the life of a bright working-class boy called Tom Smith. Note the ordinariness of his name. He was a clever lad who had been able to get to public school with the help of his local vicar and lots of hard work. We learned about fagging, a system of service in those places where young boys were the servants of older boys. They were always making toast for their man and running errands. God help them if they were less than perfect. The older boys had the power to beat their fags and they did so, frequently. Fortunately for Tom Smith of the lower third, he fagged for an easy-going chap called A. P. E. Carew who was not demanding and had a fine line in drawling speech. We grew familiar with these small but vital details of initials. We knew that in the county cricket sides the placing of the initials was a certain sign of the player's status. By that I mean we knew whether a man played for love or money: initials in front, N. W. D. Yardley, an amateur; Compton D. C. S. was a pro who did it for a living, and didn't use the same changing room. Gentlemen versus Players. Those were the days.

So we had words on our tongues that only applied to the fantasy world of public schools where we longed to be. In spite of the cruelty of certain masters, life there seemed one long wheeze. In Red Circle, one housemaster was called Mr Smugg. How we loved to read of young Rob Roy MacGregor outsmarting the cruel housemaster every week. It seemed to be always summer and life full of japes and visits to the tuck shop for buns and bottles of Cream Soda or Sarsaparilla, which was also called Dandelion and Burdock. Dandelions were usually associated with wetting the bed. Not one single boy in those places ever wet his bed. This made me very depressed, as you can imagine. We picked up bits of Latin and were brainwashed about loyalty.

In the *Adventure*, there was one character who puzzled us. He was called Alf Tupper, the Tough of the Track. Alf was very working class, rough of speech and lived in an abandoned railway carriage and only ate fish and chips. He was just like us except that he was a brilliant athlete. The stories were about his triumphs over drawling fellows with double-barrelled names who wore Norfolk jackets and said 'I say, you chaps' an awful lot. He was our first anti-hero, I think, bloody-minded and full of spirit, with no desire to be like the drawling enemy. These stories swamped our imaginations and reinforced our mistrust of girls and our patronizing attitudes towards foreigners.

The *Champion*, out on a Friday, was dominated by Rockfist Rogan of the RAF. Boy, he was the terror of the dirty double-crossing wild-eyed Huns. He feared nothing didn't our Rockfist, he could take on three German planes at a time, shoot down two, see the third off with the Kraut pilot screaming, '*Gott in Himmel!*' as he gratefully made his escape. Rogan would then have his eggs and bacon, crack a few jokes and spar a few rounds in preparation for his fight that night against the heavyweight champion of some Highland Regiment or other. Gosh, what a man was he. So my imagination was filled with the voices of cowardly Italians, (*Mama Mia*), or Germans, (*Gott in Himmel*), or the whispers of mad priests asking me 'and did pollution take place?', or my mother's exhortations to know my place, keep my bowels open and always polish my shoes – feverish stuff.

When I was about nine years old I was struck with abscesses on the back of my left leg. They got so bad that I had to stay in hospital for several days. The pain of having my abscesses squeezed was really very severe and it upset me terribly. The nurses chosen for this ghastly job had tremendous thumbs. I think that most nurses in those days had powerful thumbs but the squeezers were very special. I still tremble at the sight of highly developed female thumbs. The squeezing nurses always seemed to work in pairs. One would hold you down while the other with raised thumbs and flickering tongue would approach and, with sacramental precision, would complete the torture. These squeezing sisters always seemed to be red-headed and very freckled. And when they had squeezed all the pus-filled children in the dressing station they would cruise the wards to back up other nurses. Especially they were useful to their ward sisters when it came to making the children eat up their food. One day I was ordered to eat up my cabbage. Being rather undisciplined and mostly used to jam butties and sweet tea I refused to obey the order. At my refusal to eat up my greens, the two ward sisters glanced at each other and clicked their fingers and, as if by a miracle, two thumbs appeared topped by freckles and red hair. I was pushed back against my pillow by the finger clickers while 'Power Thumbs' slapped a wad of cabbage across my mouth and tried to force it down my throat with her magic thumbs which were a bit like tyre levers. Struggling to resist the force feeding which made me feel sick, I began in my fear to fart like a buffalo. The finger and thumbs trio of freckled harpies were appalled by my grossness, involuntary though it was.

'Stop that stink,' they screamed, 'stop it.' But I couldn't stop it. Like a lost and panic-stricken tug boat in a thick fog I farted on in various keys of terror. Gasping for breath, the cabbage squad retired and conceded defeat.

After the healing process was judged complete, I was pronounced well and was sent to a place called Olive Mount just outside Liverpool. It was a convalescent home for faded children. I was glad to escape from hospital and glad not to have to go home either. At Olive Mount the discipline was strict but the place was wonderfully clean. I had a little locker all to myself and was given a toothbrush and a face cloth. That was all I had so it wasn't hard for me to keep my locker tidy. The food was tasty and when the servers saw the effect that a bucket of cabbage had on me they did not insist I eat any. So I was happy there for a little while.

The desire for change, the need to escape from one place to another grew more intense as time went on. I wanted to escape from home into the church because I preferred the smells in the church to the smells at home. The overriding smell at home was one of feet, neglected feet. And on Fridays when we had salted fish for supper the smell hung about like an unwanted relative. It simply would not leave us. By Monday, which was washing day, the salt-fish smell then joined the smell of soap suds coming from the kitchen copper where the weekly wash simmered away. So, suds, salt fish and unloved feet were the dominant odours all over the house. To these smells was added the scent of stale tobacco for everybody smoked all the time. So I always wanted to leave home because the smells I have just mentioned outweighed my love for my mother.

FIVE

BECOMING A PROFESSIONAL LIAR grew out of my obsession with God's business. I grasped very quickly that life in the House of God was more interesting than life at home. For one thing God was a stranger and I always got on very well with strangers. Another attraction was the cleanliness of the church, the lovely smell of the floor polish, the altar rails all smooth and shiny, our highly decorative lace surplices, washed and starched by nuns for the greater glory of God.

My own home always made me feel ashamed. My poor mother was mostly too tired to clean our house after spending most of her day cleaning other people's houses. And then in the evening, after a day's scrubbing, she would do a shift at the Sefton Arms pulling pints. Nearly all the women I knew were always tired. How could it have been otherwise? They worked in the munitions factories on long shifts and then came home to all their household tasks. And often without the support of a husband because of the war.

Because of the bombing we were often as many as fourteen people in our house. The whole place became a sort of billet at night. But I remember liking the great chaos. And the refugees from the bombs were all very nice and talked and talked all the time, which pleased me. There was Mrs Fogarty, a widowed lady and very respectable; her brother, old Joe Fogarty, a docker, who only shaved once a week; there was big John Fogarty, her eldest son; and handsome young Joe Fogarty who shaved every day and was killed a little later in the war. There was Annie, my mother's sister, and her husband and children and, of course, my grandmother, Ninny Fleming.

Keeping clean in a family of fourteen people wasn't easy. In the mornings the smell of Lifebuoy soap filled the house. Actually the smell of soap pervaded the whole of Liverpool most of the time. At school the smell was of Derbac soap, the instant slayer of lice. The lice were hunted by a special squad of highly trained women who were chosen for their eagle vision. Sometimes they could tell you had lice when you were thirty yards away. Being a Lice Lady was quite a good job in those days as so many of us were lousy a good deal of the time. It was a very common sight to see small groups of children standing on a corner with jam butties in one hand and the other hand busily scratching away at the tops of their heads like miniature Stan Laurels. But nobody seemed to mind at all. Whenever I see the visual cliché of a character scratching his head as if in thought, I am translated back to my happy lousy childhood on the street corners of Liverpool.

At school, we were very preoccupied with cleanliness and Godliness and leprosy and the sufferings of waifs and strays in Africa, while our Guardian Angels perched on our shoulders sneezing away in the clouds of dandruff and falling lice. We often heard stories of saintly priests who sacrificed themselves among the lepers of Africa. We became obsessed with Africa and the sufferings that went on there. We worried more about the black people of Africa than we did about our neighbours around us in Liverpool. Fr. Nolan, our parish priest was forever haranguing us about saints and lepers. In singing we had nymphs and shepherds, but from Fr. Nolan we got saints and lepers. His favourite leper man was a Fr. Damian who simply adored lepers. As he couldn't find any in Liverpool he'd buggered off to Africa where the place was crawling with them. There he hugged them and they made him pots of tea and brought him water every night to wash his feet. It sounded a great life to us, supping tea and hugging friendly lepers. Once, so the story went, after a long day's hugging, the time came for the feet washing. By some accident the water was boiling, but Fr. Damian didn't notice because he'd caught leprosy. It was only the look of horror in his servant's face as he happily wiggled his toes that made Fr. Damian realize what had happened. But he didn't mind. 'And he became happier and happier,' said Fr. Nolan, giving us the gimlet eye of the frustrated, God-stealing missionary. 'And why? Because Our Lord loves a leper, because He made them lepers in His mysterious wisdom and not only does he love a leper, He loves a leper lover.'

Fr. Damian was always hoisted up as an example of self-abnegation. Self-abnegation, what a phrase to use to infants. Stories of leper colonies and of dodgy saints who liked licking scabs. It was all so romantic to us and I longed to take part in the great work of enlightening the benighted natives of just about anywhere in the world. We weren't frightened of disease, we longed for it. We scoured the streets for lepers whenever we were out scavenging for salvage, but we never found one, not even among the supporters of Everton Football Club.

But when leprosy finally arrived in our house in the form of scabies, Fr. Nolan was nowhere to be seen. The neighbours were informed of our infection, and in turn informed on us to the rest of the parish. There was no Fr. Damian to come and make pots of tea for us and give us a hug. We were on our own, my sister and me and our Mam. Daily we walked to the hospital aware of everybody avoiding us for fear of the plague of scabies. Neighbours gone, Fr. Nolan gone, and banned from the church as well. For all we knew our Guardian Angels had buggered off, too, in fear of the dreaded scabies. We couldn't be sure of that of course because, as you know, angels, particularly Guardian Angels, are invisible.

The smell in hospitals in those days was of surgical spirit mixed with iodine and a kiss of formaldehyde. It was quite overpowering and made people hysterical with fear. I knew lots of people who refused to go to the hospital for treatment just because of this awful smell. They preferred to die in their own backyards. The smell in hospital just made them sick, and that was that.

As if the high hysteria induced by the surgical spirit were not enough, the appalling screams of unseen children caused us to free fall into complete panic and we clung like petrified kittens to our Mam. All to no avail. We were stripped naked in preparation for the treatment. The screams of other children not far away now made us forget how much God loved us. Mam was just as terrified as we were on that first day. There was nobody to comfort us in our terror. We were dragged off roughly into the steamy rooms from which the screams were coming, seized by shadowy figures with strong hands and plunged into scalding baths. They weren't, of course, but they seemed so. Dunked in, good and deep and long, too, we shrieked to send the message to the other children outside not to come in. Wasted screams, ghastly pale mothers in agonies of confusion and helplessness and very rough nurses. We were lifted out and rubbed down energetically. The shock eased and the near-ecstasy of feeling clean was interrupted by the searing pain of surgical spirit being painted all over us with wide brushes. The cold spirit on our hot little bodies caused the screams to rise – 'I want me Mam, I want me Mam' – and the nurses shouted louder to calm us down. It's hard to calm a child you're hurting. Then the pain would pass and the sight of Mam would be some comfort to us as we got dressed in our newly autoclaved clothes, reeking we thought, of freshly roasted fleas.

Sometimes kind people waved to us in the streets but mostly we were ignored. And this daily terror went on for weeks. We learned to scrutinize the piece of paper given us by the examining nurse on which would be scrawled a terrifying S or a more comforting C. The S for spirit filled us with dread, the C for calamine lotion would make us grin and with cheeky relief we'd show it callously to some poor sod who'd drawn a big S. To us, S was for agony and C for relief. Finally it was all over and we were pronounced clean and we resumed our lives in the parish. The pain of surgical spirit had been bad enough, but to be banned from the church, especially from Holy Mass had been a terrible event. When people have very little and are so very ignorant as we were, not to go to Mass made us despair. Our religion was the only thing in our lives that made us feel important. Being a Catholic made us feel tremendous. We were very conscious of being the chosen ones. And although a Catholic can't be a vegetarian because of his habit of eating the flesh of Jesus

28

and drinking His blood, being a cannibal was considered a small price to pay in return for being a member of the one true faith.

The main thrust of a Catholic education all those years ago was self-loathing. The more you despised yourself the better you were.

'You are nothing,' cried the teachers and priests, 'and never forget it. You are nothing.'

Sometimes I would catch the eye of the priest and he would point to me and ask: 'What are you, Tommy Baker?' And I would yelp, 'Nothing, Father, I'm nothing and don't you forget it.' Then there would be a pause and Father Moriarty would point again and raise his hand and say: 'Good boy, Tommy Baker, and how do you say that in Latin?' I would leap to my feet, and pounding my left breast with my right fist I would cry out: *'Domine non sum dignus.'* As you may guess, I was a very abject child. The sense of unworthiness that was hammered into us from the word go would deepen in me and would remain. To teach children to hate themselves strikes me now as grotesque and yet in my childhood it was the received wisdom. 'Never forget that you're nothing,' Miss Egan told us. And I learned that lesson well and still feel the result of the long practice of her advice.

Once, trying to curry favour with a teacher who asked me what I was thinking, I said: 'I was just thinking I was nothing, Miss.' Miss Lynch looked at me meaningfully and I was convinced that I was nothing. And this bending of our wills to authority gave us an irrational regard for the very authority that was annihilating us. We wanted to please our superiors. And wanting to please people, to only tell them what they wanted to hear became very deeply a part of me, as it probably did with most children who felt uncertain of the tactic needed to avoid a blow.

I had the greatest admiration for a boy called Tommy Ryan, a lad destined for the priesthood, they said. He was Miss Mallory's favourite pupil. No matter the problem, Tommy Ryan was called upon by Miss Mallory. Ryan spent a lot of time with a lad called Brian Jones who was always dressed in green and had a wooden leg. A peg leg, like pirates had in Saturday morning films at the Regal cinema. It was shiny brown and nearly filled the leg of his short trousers in the way a well-muscled arm nearly fills a short sleeve. This wooden leg set Jones apart from the rest of us. We were so envious of it. Secretly I prayed for one of my legs to fall off so that I, too, could look and move like Brian Jones looked and moved. His right shoe was always very highly polished and as he swivelled, hopped and crabbed all at the same time down the church aisle after communion, he was the object of many furtive and admiring looks. His left shoe had, of course, been sent to Africa. How I envied Jones his wooden leg. Even today more than fifty years later I feel jealous. I realize that I still want a wooden leg, though now I'd have to wear knickerbockers to show it off. It would guarantee me a part in *Treasure Island* every Christmas. When I played Long John Silver at the Mermaid Theatre I thought of Brian Jones at every perform-ance. Peg Leg Jones, we called him. I would dream of having a wooden leg, one eye and a hook for a hand. That would have set me aside and might have led to Peg Leg speaking to me. As it was, Jones hopped along beside Tommy Ryan, another boy set aside from the rabble. Tommy Ryan was said to destined for the priesthood; indeed, I heard he became a bishop and had to flee to South America – Bogotá as it happens – but I travel too quickly for the tale.

But Peg Leg Jones! Just get this. He was a great farter, a farter in million. And this is important. All boys given the chance would like to be professional farters for it is a capacity to fart that gives a lad his first true sense of status. Before he becomes a member of the SAS or a paramilitary group with a cause that lines up with his adult psychosis, he must first start as a farter. I suspect that there are no exceptions. Well, some have greatness thrust upon them as the poet says and Peg Leg Jones was in that tiny group. Several of us were competent as farters, as we were as whistlers, or pitchers and tossers, and Jones was no slouch as a tosser either. Oh, but as a farter! There were some who could fart wetly or trump, as they say; others could pump as though whistling through gooseshit. And these few variations were all more or less noxious. But Peg Leg Jones could produce the vilest smells that ever you suffered. And his product, when he wished, was perfectly silent. It was in a register higher than humans could catch. Sometimes a dog would be found dead near a crossing, run over after pausing to decode Jones's high-register signal. I may be exaggerating but, when Jones let rip, it seemed that the green and cream paint on the walls at Saint Swithin's school would curdle and bubble and run a bit. But these details were as nothing to what followed. Our teacher, Miss Mallory, who had a long face, rather like a horse that has been baptised and can't conceal its glee, would in a split second be transformed. Now she would look like an Orangeman's horse, all tortured and filled with the agony of the true heretic; in a word, she would resemble a horse that had lost its faith. And there are few sights sadder than a faithless horse. Neighing hysterically, she would squeal for Tommy Ryan. 'Somebody's just committed a sin,' she'd whinny, 'where's Tommy Ryan?'

'Here, Miss Mallory,' he'd call, 'shall I sniff him out?'

'Do that, Tommy, there's a good lad,' she'd answer. 'And show no favour, nobody's to be spared.'

And Tommy Ryan would come out in front of the whole class and survey us like the young slaughterman that he was. With the eyes of a future prelate, unconsciously miming the holding of the crook, he would plunge in among us like an ecstatic ferret but all the while keeping well away from the source and making sure we all knew that we were at his mercy. We held our breath, not just out of fear of Tommy's power, but because a deep breath in the vicinity of Peg Leg Jones would have required the last rites. And Tommy the corrupt, bishop to be, and bringer of shame to our Holy Mother the Church, and look out Bogotá, identified *me* as the stinking sinner!

'Get behind the blackboard, Barabbas,' snarled Miss Mallory. And I crept into the shadow of the blackboard and within a few minutes was forgotten. And I stood there and wondered how Tommy the vile could be so hard and what did he say when he confessed weekly to Fr. Barry.

Each Wednesday morning after playtime, Horseface would cry

out, 'Tommy Baker and Tommy Ryan to confession.' Why Brian Jones wasn't with us I can't remember. Perhaps if you had a wooden leg you didn't have to go to confession. And so the great liar would lead the way and be in and out of the black confessional box where all the information about our latest crash from grace would be recorded.

'What do you tell him, Tommy?' I'd ask, meekly. And, like the Steerforth of Saint Swithin's that he was, he'd say airily, 'Oh, I tell him about my impure thoughts, murders and odd other mortal sins, things like that.'

So I learned to classify sins, to find words that might suggest what I felt and thought. And gradually, from Tommy and other boys, I invented my own criminal record and began to believe it. I wanted to be a sinner. It was the only way to be sure that God would love me. I wanted to steep myself in sin and then to repent and cause joy in Heaven. Within a few weeks I progressed from:

'I was disobedient, Father, and also I looked sideways at me Mother, and also I only washed one of me feet last night,' to:

'Pray Father, it is a week since my last confession and since then I've had an impure thought and a deed, too.'

I heard the click of beads and caught the whiff of wine, 'God's blood' came the thought. Most Catholics were a bit baffled that the blood of Christ smelled like cheap sherry.

'And an impure deed, too?' crooned Fr. Barry. 'And did pollution take place, eh?' and I heard the phlegm jump in his scrawny throat for he was a Capstan Full Strength man – nothing but the best when the poor are paying. The pollution question seemed to please him so much that I readily agreed.

'Oh yes, Father, it did,' said I.

'And did you take pleasure in it as well?' keened the anointed one.

'I wasn't too greedy,' I said, worried about this pollution that might have taken place. He sighed, did Fr. Barry and I think I heard his upper denture drop to the lower set.

'Anything else?' he asked.

'Yes, Father,' I said.

'Well?' asked Fr. Barry. 'What else?'

'Murder, Father,' I said. 'I've done murder.'

There was a pause before the next question.

'How many times?' he asked.

Very quickly I jumped in with, 'Three times, Father.' And the sense of serious sin filled me with importance.

'Three murders since last week?' queried Fr. Barry, 'Anyone we know?'

Possessed by the genius of Tommy Ryan I said, 'No, Father, they're all from St Teresa's.'

This shifting of the scene of the sin to the next parish seemed to soothe Fr. Barry and he said, 'Well that's all right then. Remember that Jesus loves you and stay away from St Teresa's.' He was merciful to me that day, was Father Barry, and later I grew to love him for it.

In the days before penicillin people seemed less complacent than nowadays. A nail in the shoe at a Saturday night dance in 1942 could result in a sore foot Sunday morning. By mid-afternoon the foot and lower leg would be very swollen and an early night would be taken to ease the pain. Monday morning, lower leg very swollen and dancer has a high temperature. By late Monday patient is slightly delirious. Tuesday, septicaemia, and fox-trot Charlie is intermittently incoherent. Wednesday, the last rites and family gathering. Just before midday on Wednesday, Charlie dies roaring. Saturday sees the funeral at about four o'clock followed by ham and Guinness at the house. That evening at the parish dance, many conversations go like: 'And I was only having a drink with him last week on this very spot.' After the dance, at goodnight time, 'See you next week, God willing.' But there seemed no hard feelings in those days. Of course, for a lot of people, death was a welcome change. Grinding poverty takes the edge off most things including life. And to be fair, they (the poor) were going to see God. And that sweetened the pill a bit.

What would we have done without the sermon on the mount? It was our great comfort and helped us to make sense of suffering which, I suppose, is what religion is for. Certainly people had faith.

33

I remember my grandmother dying in ecstasy. Faith banishes fear, and the practice of religion often brightens life up if you're skint. If you are beautiful and have a few bob and lots of people want you and love you and laugh at your jokes and ask you to dinner you don't need God. But you do need Him when your looks go and nobody wants you. Then religion should be dramatic not vague and milky. Real life is hardly possible without real drama; and if we can't have real drama then we'll invent it. By 1943 I was doing two or sometimes three funerals a day come November. A good outbreak of flu would clear out a fair number of grannies in most streets. And granddads, too, though they often seemed to favour strokes. As an altar boy I was right in the thick of it swinging my thurible with a will.

Without realizing it, I was addicted to the smell of incense, I just loved it and wolfed it up. Or down. The visions I saw were less a result of piety than incense trips and hunger. The charcoal came in large discs about the size of a Bendick's bitter mint. I used to blow hard on it when I lit it in the sacristy before the services, so that when the priest put on the incense the cloud of smoke arose like a gigantic mushroom and we were all engulfed. It actually took away the hunger pangs. A dedicated thurible swinger who sipped God's blood and ate God's body every day could get along on very little food.

Fasting was a way of life for boys then. If you were intending to gobble God at morning Mass, then from midnight not a morsel or a drop must cross the lips. For fear of breaking the fast we didn't even brush our teeth. And after one funeral, wearing only the skimpy cassock and surplice and, because we were fasting, and feasting only on incense smoke, we'd go to the next funeral with a change of priest but the same hunger. Meantime, the holy Father was in the warm presbytery at his hot toast and pot of tea. It was not uncommon for a boy to faint from hunger though I never heard of a thurible swinger going down, thanks to the holy smoke, I suppose. I cannot say that I resented this regime even though I was hungry. The drama that grief produced helped me to get through the dizziness.

It was at a funeral that I found my true vocation as a faker. Baker the faker. It happened at the third funeral of a cold day in November in 1943. It was the funeral of a child by the name of Audrey Cheeseman. She was about eight years old and the cause of death was diphtheria. I was fading a bit for want of some food. Even the cause of her death couldn't ease the pain. The rain was slashing down, like stair rods, as they said then. I wobbled a bit at one point and even the word tracheotomy hardly sustained me. After pollution it was the only other big word that frightened small boys. We often talked of cut throats before funerals of children. We were all convinced that when diphtheria arrived then the doctor had to cut your throat. So when you woke up with a touch of tonsillitis then you usually hid the breadknife if your mother mentioned the doctor.

Anyway, there I was at the graveside trembling a good bit and trying to flick the rain from my eyes and sniffing hard as I strove to keep my incense burning, and my shoulders shook with cold. As the funeral came to an end and we turned towards the old church I felt a hand grip my arm, slide down to my wrist and slip a warm hard object into my incense control hand, my left one. It felt very like a large coin. Piously rolling my eyes, and shaking a bit more for good measure in the hope that whoever had slipped a hard object into my left hand might slip another hard object into my right, I hoped that nobody had seen what I can only call 'the incident'. In my corner of the vestry I opened my hand to discover a florin. This was a stupefying tip for a server and I was amazed and afraid. But not for long. Why? Why? Why such a big tip? And then it came to me: old Cheeseman thought my shaking shoulders and rain-filled eyes were tears for Audrey, his daughter! The penny dropped. That florin changed my life and got me going as an actor. From then on it was tears and snot all the way. And while the others occasionally copped for a threepenny bit I sobbed my way to florins. I was sniffing incense, swallowing God and on the top money, too. I was nine years old.

*   *   *

35

Of course, all my church-going led to great mockery from the street-corner boys. Whenever I was near them, they used the vilest language they could think of just to torment me. They knew that even to remain in the company of blasphemers was a sin, a mortal sin, and they were determined to drag me to hell with them. I am a very timid soul as you will know, and like most nervous people I greatly admire courage. My street-corner acquaintances were full of courage. They feared nothing: not the Devil himself, not even God. This used to astound me. They were certainly not afraid of sin, or hell, they didn't give a damn. And they were clever. They used to get at me with their devilish interpretation of what we were taught at school.

'Jesus loves us more than He loves you, y'know,' they would sneer.

'How come?' I would ask. And the dagger of their logic would strike me with: 'Because, Jesus loves sinners, y'daft bugger. He died for us. He was crucified for us, you know, not you. He didn't die for the likes of you. No, He died for us.' And they would skip off down the street singing with terrific gusto: 'Jesus died for us, Jesus died for us, Eee aye ee addio, Jesus died for us.'

I would look after them with such envy. There was something terribly disturbing in what they said. All the stuff about joy in Heaven over one sinner. Truth to tell I was desperate to be sinner. I wanted to steep myself in sin. And often I would listen to their dirty talk when I knew quite well that it was a sin. And while I was afraid, I was excited, too. That's the problem with virtue, isn't it? It's dull. It might be good but it ain't exciting. How can we make goodness exciting? I don't know.

So when they talked of Shilling Kate of Skelhorn Street, my breath would come short and my whole body would tingle. And now when I think back over all those hours of going to church, all that kneeling down and listening to various lunatics telling me the meaning of life when I could have been tingling on the corner, I could open a vein. I'd give anything for a tingle right now, wouldn't you? But to get back to Shilling Kate of Skelhorn Street. They said she'd do it for a shilling. They said that Nick Whiteside had been there and shagged her for a shilling up against a Ribble bus in Skelhorn Street, right next to Lime Street Station.

'But didn't anyone see them?' I asked. 'Oh, dozens,' replied Willie Rotherham airily. 'But in Skelhorn Street they are all doing it; they're used to it.' I was amazed, and so excited. I was sick with desire to do IT, whatever IT was, to Shilling Kate in Skelhorn Street, and up against a Ribble bus as well.

'Do you have to be sixteen?' I asked. And Willie said stiffly and with a sneer: 'Even when you're sixteen you won't know what to do. Anyway, isn't it time you buggered off to confession again, you've been listening to dirty talk and that's a sin,' and with a vicious leer, 'a mortal sin.'

I would slink off home, a failed sinner. Even Willie Rotherham could see I had no future as a sinner. The Devil was my first inclination but I was too tall and too frightened so in a sense I had no alternative to God. All I could do was listen carefully to the dirty talk on the corner. It gave me something to confess to Fr. Barry and I daresay it broke the monotony for him as well.

Years later, after I'd betrayed God and blown the whistle on His mother, I asked in the Sefton Arms if anyone knew what had become of Shilling Kate but strangely nobody was certain. A chap called Ronald Fogarty who still lived with his mother and was, therefore, looked at sideways said she'd gone into a convent. But another fellow who was a Knight of St Columbus contradicted him and claimed she'd opened a fancy goods shop in Bold Street. I never did find out. These memories crowd me sometimes and it downs me a bit that I'll never know what happened to those people from my own and my mother's childhood: Shilling Kate, Woodbine Emiline and Maggie Bloch, an old German woman who ran a takeaway scouse* shop in Athol Street. What a thought, selling scouse to scousers. But she did and she did well, too, right up to the beginning of the Great War. The scousers then lost their sense of proportion and

* For those from the Home Counties, this is a stew.

37

their sense of humour as they blamed the war on Maggie and did her windows in.

Woodbine Emiline, so called because she would do the deed for a Wills Wild Woodbine, was very ugly and very bandy, they said. But she served the poor, the randy poor who had nowhere else to go to fornicate. And because she always smoked her fees – she was quite feckless that way – she had a terrible cough, so bad indeed that she kept a spittoon near the shed door – proving that she wasn't lacking in fine feelings. Sometimes she'd make thirty fags a day. Not bad going for a bandy scrubber between the wars. But she never worked Good Fridays or Boxing Day.

There were mysteries as well. My uncle Tom's wife, Ella, just disappeared one afternoon; he found the baby's bath water was still warm when he got home from Tate and Lyle's sugar factory. And by tram and on foot he rushed to Lime Street Station in the hope of catching her before she took the London train. He was too late. He accepted his misfortune and scarcely ever spoke again. And there was Pat Heinz, of course, the one who was in love with my Auntie Louie.

Occasionally I think of Dr Crippen, what a man he was. In those days murder and the trials of the accused were the opera of the working classes. My grandmother was a great fan of Crippen and thought Ethel Le Neve hard done by. Personally I thought Mrs Crippen hard done by but I never dared to say so. There seemed no great contradiction in doing the nine first Fridays in devotion to the Sacred Heart of Jesus and believing in the innocence of Dr Crippen. The theatre couldn't match what was going on in a court of law or at football grounds. The theatre has never been able to match what goes on anywhere, that's why so few people go. What's the point of going out to the theatre when you can stay home and wonder about what happened to disappeared bridegrooms, and hear stories that stay with you for the rest of your life? A few Guinnesses, a few pickles and a tale or two in front of a big fire. What could be nicer? The theatre? Stow it. 'Pass the pickles, Lil, and tomorrow we'll go down to the Pier Head and watch the *Mauritania* sail for

America.' And if you get fed up talking to each other, well, slide a video on and go to *Casablanca* with Bergman and Bogart. How can the traditional theatre compete with the drama of a rock concert or even with the drama of a well-run pub? In the early 1950s in Liverpool the Playhouse was putting on plays like *I Killed the Count* and wondering why it didn't bring in many young people. Playhouse: 412 people, Liverpool FC: 71,000 people; Liverpool Cathedral: 611 souls, Everton FC: 72,000 souls. Conclusion? Wrong Gods. Paddy's Wigwam* 813, Liverpool Empire: 3000 souls twice nightly. To be fair Donald Peers† was top of the bill and he certainly couldn't hold a candle to Albert Stubbins for thrills. Whether Albert Stubbins could hold a note is not known, but he certainly played to big crowds and was a great centre-forward for Liverpool.

* So-called as a result of the compromise design for Liverpool Cathedral.
† Donald Peers, 'In a shady nook by a babbling brook'.

SIX

ON A SATURDAY NIGHT during the war and after a few bottles of Guinness had been sunk along with a few pickles and some Cheshire cheese, old memories would surface of times remembered and good deeds done.

'Do you remember the day Willie and Barney went out to drown the dog?' someone would enquire. This would provoke the warm laughter of recognition; cruelty made mellow by Guinness and the passage of time.

'He was a big bugger.' They were talking about the dog now.

'We had to get a special sack from Tate's.' They were now talking about Tate and Lyle, the sugar factory, where so many people in Liverpool worked.

'Yes, we had to find a bloody big sack for that dog, what was his name, Jane?'

'Bruce,' my mother would say while she poked the fire. Cruel stories always provoked her into a fierce fire poking. If they were not cruel my mother would elaborate with a will; she was a great improviser, she had to be, she was a good Catholic. The dog had been caught red-handed shitting on the steps of St John's Church by Fr. Lynch, the parish priest, and Willie and Barney had been ordered to drown it. Fr. Lynch had appeared from nowhere, spotted the crouching shitter, cursed him and condemned him to death.

Appearing from nowhere was a great skill priests had in those days. For a priest who could not appear from nowhere had no chance of robbing the unemployed men as, on their knees, they played pitch and toss. And a priest who couldn't rob the poor had no money to bet on the horses and no status among the jobless of the parish who loved to be robbed by a priest. What do you mean God's got no sense of humour?

'Let it be destroyed,' announced Fr. Lynch, 'tis a sinful and Godless dog.' And so with the black biretta on and the dog being unable to speak for himself, not that it would have made a scrap of difference, the avenging judge swept back into the church knowing that his sentence would be carried out. And Bruce, in a special sack because of his size and with three pieces of coal to weigh him down, was dumped in the canal by Barney and Willie who then went on to the Trafalgar for a couple of draught bass.

Well, what with the drawing power of the story, especially the death sentence from the Revd Judge Lynch OMI, Oblate of Mary Immaculate, and the embroidery added by Willie as he swiftly realized there was free drink in this tale of a dog condemned to death by the parish priest and no chance of an appeal, the afternoon session drew to a close before Willie and Barney set out for home. On arrival at 13 Arlington Street, humming *'Ave maris stella'*, for they always lurched into Latin after a drink, they pushed open the door and entered into . . .

'Like a bloody cesspit,' my grandmother would crow, taking out her teeth to laugh the heartier and gulping down the Guinness with bliss at the memory.

'The mud in the room was inches deep, inches, and there was the bloody grinning dog behind the door.' My mother ceased to poke the fire and got up to go to the kettle to make tea. She knew what was coming next.

'So the dog survived?' urged Ernie, my Auntie Molly's husband, knowing he was cueing the savage narrator.

'Survived,' shrieked Ninny, like a jay taken by an unneutered tomcat under a thick berberis. 'Survived? Only till I got home from Tate's and tied the bugger's legs together.'

'What happened then, Ma?' breathed Mrs Robinson, a neighbour, also a good Catholic and therefore bloodthirsty.

'What happened then?' screeched the demented matriarch. 'Why we took him back to the canal and did what Fr. Lynch told us to do, the will of God.'

'Well, you've gotta laugh,' wept Ernie as he raised a buttock and eased a fart that must also have reminded them of the old canal. They were all good-living people. They would have done anything for God.

My mother had led a very sheltered life. I suspect she had never been out of Liverpool. Come to think of it, she probably knew very little of the city at all. As far as I can remember she never talked about a play or a book or a holiday. At the outbreak of war in 1939, she was thirty-three years old. She had twenty-seven years to live and an awful lot of hard work and worry ahead of her. But she was sustained entirely by her religious faith. The saints were the counsellors in those days. They didn't speak to you directly or appear to you but they were there all right. Everyone had her favourite saint. St Anthony to find things, St Joseph if you were having trouble with your joints, or St Chad if you were a commercial traveller. And the Blessed Virgin if chastity was threatened.

There were other holy icons who were not yet saints though usually well on the way. The three steps to sainthood were: Venerable, Blessed, and then, if enough miracles were forthcoming, SAINT.

I recall a fragment of conversation between my mother and a woman down the road who was having anxiety with her son, Freddy.

'I don't know which way to turn, Jane,' said Mrs Spilsbury. 'I think it's going to have to be Saint Jude.'

My mother was appalled.

'Saint Jude, Madge? Jesus, Mary and Joseph, not Saint Jude.'

'Why not?' asked Mrs Spilsbury. 'Nobody else is interested.'

'What about the Sacred Heart?' suggested my mother.

With a sigh Mrs Spilsbury laid her hand on my mother's arm. 'Jane, I have harangued Him,' she said, 'harangued Him day and night. I've done the nine first Fridays just for Freddy and not a light.'

Not to be proved unhelpful my mother stroked her forehead

gently, and then with a little gasp as if to say, 'Of course, why didn't I think of it sooner,' she looked both ways in the style of Max Miller and said, 'What about Blessed Martin of Porres?' She pronounced it Paws. 'Have you ever tried him?'

Mrs Spilsbury, intrigued, folded her arms and said, 'No. Why? Is he any good?'

My mother opened her mouth in horror and then covered it up as she repeated: 'Any good? Any good? Merciful Christ, Madge, look what he did for Katie Welch.'

Mrs Spilsbury looked impressed, and lowering her voice and doing a Max Miller too, said, 'Oh, was that Blessed Martin of Prawns?'

My mother nodded very knowingly as, quite convinced, Mrs Spilsbury made up her mind and said: 'I'll give him a chance.'

'You won't regret it, Madge,' said my mother. 'As God is my judge, you won't.'

Mrs Spilsbury went off, comforted. Two days later it was told all over the parish that Freddy had gone to confession! Three days later the details began to emerge. It would seem that Freddy was seeing, as they said in those days, the wife of a sick policeman. This policeman was a Protestant who had fallen head first into his helmet and that was the rub.

Within a week the affair was over, St Jude had been bypassed and Blessed Martin of Porres was the flavour of the month.

I never did find out what it was that Blessed Martin of Porres did for Katie Welch.

Home from Fremantle, Australia, Dad was full of adventures. To Mam's amazement he said there were Catholics in Australia. And, even more amazing, two of them, a couple, had befriended him. The woman was a teacher and her husband, Joseph I think his name was, a carpenter. And on the way back from the Stations of the Cross at St Malachy's they'd met Dad and taken him home. Monica, the woman, had done Dad's dhobi and even ironed it. 'Washing dries in about eleven minutes over there,' said Dad, ever the one for the minute. Mam gasped. That pleasure could endure for eleven minutes staggered her. Where we lived, the washing never dried, which was later accepted as the explanation for bandy legs among the men.

'They couldn't have been nicer,' said Dad, producing a small photo of the distant couple standing in what looked like an orchard. 'They're the nicest pair I ever met.'

'No children?' enquired Mam, peering closer at the photo in the hope that among the apple trees she might spot the inevitables.

'No,' said Dad. 'But Joseph told me they've done every conceivable thing they could think of and not a light.' Mam's eyes glittered with tears. Poor people love to cry, it makes such a change from laughing which can make them tired if they have no savings.

'I'll say a prayer,' she sniffed. 'Isn't there anything we can do?'

'Well,' said my father, 'I did tell them that they could have one of ours.'

'Bless them,' said Mam, 'and what did they . . . what did you say?'

'I said that perhaps they could have one of ours, I mean we have got three,' Dad said, as if Mam couldn't count.

'You told them that they could have one of ours?' repeated Mam, suddenly looking as if she had a special vocation. 'Which one?' she asked as she glanced down at me. 'Well, which one did you have in mind to give to your bloody Australians?'

The talk of orchards and chickens and the sun had got to me. I listened with great care, perhaps this was my chance. I could imagine myself up the trees. I could imagine carelessly tossing apple cores over my shoulder without fear of the usual near riot. Over here a lad with an apple would be followed by perhaps five other lads each one hoping he'd cop the core. Oh, how I wanted to get away from them all and start again; I was young and I was restless.

My mother's legs sagged as she swung towards me. 'You don't want to go to Australia, do yer?' she squawked, holding out her arms and looking dull.

'Yes,' said I, unaware of her pain. And, unable to keep the

44

anguish to herself, she shared it with me by hitting me so hard I skidded across the room and crashed into the sideboard. The front cupboard doors were carved with grapes and a curly foreign pot, not intaglio. My poor head hit the bunch of grapes with such force that years later the dent in my temple had to be entered on my passport as an identifying mark.

My trip to Australia was postponed for thirty-three years and the house became silent. And that was the second terrible blow I received from me Mam who would have died for me. It didn't stop me loving her.

During the Second World War my father was away from home for two years. When he came back we were so happy. He had a tremendous cough and we had missed it terribly. It was a deep, resonant, Capstan Full Strength sort of cough, the sort of cough that tells you that he had always been in work. An out-of-work man who smoked Park Drive, for instance, would never have been able to cough with the authority of my Dad. So for a few hours we were happy at the arrival of Dad and his cough. Then me Mam opened his dirty washing, his dhobi bag, as they used to say, and found all her letters to him, all twenty-four of them, unopened among his dirty clothes. Two years' letters unread. She was very nettled by that discovery.

'Why didn't you throw them over the side?' she asked him. 'At least I wouldn't have known anything about them.'

I could see by the way Dad looked at her that he wished he'd thought of that. But he hadn't, and the wound remained festering in Mam's heart. It is the same now with me, somehow letters don't get opened. Fortunately, my wife is fearless and can open any envelope, even a brown one. Who was it that designed brown envelopes? I feel sure that he hated people whoever he was. I wonder where he's buried?

I shall never forget the expression on my father's face as with scalded balls he tried to find the budgie in the coal scuttle. His howl of anguish as he abandoned his suffering knackers to rescue the bird was very shocking. For one thing it broke the silence in the civil war between him and my mother. In those days, just like these days, it was very common for married people suddenly to discover that they didn't know each other. This discovery usually led to acrimony – the discoverer feeling cheated, ill done by. 'Why are you looking at me like that?' was a common question in the war of attrition that followed. Answer: 'I was just wondering what on earth I ever saw in you in the first place.' A plate might be smashed at this point as the victim of this remark vowed revenge again. When my mother realized that she didn't know my Dad and didn't like the sight of him anymore her disappointment was expressed in silence. A profound silence that endured for nine years. Trappist monks take a vow of silence, though the only time I ever went to a Trappist monastery, on a shopping trip naturally, the buggers were chatting away like Rat and Mole on a picnic. But then you'd expect that from idle monks who, if they hadn't climbed aboard the well-sprung gravy train called 'The Vocation Choo-Choo', would have been seen in Bold Street, Liverpool, selling copies of the *Big Issue*.

No, when my Mam decided on silence that was it. Not a smile went in my father's direction, not even a glance of contempt, nothing; he had ceased to exist. Now ashore, my father worked nights at Jacobs' biscuit factory and she worked days at Bird's Eye frozen foods. This kept encounters very brief.

But let's get back to Father's scalded balls. In his solitary confinement at home, no words, looks or comfort, he turned all his unwanted affection towards a budgie. Unable to express his feelings for people, he was able, like most men, to sustain a very complex relationship with a pet. Lots of men in our street did the same. The object of affection was usually a dog, though one man I knew, a tall man who blinked a lot and had a terrible stammer, kept a tortoise. It's name was Gladys but he never really managed to get the name out and Gladys didn't seem to mind. Tortoises are good pets for the timid, especially timid men with houseproud wives. But dogs were the objects of most fellows' feelings. On a Sunday, at two o'clock as the pubs closed, it was nothing to see nine men and their dogs in Indian file and all drunk. It was a terribly sad sight to see a drunken bulldog trying to lead his plastered owner back to lunch. Sitting drinking for two hours with his whippet or lurcher (lurchers were very popular with Roman Catholics for some reason) would give a man time to plot the spoiling of the Sunday dinner.

And it was after lunch in the Gethsemane of our kitchen one Sunday that the scalding of balls came to pass. During lunch, my father would often put a whole roast potato in his mouth and then blow like a melancholy grampus, trying to cool it. This was an appalling sight, especially to my mother who had once worked as a chambermaid at the Exchange Hotel and thought she knew how the best people behaved at lunch. Her head would go down and she would reach for the carving knife. Knuckles white, she would struggle to control herself. Even an Orangeman would have guessed from her expression that the Fifth Commandment was on her mind. And she would mutter as Dad's blowing changed key and began to sound like a sad foghorn in the Mersey in November.

After he'd finished his dinner and knowing how much he'd made my mother suffer, he would suddenly feel affectionate and get the budgie out of its cage. What a bloody palaver. My father had been given the budgie just after Christmas following Mam's *fatwa* and had called it Herod. Oddly my mother didn't seem to spot Dad's malice in this detail or, if she did, she never mentioned it to me or my brother. Anyway, after dinner Herod would hop from his cage and on to Dad's finger, then on to his shoulder while Dad, carrying his great mug of tea, got himself comfortable by the fire and ready for the next stage in the Sunday roasting of the peace. So that the picture be clear, I must tell you that Dad liked his tea strong, very strong, and no sugar. He would lean forward and Herod, with all the agility in his genes, would hop from shoulder to biceps, to forearm and wrist and then, with the neatest little leap you ever saw, he'd hop on to the rim of Dad's mug of tea and sit there as innocent as could be. He could not have known that his destiny was coming along the road on a bike. If he had, he would not have been responding so cutely to Dad's 'Who's a pretty boy, then?'

47

Swaying backwards and forwards Herod was, well, flirting is the only word that comes to mind. And while Dad supped his tea noisily, and made a sound like pebbles being shovelled into a zinc wheelbarrow, my brother John parked his bike, opened the front door and – how could he just let it go like that? He let the door go, and bang! It went off like the one o'clock gun, sending a column of air down the narrow passage between the front door and the kitchen where Herod was performing on the rim of me Dad's mug. The blast was too violent for a budgie to keep his feet and little Herod plunged head first into a big mug of very strong Liptons' tea.

Father, in reflexive terror, threw up both hands, thus allowing the scalding Liptons' to fall into his lap and souse his balls. But at least it got the budgie out of the tea. The falling mug jerked Herod with really quite a lot of force into the coal scuttle, which, half full of slack and nuts, didn't give him a soft landing. All this happened so quickly. From 'Who's a pretty boy, eh?' to the flirting of Herod, to the arrival of my brother and the blast of air that pitched Dad's love into scalding tea and then into the blackness of the coal scuttle seemed a mere fraction of a second. I saw it all, from the torture of Dad's slurping to the bird's silly carry-on, to the catastrophe itself. And I saw my mother's face change from Deirdre of the Sorrows to a vision of bliss as the hated object of my father's affection fell to its doom. Well, not to its doom exactly, but it never spoke again, or flirted again, and certainly it never danced again. It seemed to lose all zest for life and not long after it seemed to volunteer itself to an easy-going cat we had, called Innocent, after a famous Pope, I believe.

A few weeks later, the man who gave Dad the budgie, a short man with a glass eye who was keen on stamps and lived opposite to us, won a suitcase in the parish raffle. He hadn't got on with his wife since the day he'd set eyes on her, so he packed his new suitcase and went away. His wife, who hated him and was called Eunice, pined. Within sixteen weeks she was a different woman. She had the dog put down, became very pale, and died. She left no will so her husband came back with a nice girl called Marge. They settled down and seemed really quite happy to the great annoyance of the neighbours. But when he offered Dad another bird, it was refused. Not long after, Innocent the cat was run over by Price's bread van. So poor Dad lost his Herod and his Innocent in quite a short space of time. It downed him rather though me Mam was in very high spirits for quite a while.

SEVEN

EVERY ONCE IN A WHILE some man would come to the school
to talk to us about our future. On one occasion it was a man from
the Coal Board. He said being a miner was a good life and would
anyone like to go down a mine to have a look, no obligation, so to
speak. I put my hand up. A few weeks later, a dozen of us were taken
down a mine somewhere near St Helens. It broke the monotony of
long division and the darkness was comforting. But all the laughter
from the black-faced demons already at the coal face did not
convince me.

So next time, I put my hand up for the man who said that
farming was a good life, and for the man who said Australia was a
good place to be. If there had been a sergeant recruiting for the
Foreign Legion I would have put my hand up. When a little round
man came to talk to us about being a hero for Christ, about labouring
in the vineyard, and saying that many are called but few are chosen
I kept my hand up. What he promised seemed to combine farming,
grape picking and going to heaven. Oh yes, I put my hand up. But
oddly enough nobody else did. A few days later the little round man
came to talk to my mother about my renouncing the devil, the world
and the flesh. To have a son or daughter in religion conferred great
status on a working-class mother. How they reconciled the teacher's
assessment of my thickness with my potential usefulness in the
vineyard of God I don't know. Neither did my mother.

'Are you sure he'll please Our Lord?' she asked.

The round man described the life of sacrifice to us. 'It'll mean
getting up early and praying a lot,' he said. 'We don't even speak

when we're eating,' he added mysteriously. I couldn't understand that last point since it was absolutely forbidden to speak at meals in most houses I'd ever been in.

I was an affectionate boy in those days and I was quite willing to show God some, if that's what He fancied. I certainly wanted to please Him. Once during a series of sermons lasting a week in our parish – a retreat, it was called – I recall a priest talking about adultery, one flesh and not being put asunder. It was a Friday evening, Sixth and Ninth Commandment night, the church was packed, naturally. Committing adultery or coveting the neighbour's ass was always good for a shiver. The resident priest, Fr. Jameson, had done the warm up and retired to the seat reserved for him at the left of the sanctuary. The pulpit was empty but lit interestingly by the candles. There was a profound silence. Then, as if from the other side of the universe, we heard the sound of dragging feet and stertorous breathing (some priests were fifty-a-day men, adultery experts favouring Sweet Afton*. And then came the chink of rosary beads. These noises came nearer – the sound of the terror for tonight as our man dragged himself up the steps of the pulpit. Two claw-like hands appeared over the edge of the pulpit and a terrifying Old Testament figure came into view. This was our appointment with fear and the old frightener up there was our very own answer to Valentine Dyall† the Man in Black with a cassock on and a huge crucifix tucked into his belt. He glanced down at us; we were seized with awe and shrank within ourselves. Just the sight of him reminded us of how unworthy we were. His gaze swept over the whole congregation. This way and that he looked about, and all in silence. He rocked forward a little and then drew himself up to his full height. He towered over us like Ivan the Terrible and drew out the crucifix from his belt. Then holding it before him as if to bless us, he raised it up and, with the sudden strength for which prophets are famed, he spun round towards the altar and from his great height he hurled

* Popular Irish cigarette.
† A great radio actor of my childhood.

the crucifix across the altar rails! It landed on the marble floor with an amazing crash and slid at speed about ten feet before crashing into the credence table, rattling the cruets and nearly severing the table's legs. We were appalled. But our man slowly turned back to us and hissed, 'And that's what you do every time you commit a sin against holy purity.'

He then rapidly ran through the party line on chastity, how long a kiss could be sustained before it went from a venial sin to a mortal sin. The time was calculated from billiards, and the interval allowed was the duration of a canon shot, not long if you were a keen kisser. Oh, those Passionists hated kissing. Of course, they knew nothing of the fancy stuff they did in France. Or if they did, they didn't let on. That night dicks were slaughtered and quims dried up in their hundreds as the queue for confession stretched to the edges of the church. It was wonderful, and I miss it still. The feeling of self-loathing and a desire to be a slave to someone, anyone, as long as he knew what life was about and didn't mind if you were thick, stayed with me and led me to the religious life in the Channel Isles.

So off I went in answer to the call of God to labour in His vineyard. We just loved all this imagery of vineyards and shepherds and goats and talk of leaving family and friends and all worldly goods. Of course, poverty, chastity and obedience seemed no great hardship at the time of my decision. What did poverty mean to me? After all, I had been raised in considerable poverty. Most of the people I knew were poor. In a sense we gloried in it: 'Blessed are the poor; for theirs is the kingdom of heaven.' You see for us being poor was a blessing, poverty was the key, it was the pass into eternal life. The rich just could not grasp this simple fact. We felt sorry for the rich, we prayed for them. 'We are so fortunate to be poor,' my mother used to say. 'We may be sinful,' said Mrs McHale next door, 'but at least we're not rich.' If someone died in agony having lost two legs in an accident at the docks, there would always be the comfort of: 'Well, at least he wasn't rich.' This was an amazing state of mind. All suffering was understandable to us. All pain was a blessing because it was the will of God. There was no fear because faith banishes fear. Fear itself is afraid of faith. So you see I joined the rest of the labourers in the vineyard and really looked forward to being poor and staying poor. The paradox of all this is that if the church needs anything, such as money, why then the poor provide it. That's what keeps them poor. And preventing the poor from being rich was a good deed for which God blessed his sheep. Neat, eh? God keep me poor I prayed; and He did. He's so good in that way, He never once let me down.

Then there was chastity. Yes. 'Good morning, Brother, how's your chastity?' 'Oh, can't complain, cock, how's yours?' It has to be admitted that purity is a bit of a bugger. Whichever way you look at it you're on slippery ground. Even to think about it is a sin. A hard heart is an obstacle to getting to heaven, but so is a hard cock because a forty-five-degree hard on is a real scrambler of good intentions. It's also embarrassing with God and your Guardian Angel on hand, so to speak. In fact it's almost impossible to do a good deed with a stalk on. Talking to God in this condition is a monk's nightmare. You can't just shoo a firm dick soft, you know. And, of course, handling him is strictly forbidden, it's a mortal sin. What to do? Well, in some orders you can take the offending organ to another monk who has been specially chosen by the Abbot to deal with this problem. Usually he was the one with really sharp teeth. That's right, it was his job to bite your dick. This practice led to the old proverb: once bitten twice shy. Even pious monks were loathe to have their stalks docked in this way and they just had to put up with the engorgement if they couldn't face Brother Richard. Some people wonder why monks walk with a slight stoop. They walk like that to hide their truncheons. The bigger the engine the greater the stoop. Monks age very quickly for this reason. They also miss a good deal of what's going on around them. But nature won't be thwarted. Why do you think monks never turn their backs to a window? Especially a third-floor window? I'll tell you why. After six or eight years of chastity something's got to give, and when a chap ejaculates eight years' worth of the goods, he's likely to be blown back a yard

53

or two, hence the narrowness of the high windows in a monastery. There is a good deal of tension in houses of chastity.

The vow of obedience is not easy for anyone with an imagination. In the army it can be fun to obey blindly as long as your life isn't in danger, and there are always fellows around who can share the contempt you feel for authority, but not so in a monastery. For a start, the obedience must be unquestioning otherwise there is no merit. Even if you know the order is quite daft, you are told that God has His reasons. This rule makes things easier for the superior monks who derive their authority from God Himself. The great injunction of the New Testament is that we love one another but the monastic rule may also add that no friendships are to be cultivated. Fraternal love doesn't include a special pal. We weren't allowed to go around in pairs: rarely one, never two, always at least three; that was the rule. So someone is always cast as the gooseberry, three's a crowd. At home I was quite used to being ordered about by everybody: parents, teachers, neighbours, priests, especially priests, policemen, shopkeepers and nuns. So when I was reminded that great store was set by obedience, why, I just smiled. I couldn't wait to be tried by God's instrument whoever he may turn out to be. At my lowly level his instrument turned out to be just about everybody. For a time it was all worthwhile, just to be in a frock.

The soutane was great to wear. It carried all the authority of the church. It made me feel special; it kindled a desire to be a martyr. This pleasure was faintly odd because the priests in Liverpool didn't wear cassocks outside the church; not that I cared about that as I spent nearly all my time inside the church. It was in the church that I got to love shadows and dark corners, musty cupboards and creaking floorboards. I was a perfect recruit for the Addams family. Cobwebs made me whimper with joy. The smell of cheap sherry on the Father's breath comforted me and the thick stupefying smell of incense that Browning noticed fuelled my fantasies, it was like inhaling zabaglione, it quite scrambled the senses and made me think that I could understand the language of the liturgy and, indeed, that I could follow some of it.

My favourite words were 'Hic est enim calix sanguinis mei – this is the chalice of my blood'. I tried to use that expression in Latin once at a transfusion centre but the nurse was a Prod and didn't follow my joke. She just said, 'Pardon?'. But by that time I'd lost my faith and didn't really care whether the nurse got the crack or not.

The first thing that happened on entering a religious house was that you lost your name. My name was Tommy in those days but who had ever heard of Brother Tommy then? Now monasteries all over the world are crawling with Tommies and Willies and Tweaks and Larrys; most of them don't even wear frocks anymore, except on masquerade days. But then, your name was changed. Then, it was virtue to leave father, mother, brother, sister and so on and change your name, too.

In the old days, thousands of young people joined the army to get away from their roots and make a new start somewhere else. In those days you didn't leave home until you got married; and often you didn't leave home then because you had nowhere to go. So we yearned to be old enough to go and die for something, anything, rather than go on living at home. There are lots of times when you're poor and uneducated that death can seem rather attractive.

How, if you were less than eighteen, or you were a girl, how did you get away from them all? Why, you suddenly felt you wanted to go and work in a vineyard. Not any old vineyard, His vineyard, God's vineyard. A girl, be she never so plain or young, could quickly become a bride of Christ. She'd have all her hair cut off, take the veil and spend the rest of her life looking down at the floor as if she'd lost something. That was called being modest. We never saw her again, or if we did we wouldn't recognize her because they all looked alike. People would talk of her mother as having been chosen by God to give Him a bride. It was a very great honour to have a daughter in religion. There is a soap opera to be made about the dramatic jealousies that led to exquisite acts of spite in those famous convents. Saint Teresa of Lisieux recounts some of them. As children we knew about the little Flower of Jesus and her suffering among the Carmelites.

But for a boy to go to God as a priest or a monk or Christian Brother, gosh. This gave even bigger status to the mothers of such boys. Priests were superior to nuns for the very simple reason that they could perform the miracle of Transubstantiation, the transforming of bread and wine into the body, blood, soul and divinity of Christ during Holy Mass. It is impossible to exaggerate the esteem in which priests were held by the faithful. Today we understand the star status of film actors or sportsmen or rock musicians; they amaze us and excite us. But everybody has got to love somebody, as the song goes. We are all fans of something or someone. Even God has His fans and, of course, His fan clubs. The biggest and most powerful fan clubs were the great religious orders. The great conventions took place, and still do, at the great shrines like Lourdes or Fatima. The smaller and daily conventions take place every morning and afternoon in all the Catholic churches in the world, and especially they are expressed by Holy Mass. Sometimes when I'm in the West End I go to St Patrick's Church in Soho and I kneel there and try to recapture the joy I once felt when I crouched in the presence of God and felt certain of something. Where did my once-strong faith go? The betrayal of my faith has led to the deep self-loathing that I feel now. But that's now. What about then?

I wanted to call myself Sylvester. I thought it sounded good and my mother often talked about St Sylvester's in Liverpool. Yes, Brother Sylvester pleased me a lot. So that when I reached the mother house in Jersey, Maison Bon Secour, the house of succour, my happiness was complete. I was determined to be good. We say, don't we, 'she's a good girl' or 'she was a good mother' or 'he was a good man'. We still mean it, too. To be good in the moral sense still draws us to admiration. I wanted to be a saint. You can laugh if you like, I won't reproach you, but that's what we all felt, all forty of us in the novitiate of 1951. The discipline was very severe. The popular idea was that silence, lots of silence, deep silence, eternal silence it seemed to me, was good for the soul. I found it very hard.

The day started at about four thirty, I think. Odd, isn't it, that in a house of religion where silence was the great idea, we were roused in the morning by what I can only call a fire alarm. The shock was appalling. But one can get used to anything. It didn't occur to me to complain. Complain?

That dormitory where forty apprentice saints passed seven and a half hours' sleep was an anxious, damp place full of fumblings in the dark and pretend blindness in the daylight, for after silence the great virtue was modesty. After a year in that place I still didn't know any body by sight. I think I only saw the sky about twice and each time was only for a moment before somebody shouted, 'Modesty'. When we went to bed at night at eight thirty, we were allowed perhaps three or four minutes to brush our teeth and swill our faces. Then we would all glide, walking wasn't permitted, each one to the foot of his bed and there you would turn into a statue until the last glider had arrived at his bed. What a sight it must have been. I never saw it myself because of the modesty rule. When I cast my mind back I sometimes doubt if I ever went to Jersey at all. I never saw anything. Bon Secour? It should have been called St Dunstan's. Well, there I was at the foot of my bed and as far as I knew thirty-nine other statues were there at the foot of their beds. And then, on a signal – two ominous hand claps from the supervisor – the room was plunged into darkness. Silence, gliding and darkness. And, as the blackness fell, the fumbling started.

The reason for this little ceremony of the sudden blackout was that we should not catch a glimpse of each other as we got into bed. Yes. This dark spell would go on for about two minutes during which you were required to get your clothes off, tuck your socks under the mattress to keep them dry for morning, lay your soutane across the bed, hop in, get flat and fold your hands across your breast as if you were dead. There would be two more spooky claps from the man in black and the night light would come on. And so we would all lie there bathed in Hammer Horror red light as Brother Audifax (feast day 9 January) cruised or rather glided like a great black pike in that lake of a dormitory, glancing at all the beds which,

57

like little islands, protected us for the next seven hours. I don't know if Brother Audifax (why did he want to be called Audifax?) ever slept. I don't know where he was kept during the day either. But no matter at what time you might wake, the pike was gliding among the beds, as though waiting for some poor soul to fall out and then, tearing him into fragments, eat him. This lying there like figures on cathedral tombs was to maintain our modesty in the eyes of our Guardian Angels who were also there, though we couldn't see them – yet. And if by any chance you should move in the night and make the bed springs creak, why then with a little plop and gurgle Pike Audifax would materialize at your bedside and hiss, 'On you knees.' With two well-practised moves your bed would be unsealed, your soutane flung over you and on your knees you would remain until the gliding pike arrived out of nowhere and nudged you with his prickly gills which was the signal that you could go back to being a dead knight on the tomb of your bed.

Sleep would finally release me from the worry of making the bed springs creak. At four thirty the fire alarm would yell like a lunatic and Audifax would applaud it with the devotion of the bigot. I never heard anybody clap so loudly; what a spanker he could have been in another profession. And after the yelling of the bell and the clapping of our enemy of sleep came the morning fumble. Because of my thyroid condition I am able to see through a wide arc. What an amazing sight, forty young men struggling to get their trousers on in bed. The bed springs went mad with the joy of being able to creak freely; Audifax glided every which way darting razor glances in every direction in case one of the forty contortionists was taking pleasure in the morning wriggle. As though on silent skates he whizzed among us calling up the Holy Ghost. Yes, we called up a ghost first thing in the morning, and in Latin. 'Veni, Sancte Spiritus', moaned the slithering pike as he swivelled among us, and we were all of us curved like butchers' hooks to hid our piss-proud dicks as we responded: 'Come, within our bosoms shine, for where Thou art not, man hath nought.' There is no sight so unmysterious as forty young men struggling to pull on eighty damp socks in the presence of some demented, railing maniac while chanting aloud, 'Melt the frozen, warm the chill, bend the stubborn heart and will.' Some mornings I suspected I could hear God tutting at the indignity of it all. We then rushed to ease our bladders and wash our haggard faces before the wild bell yelled again to call us to morning prayers and meditation. It was like living in a bloody fire station.

We would gather in the beautiful dark chapel. This was an exciting moment for me. I would watch in astonishment as from all doors, there were about seven, black clad figures would enter at speed but in silence to call again on the Holy Ghost. We gave Him no peace. Then we would be invited to think of our last ends. We'd only just got up and we were thinking of our last ends. 'At any moment we may die and enter into our eternity. At death we shall be judged according to our works.' In moments of weakness and tiredness I longed for death in any form just so long as I could lie down. How weak I was. It makes me go pink just to think of it; and that was nearly half a century ago. Of course, I had not yet read *The Dark Night of the Soul*. I did not understand that depression and self-doubt were to be welcomed as gifts from Himself. It meant He was interested. It meant you were in with a chance. Later, in my madness, I would pray: 'Come O holy depression, and fill me with terror.' This excess later spilled over into my style of acting and makes me virtually unemployable. After a quarter of an hour of common prayer we would all rise and disappear through our special door towards a common room where we would sink into forty minutes of meditation or mental prayer as the old hands called it.

This mental prayer would begin with what was called a colloquy or loving conversation with the Saviour or the object of one's spiritual affection that morning. To tell the truth it was always Morpheus – we were all so shagged out. But I did the best I could. I would call to mind the suffering Christ in the garden of Gethsemane during his agony. This could be a little risky if your thoughts wandered to the Apostles who were there with the Lord; for as you know they fell asleep. Yes, they actually fell asleep when Christ was in His agony. I tried to dodge that bit or I would have followed suit and dropped off. It always baffled me that St Peter himself could not stay awake at that moment of near despair. The story is so beautiful and I suppose the sleeping Apostles should comfort us in their example of human weakness. Meantime these thoughts were interrupted by the nasal clicks of some insensitive wanker called Boniface. There was I trying to make contact with Jesus in His agony and this tosser Boniface was clicking in his nasal passages. For the next thirty minutes I meditated on how I'd like to torture Boniface. I nearly went as far as to wish that he might fail in holy purity. But this made me feel such an apostate that shame engulfed me and I toyed with the notion of talking about it to Fr. Galleotti, our ghostly father. But I didn't. And as I vacillated between the garden of Gethsemane and the desire to murder Brother Boniface that bloody yelling fire bell wrenched me back to self-disgust. And as I slid along to Mass in line with the other forty I would sometimes wonder what they had been thinking about during meditation. Did I make clicking noises? Did I rock back and forth like Brother Casimir and moan occasionally? Surely not. Did anyone secretly want to kill me? Did anyone want to tempt me into a sin against holy purity? And if he did and it was Brother Felix, would I be able to resist? Would I want to resist? This thought made me shiver with pleasure. I mean shiver with fear. Or, to tell the truth and shame the devil, it made me shiver with both pleasure and fear. It was ecstasy and, therefore, made me feel guilty. It wasn't yet six o'clock and all this turmoil. How was I going to get through the next fifteen hours without a fall?

EIGHT

THE BROTHER SUPERIOR, also called the master of novices, was a tall, bald man with sandy eyelashes; he had, as I thought, a rather insincere stoop and was in the habit of clearing his throat a lot as though he was about to make an announcement. When he looked at me it was as if he suspected I wanted to slap him. Curiously, that was exactly what the devil was always telling me to do; but I resisted him. Stooping Sandy, whose monastic name was Etienne, always encouraged the very keen members of the novitiate to call out reminders to the more timid ones of what our ideals were: to be modest, by which was meant we should not look at each other; to be pious and meditative; to work hard and not to think for yourself; and, especially, to be obedient. The shouted-out reminders of our ideals were meant to inspire us, to keep idle thoughts away and so on. Come to think of it I suppose you could call out anything you wanted as long as it was fine and noble. It was not unusual for someone to call out at breakfast: 'Let us think of Saint Aloysius Gonzaga.' There would be a general sigh of satisfaction all round and if you caught the reference it nourished you. St Aloysius Gonzaga was famous for his chastity so just the thought of him would lower the boom of your lust. He was an easy reference and we all responded. And if another fervent young novice bawled out: 'Let us all be minims', you might not get the reference to St Francis of Paula who was big on humility. But the passion to be a minim was very common and we would all bow our heads and pray for lowliness. One cold damp morning in January, so damp we were allowed to sleep with our socks under our pillows, I tried to overcome my timidity about the calls to piety by suddenly yelling out 'Polycarp of Smyrna'. Thirty-nine young men, faces buried in tin basins of coffee were caught on the hop. I thought it was quite droll to see them all forget their modesty for a moment and glance at each other as if to say: 'Who the hell is Polycarp of Smyrna?' There was a small pause and the noise of thirty-nine gorgers ingesting coffee pobs eased and someone called: 'Let us not be obscure.' This rebuke from a particularly plain tormentee to judge from his clogs irked me a bit and I countered: 'St John Bosco?' Plain clogs riposted with: 'Joseph Cupertino.' The sandy master of novices tapped the rim of his tin bowl and hissed: 'Let us have silence.' And the silence descended. The obedience was absolute. You could nearly hear the building growing older. I never called out again, though I was often tempted to. The devil ricocheted in my head and did his damnedest to provoke me. He kept suggesting I shout: 'Everybody get his dick out.' But I never dared.

Once at collation, a few months after I had been urged not to be obscure, I inadvertently, oh very inadvertently lost complete control of myself and glanced up at the novice sitting opposite me. He'd been sitting there for at least six months because I recognized a broken button near his throat but I'd never looked past that broken button and into his face until now. As I looked at him (in my weakness), I was quite shocked at how beautiful he was; but not only beautiful, interesting, too, in the way I imagined the devil might be interesting if one could only catch a glimpse of him. As I looked at my opposite novice he seemed contemplative – by that I mean he was being modest and looking into his lap. I longed to look into his lap with him. I longed to lay my head in his lap. I wanted to be in his lovely lap forever. I wanted to be his lap dog. But even before I could enjoy that thought the ugly bugger next to him read me real quick and shouted out: 'Be modest, let us all be modest, let us not look at one another.' The ugly ones always wanted the others to be modest. He was called Linus, I think, the ugly one, and taking him at his word I never looked at him again. Compared to him the floor was mysterious. It was a strange life only loving someone's buttons or fingers or feet: the part for the whole, so to speak. I would have liked to possess that broken button and suck it in chapel during the meditation on our last ends.

I once spent about half an hour looking at a chap's clogs and felt quite affectionate towards them; he was in them, of course, but I never saw his face and I never once shouted out a call during the remainder of that whole year. All I wanted to do was to stroke clogs and suck buttons. Somehow the idea of calling out 'Let us recollect ourselves' didn't appeal to me, though I was often tempted to cry out, 'Let us *love* one another.' It was indisputably a good thought but it might have been misconstrued by Brother Linus or old Stooping Sandy.

From morning till we dropped there was work to be done. The whole point of that year was to learn humility and practise obedience. The whole bloody point was the annihilation of the self. I suppose that's where I lost myself forever. We sat in silence at meal times while somebody read to us from the lives of the saints. And afterwards we washed up the dishes of the whole community, there being about sixty senior brothers around the place. We had no contact with them at all, and we knew nothing about them or their duties, though I knew all their clogs by sight. Odd, isn't it, you'd think one pair of clogs was just like another, but no, each pair was special.

When I say there were about sixty senior men I'm going by the number of feet I counted as I went about my duties. They all wore clogs and as I was aching with loneliness I formed passing fancies for different clogs. Once, just outside the kitchen where I had the honour of washing up the monastery porridge pot, I noticed to my amazement four clogs, which equalled two monks, and five rather shiny ankle-band shoes of the kind that my grandmother used to wear. What were two and a half grandmas doing near the kitchen? There was nobody I could ask and it remains a mystery to this day. Some nights, lying on my tomb bed while the black pike hovered around us, I got to thinking that five shoes could have meant that one of the grannies might have been a one legger. That kind of thought often came to me without invitation as I lay there hoping for sleep.

Once, playing softball on a gravelly courtyard in front of a statue of the Sacred Heart of Jesus, I struck the ball so hard it flew across the yard and struck the Sacred Heart in the eye. There was a terrible silence and as I looked about as though to say, 'Sorry, I didn't mean it,' I noticed several of the others were already weeping in sympathy with the statue. We sometimes walked up and down this court in the evening at about seven o'clock. This occasional walking was organized in a strange way. As we stumbled modestly on to the court an assistant to Stooping Sandy indicated with his clicking fingers where we were to be. No choice at all. We would line up in threes facing each other. Then on a signal from . . . God, I suppose, we walked modestly forward while the three fellows opposite walked modestly backwards. When they hit the back wall at the far end of the court, we walked backwards in our turn and the other three looked forward to us smashing into the wall at the other end of the court. Even monks need their little pleasures. The conversation during this to-ing and fro-ing was numbing. We were encouraged to put ourselves into the shoes, or rather the clogs, of various holy persons from the past. 'What do you think Joseph of Arimathea felt at the foot of the cross?' I used to pretend I was in the next world and don't remember saying much. Sometimes I wanted to ask them what it must have been like for the guests at the marriage feast at Canaan when Christ turned the water into wine. But I didn't dare. The first miracle of Christ's ministry has always been my favourite.

And so as I told myself that I was happy to be in this infernal house of God I gradually got used to the terrific regime. Of course, I had no way of knowing what the others were feeling or thinking. Discussion of feelings was not allowed. Every few weeks one of us would disappear. It would be a terrible shock.

> 'Thirty-nine little novices all went off to church.
> One disappeared and all their hearts did lurch.'

This would be noticed in chapel when for a moment on the morning of the disappearance there would a gap where some poor soul had prayed the night before. Just as I was trying to work out who had gone, Stooping Sandy would appear and shoo the others along. The holy books of the disappeared one would be snatched away, the gap would be filled and that was that. The same process would take place in the large study area. We were told nothing. We asked nothing. To ask a question would have meant disappearing and I feared to disappear. I simply felt sad that I could no longer see a familiar pair of clogs or a beloved neck. But there was nowhere to weep and nobody to talk to. It was years before I experienced missing the front of anyone. I wouldn't have known a front if it had been pressed against me. That was a long way away. It was to be a long time before I even saw a complete person and when I did I didn't know what to do.

Once when I was on laundry duty I had to go and fetch the clean rough sheets for the dormitory. At the far end of an immense corridor, perhaps two hundred yards long, I rang an old brass bell and waited at a highly polished door on which was a brass plate so worn I could not read the vital information on it. I listened carefully. Sure enough there was the sound of fumbling. After what seemed about two days and nights the door was eased open and the top of a head appeared all covered in a black cotton veil. It was possibly the top of a tiny nun I thought to myself. A hand stretched out towards me and I placed the requisition note for seventy-eight sheets, thirty-nine pillowcases and thirty-nine towels. I'll never forget those towels. They were as coarse as cheese graters; we didn't need to shave. The note was enfolded in one hand and another hand came out from somewhere and beckoned me in. I stepped inside and made as if to advance. The figure in black hissed in my direction and I froze. It then did a dreadful little shuffle and a hop. I looked at it and it looked expectantly back at me and repeated the hop and shuffle. It obviously wanted me to do the hop and shuffle, too. The hand cocked impatiently as if to say: 'Well, what are you waiting for?' So I did a terrible hop and a vague shuffle, very vague I'm afraid as I'm not too immense at ballet. The figure in black hissed with fury and repeated its ghastly dance of death clucking as it hopped. Hiss, cluck, shuffle hop, hiss cluck shuffle hop. I raised my hand, the gesture saying: 'Got it, got it!' The black-clad Sister Terpsichore* paused and watched. So I went into my shuffle and hop with a little hiss and a bit of a cluck, too. This did not go down well. Later I would feel the same degree of helplessness in front of John Dexter† when he would say: 'Go on, then surprise me.' The dancing thing in front of me now gurgled in between the hisses and clucks. Like Aaron throwing his rod down she pointed towards my feet. I leapt back and saw before me two very neat little mats about fifteen inches by eight, like small off-cuts from an old dark-green carpet. The little demon in front of me jumped back and revealed two identical mats between its feet. Then with a scolding shake of its hand as though to say, 'This is the last time,' it performed the hop and shuffle which got it on to the mats, and then, with the most shocking change of style, it skated off quite lyrically towards the far end of an enormous room around the walls of which were high cupboards and in the middle of which was a table maybe sixteen by seven, though I could be mistaken. The black-clad skater seemed to do a pirouette and with a hiss watched me set out. With more of a yelp than a cluck, I leapt aboard my mats and skated towards my tutor. Its hands jumped with pleasure and I distinctly heard chuckles from among its veils. It looked down at the high gloss I had produced on the floor and nodded vigorously. It was pleased with me. Hideous as it seemed, I fell instantly in love with it and set off westward across the room, eased southerly and, swinging to the east, got up speed before sharply turning north and heading back towards my teacher producing a marvellous gleam behind me. I had become a floor polisher. And suddenly I wondered if this was what God wanted of me. Did He mean me to be a minim among polishers? My lips were tumescent with affection as I panted to a

* Goddess of the Dance.
† World-famous director and one-time actor in The Archers.

66

halt before my new love. Her chuckle became a chortle and the hidden head nodded to me in approval. I skated away again and did some fancy turns for my mysterious new love. And I remember laughing aloud and being shocked by the noise for laughing was forbidden. The dark figure held out its hands and for a moment I thought it was proposing a dance. Oh, all things bright and beautiful! At that moment two other ghostly figures skated into sight and coughed. My tutor seemed suddenly old and defeated and turned towards a cupboard behind her and began to load me with the linen I'd come for. Back and forth I skated polishing the floor the while until seventy-eight sheets and thirty-nine pillowcases and the same number of towels were stacked outside the mysterious door to the linen studio. I never did the bed-linen run again but I reproduced the hop, shuffle and glide in *She Stoops to Conquer* at the National Theatre years later. Jack Tinker in the *Daily Mail* hated it, thinking it rather overdone. I didn't care as an ex-ballet dancer wrote and told me she had seen the production and fallen in love with my legs. She said that in other circumstances she could have lived happily with my legs but that she only had a small flat in Holland Park. The Nottingham theatre critic felt pretty much the same but was a married man so I had to keep my legs to myself. I've held on to them ever since, and honestly, I can't say that I've regretted it, they've been very loyal over the years and we're still together, my legs and I.

NINE

I HAVE ALREADY EXPLAINED that I was a sniffer of incense and of floor polish from an early age. By the time I was ten I couldn't walk past a tin of floor polish without having a furtive snort. The same was true of the stupefying incense and the smoke from newly snuffed-out beeswax candles. After a while my nostrils began to flare quite naturally so that I was able to inhale larger and larger pockets of loaded air. On a good day of snorting smoke, polish and incense, the holy pictures in my prayer book began to move and the blood of the Sacred Heart of Jesus would seem to flow; I was in ecstasy.

I still have a fairly highly developed sense of smell. A gift like that doesn't fade that easily. Often when I'm on the train from Ashford to Cannon Street or Charing Cross I find myself surrounded by youngish business men who slap on an awful lot of scent. Perhaps they are influenced by those commercials that Henry Cooper did all those years ago. Sometimes you can see thirty or forty commuters on the 7.02 a.m. train to Cannon Street apparently fast asleep. But if you look closer you will notice that they are nearly all muttering incoherently and some will also be rolling their eyes. This is because they have been overcome by the smell of male scent. Once on a packed train to Charing Cross – luckily for me, the slip window was ajar – I stood next to a man who had slapped on so much perfume that it had begun dissolve the seams of his suit. One sleeve of his suit fell to the floor before we had reached Staplehurst. He didn't seem to notice anything amiss. The deadly scent continued to rot the seams of his clothes and I'll spare you the description of him by the time we reached London Bridge.

Anyway an impulse to be somewhere else, anywhere else as long as it was not where I was then was the impulse that led me to become a full-time sniffer in the house of God. Taking the vows of poverty, chastity and obedience, I moved to Shropshire to what they called a college and for a time I also enjoyed the drama of the smells. As the years went by the ardour faded but while it lasted it kept me occupied. God may be said to have smelled of starch, incense, floor polish and beeswax in those days. What He smells of nowadays I have no idea. The whiff in the rest of His house was quite different. Generally it was like the far end of a damp and very much neglected Oxfam shop.

As professional lovers of God we were not allowed out very much. The theatre was out of bounds as was the cinema. We were not allowed to enter Protestant churches and, of course, we had never heard of Sketchley or even Archille Serre*. The monks could be said to divide roughly into two groups, smell-wise. One group was made up of Lifebuoy users and the second group of Wright's Coal Tar users. The Lifebuoy gang seemed on the whole to be a very vigorous group. They gave the impression of being rather immodest and were sometimes seen to look at each other right in the eyes which was forbidden. In contrast, the Wright's Coal Tar brotherhood seemed mildly asthmatic and round-shouldered. They gasped a lot as though they really enjoyed the smell of each other. But when they crossed the path of a Lifebuoy saint the Coal Tar mystics would be seized with fits of coughing. It got so bad that the two groups had to be separated for prayers in chapel, Lifebuoys to the right and Wright's Coal Tars to the left. Of course, it was not quite so simple as that because the ascetics among us favoured carbolic soap. This brand of soap was not only merciless to germs, it also murdered the libido. Oh yes, the smell of carbolic is death to a stalk. If you were having trouble with your vow of chastity all you had to do was get your family to send you a tablet of carbolic. I've heard that the Pope has been told of this old remedy and has even mentioned it in a

* World-famous dry cleaners, disappeared in the 1960s.

bull to the British bishops. It may, of course, be too late since lots of priests have already become hardened by the use of 'Soir', the after-dark aftershave.

I lusted after new smells. I didn't know then exactly what they would be, how could I? When I arrived at God's house randy for martyrdom the only smells I was confident of were those of simmering shirts in a hot copper and the immovable stench of salt fish. Hospital smells were a constant in my nasal memory, along with incense mixed with the odour of beeswax candles. I could not anticipate the amazing and suffocating quality of Devon Violets. In an Italian fish restaurant one evening I was enjoying a pair of kippers when an uncertain blonde girl went past my table. So seeped was she in Devon Violets that she completely neutralized my kippers. Suddenly the friendly and confident smell of my fish vanished. In a flash they tasted like early Egyptian mummified kippers taken by a grave robber from the tomb of Tutankhamun. I must have looked startled because a waiter came up to me and asked if everything was all right. 'No,' I told him, 'my kippers are dud.' He straightaway tried my second kipper which was untouched; and then, not leaving anything to chance, he tried the first kipper which was nearly finished. What a food inspector that young man would have made.

'Hey, Aldo,' he cried out towards the kitchen. 'Mr Baker, he has a dud kipper. Doctor Who no likes his kipper. What you done to him?' The chef came out looking bemused and wiping his hands on his checked keks*.

'How do mean a dud kipper?' asked the chef as he walked towards my table and the waiter and straight into the noxious cloud of Devon Violets. The unauthenticated blonde must have been in the powder room and hit the compact. The chef sniffed me and then he sniffed his colleague before inclining slightly towards the blonde powder monkey about ten feet away. Then the chef staggered back a pace or so and groaned as he realized that his sense of smell had vanished completely. He made a terrible scene that was only

* Keks is an old Liverpool word much used by scouse cooks to describe their trousers.

eased by the offer of a large brandy and a Hamlet cigar. They would not take my money. What became of the blonde I can't say; but whenever I was in that street I always kept a small plastic tube of lighter fuel on me in case she reappeared. But all this was yet to come and more, much more, like fennel and dill in steamed cabbage and especially testosterone in Aldershot.

And so it was that in my desire for other smells I chaffed at the authoritarian demands of elders with names like Brother Provincial or Brother District Superior. I grew to hate them all and yet I was too frightened to do anything about it. There was no policy then of being released into the community. Religious people who left were always considered traitors and were said to go mad with their sense of guilt and their inability to cope with the 'outside world' as life away from the community was called.

To get away from the Lifebuoys and the Brothers Wright, I humbly accepted the menial task of keeping the entire community warm. By that I mean I was in charge of the furnace. I have always had an impulse for the menial task. This furnace was enormous and digging out the clinkers which were sometimes three feet across was not easy. When broken and dropped in water these clinkers released gases which made me feel quite disorientated, but I quite enjoyed it just the same. And as I struggled to keep the brothers warm I had time to meditate on how I was feeling towards my superiors. They were all my superiors.

Brother Provincial who limped a bit as if perhaps his wooden leg had originally been made for a slightly taller man, was a particular target for my new-found appetite for violent thoughts. I loathed him. As he walked there was a slight creaking noise from under his cassock. This noise made it impossible for him to creep up on his inferiors without warning. We used to whisper to each other about this creaking. One timid little soul called Nathaniel thought the creaking was from the harness of the wooden leg. I didn't agree with this opinion at all. In fact, I wasn't certain that Brother Provincial had a wooden leg. The creaking might have come from a too-tight truss, because he always wore a distinct frown, the frown in my

71

view of a man who might be trying to ignore his rupture. So repressed were we that these forbidden speculations fuelled our imaginations to feverishness. My own uncertainty about the wooden-leg pro-position led me to admit to myself that I was not certain that anybody else had legs at all. After being frocked from my Adam's apple to the floor for so long my legs, like my thoughts, had grown used to the darkness. And as we were covered up even in the showers our legs never met each other. It was not until I went into the army that my poor legs actually met and got to know each other again. But my desire to kick the poor Provincial in his harness grew more and more powerful. I guessed that if I did suddenly kick him then I would be thrown out. I was so afraid of what the outside world was like that I was in despair about how I could survive it. The thought of returning to the smells of my childhood revolted me. What could I do? What was I good for? What skills did I have? The answers were, nothing, nothing and none. I shivered at my hopelessness. The thought occurred to me that I might throw a burning clinker into one of the old corridors and burn the whole place down so that we could all escape God's clutches. I dismissed that thought as one of pride. Who was I to take a decision for all the others? I wondered whether these thoughts, particularly the red-hot clinker ones, were not just impulses to get to hell early.

Every year during the few weeks before Easter the whole com-munity sank into utter silence as we entered into our annual retreat. This was to be my last retreat. It was a period of deep self-examination. We were exhorted to examine our motives for every-thing in our daily lives. Now the impossible injunction which is laid upon Christians in general and on professed religious persons in particular is: 'Love thy neighbour.' Of all the injunctions in the New Testament this is the heaviest, the hardest and the most complex to apply. And during the long hours of meditation I discovered to my horror that all was not well in the charity section of my heart. The cupboard was bare. I had had enough of religious life. So deep was my resentment of authority that I realized I had an intense desire to break all the Commandments. All of them. Especially I had an urge to kill, steal and bear false witness. Adultery could wait until the opportunity arose. Prudence, Justice, Fortitude and Temperance just seemed to me to be a firm of crooked canon lawyers.

During this long retreat from worldly thoughts one was allowed to speak to the visiting priest whose job it was to reinforce the teachings of the church and to encourage vacillating monks to stiffen their resolution. In my case it did not work. Something was happening inside my head and there was nothing I could do about it. It was a very frightening time for me. I imagine it was a little like the onset of an illness. The symptoms were becoming more and more evident and more and more disturbing. And just as most people try to ignore the signs of illness, so I tried to ignore my symptoms of fading faith. The influence from my first year in Jersey was still deep in me and after nearly six years I was very institutionalized. The thought of the outside world that I wanted so badly made me very afraid. But I felt I had to have it no matter what the cost.

So when I had the chance I spoke to our visiting spiritual guide, Father Bernal, about my fears. He was a gentle soul very willing to hear me and to advise me on a course of action. When I told him about my doubts and about my desire to break the Commandments, especially my impulse to kill, he cleared his throat and looked as if he wasn't certain whether he should hear my confession or call the police but he concentrated on what I had to say. When I realized he was not about to condemn me or even just chase me out of the place I was able to be reasonably calm as I let him hear what was in my mind. He sniggered as I told him of how I'd thrown some rabbit droppings in the Brothers' soup a few days before. A very small and not very serious attempt to poison the lot of them. 'Did you eat the soup?' he asked me.

'No, Father,' I told him, 'I was the reader that day.' He nodded, and I suspected that he was casting his mind back because he then asked me:

'Was it oxtail soup, Brother?' I told him no and he seemed relieved.

After several meetings with the old man, he began to talk back to me. He called me Tom, which brought back the memories of my other life. And as I told him of all the tumult inside me he nodded and said softly: 'Tom, Tom, I think you're in the wrong place.' That's what I wanted to hear him say. My heart rose as he added: 'Do you want me to help you out?' I nodded to him with such joy that he laughed.

'I'll get it all started,' he said. I felt full of optimism, full of hope that I could at last get out of God's clutches, sign up with the devil get on the old primrose path to pleasure, even if it did lead to hell.

That same evening I was doing the pious reading at supper. As I turned a page I thought I saw Brother Provincial watching me. I wondered if Father Bernal had told him of my desire to kick him in his harness and I carried on reading from some daft old fool called Scaramelli. It was a tale about hermits who had sacrificed all for the love of God but who had remained attached to their crabs or cats or lice, I forget which, and so that after fifty years of mortification they had still finished up in hell. In God's vineyard you must not become attached to anything, not to books or particular cells or even to people; friendship itself was forbidden. And it went through my mind as I was reading all this pious claptrap that God did ask an awful lot of us. And He seemed to have this insatiable appetite for praise. Was God insecure, too, I wondered? Does He really want us to serenade Him all the time? Does He really not want us to have a pal? So it seemed to me that if you were to get on with God you had to settle for being miserable. And I read on from Scaramelli and wondered how soon it would be before I could get away. These arrangements sometimes took months. But I wondered if Father Bernal had explained that I was an arsonist, poisoner and potential kicker of my superiors. I hoped he had for I was hot to be a traitor, to get out to new smells and find some joy in life. I didn't know then that I would never find a friend, that I would go on being a traitor and that new smells would never make up for the pernicious itch in me to make change for its own sake.

For a few more days the thoughts of murder, kicking and fire-raising kept me from the notions of humility and obedience that Father Bernal was exhorting us to in the course of his three times a day homilies. As I was digging out a young clinker from the bottom of the furnace one morning at about five thirty I paused for a moment to sniff the noxious fumes. In the pause, as I leaned on my long poker I heard the dreaded creak of old leather harness muffled by a soutane and I knew that Brother Provincial was standing behind me. I turned and looked into the pitiless grey eyes of the saintly superior. He beckoned me to follow him and he led the way towards my cell. As we went along I heard the bell calling the rest of our brethren to meditation, and I suddenly realized that I would never see any of them again. When we reached the tiny room where I kept my prayer books and toothbrush, the Provincial turned to me and whispered: 'Take off your crucifix and soutane and put on these things I've brought. You are going away from us because of your selfishness.' I caught the whiff of carbolic soap, the true odour of sanctity, and I wondered if perhaps he actually brushed his teeth in it. Carbolic was good at keeping holy men detumescent, but one of its side effects was that it seemed to diminish their humanity. Lying across my bed was a dark-coloured mackintosh and a dark, lumpy, green pullover. My saintly superior looked away as I changed into the clothes of another world. It struck me that these clothes were very shabby. I realized that my trousers were rather ragged and very baggy. None of these things mattered while I was frocked up but now, now I would look a laughing stock. There was no collar to my shirt and my hair was very short in the style of a vineyard labourer. People will know that I'm a runaway labourer from God's vineyard, I thought. I trembled uncontrollably as the creaking and lop-sided figure led me towards the front door of the house. Outside on the gravel drive stood a small green van. Straightaway I realized that it was the same colour as the lumpy pullover I was wearing. The driver got out and stood with his eyes cast down as if he sensed the fear I was going through and couldn't bear to look. Brother Provincial handed me four one-pound notes and whispered: 'Ask God to forgive you and to send us someone else to do His will.' He looked grey in the face and a bit sweaty like an executioner on only his second job. I glanced towards the driver and then back to God's bailiff. He was already back at the doorway. Grey face whispered: 'The driver knows what to do.' I remember that by now I was shaking very badly, and I half held out my hands as though to say, 'I'm sorry,' but old creaky turned his face away from me in disgust and with one last creak for old times' sake he stepped back through the door and closed it quickly.

I turned towards the driver and caught him looking at me as if I were an escaped lunatic. He gestured towards the passenger seat, got into the van and turned the engine over. I got in as he'd signed me to do and said, 'Good morning.' The driver shook his head slightly and made a small movement with his left hand as though he didn't really want me in his van at all but was only taking me as a favour to God. I was so tense I could not even sit back in my seat. I just crouched there, hunched and sitting forward. I wondered how far it was from Market Drayton where we were to Crewe station where the Liverpool train would stop to take me home to my Mam and her sorrow. I no more knew how far Crewe was from Market Drayton than I knew how far Montreal was. In my fear I sank into a trance as though I was on the way to an abattoir. But the journey didn't seem long and I suppose at that time in the morning nobody except treacherous young monks in vans were on the road. At Crewe the silent driver stopped with a sigh of relief and signalled me to get out. I said thank you but he shook his head as if that was forbidden to us. I closed the door of the van and it went away as discreetly as a small hearse. And I was left outside Crewe station, with four pounds and nothing else. I hadn't even brought my face cloth. As I walked to the ticket office the few people about looked at me curiously and when I looked back they looked away quickly as I imagine people look away from newly discharged prisoners. I stood in a small line to buy my ticket and I was aware that the man standing behind me was leaving several feet between himself and me. After I had bought my ticket I went to the tea bar and got myself a cup of tea. I paid the woman and then I realized that my hands were shaking

76

so badly that I didn't dare to pick up the cup. I slid it along the counter for a few feet and when she turned to serve someone else I abandoned my tea and fled the bar and stood among some trolleys and packing cases marked Lime Street, Liverpool. And as I stood there I thought of the distress my mother would feel when I told her that I'd left the Brotherhood and of how my appearance would upset her. And the trembling wouldn't stop.

When I got to Lime Street I felt comforted a bit at the familiar sights of the George's Hall and the Empire Theatre. It was still early in the day so I decided to walk most of the way to West Derby Road where my mother now lived. I caught a reflection of myself in shop windows and dreaded anybody seeing me. I knocked on the door and it opened as if by magic. My mother was just about to leave the house to go to the shops. For a split second she looked at me in a terrible state of shock. And then, seeing my distress and my hopeless clothes, she pulled me inside and loved me. I remember trying to repeat the words of the pitiless Brother Provincial. 'They said I've betrayed God,' I sobbed. My poor mother hung on to me desperately. She must have been appalled by the realization that I had left religion. She kept making those comforting little noises that mothers used to frightened and hurt children: 'Ssh, ssh, there, there, it's going to be all right.' And as I trembled more and went on sobbing she hissed in my ear: 'I don't care what you've done you're going to be all right.' And after several cups of sweet tea she listened to my story and nodded and nodded and carried on loving me.

The news of my return flashed around the family at incredible speed and they reacted the way good kind and poor people always do: they had a whip round for me so that I could get some decent clothes and they promised to pray for me. What more could they do? And with the help of my cousin, Billy O'Boyle I went to the shops and found clothes like everybody else wore and was able to become anonymous. I went and registered for National Service and then left Liverpool for London to await my call up.

Billy O'Boyle saw me off from Lime Street Station on the next stage of escape. I felt as if I was emerging from a nightmare. My mother was disappointed that she would lose the status of Holy Mother that having a son or daughter in religion conferred upon her. But her disappointment could not lessen her affection for me. So I went to London and somehow, to my astonishment, I made out all right. I found a room in Courtfield Gardens, Earls Court, a small room, but dry and compared to the one I had in God's house, it was heaven. The next morning I found a job as a runner for the Agricultural Research Council in Lower Regent Street. All I had to do was to deliver letters and small parcels to various Whitehall departments. In those days there were hundreds of messengers in London and they were mostly a friendly crowd and soon taught me the short cuts to the various government offices.

My sense of freedom was amazing. To be able to run about and talk to people whenever I felt like it astounded me and my enthusiasm for my work amused my fellow runners. To look into shops and see people buying things gave me terrific pleasure. I was too timid to go into restaurants so I lived on sandwiches and cakes from snack bars. Quickly I began to speak an English that people could understand. After nearly six years of prayer, modesty and self-denial, and especially after all that chastity, I was slightly disabled. But my willingness to run about and do what I was asked to do made people warm to me a little. I just could not get enough of people. I think, looking back, I tried too hard, and though people quite liked me, there was something about me that also disgusted them. I found that out when I accidentally heard some of the people in the office talking about me. 'He's quite nice,' I heard a woman say, 'But there's something odd about him, something slightly disgusting.' I still have that effect on quite a lot of people I meet.

And so I ran about delivering my parcels and feeling nourished by the kindness of most people towards me. I lived on Lyons' fruit pies. If I had a pie and a tea in a cafe I was often too shy to ask for another in case someone thought I was being greedy. So I'd cruise about until I found another J. Lyons & Co. and I'd have another fruit pie and another cup of tea. It doesn't sound much now but for me it was quite an adventure. And every morning I got up

My parents' wedding picture, 1932. Dear Uncle Willie is on the left.

Below left: Left to right: Mother, Auntie Louie, Uncle Billy O'Boyle, who wanted to repair clocks, my grandmother Ninny Fleming, my cousin Joan O'Boyle in 1933.

Below right: My father at fourteen as a boy-waiter – all he knew was the Merchant Navy and dockside bars.

Me, aged twenty-two.

A publicity still from *Nicholas and Alexandra*.

As Rosinante in *The Travails of Sancho Panza* at the National Theatre in 1969; Derek Godfrey astride.

As Sir Francis Acton in John Dexter's National Theatre production of *A Woman Killed with Kindness* in 1971: Joan Plowright is dying on the bed supported by the El Greco figure of Anthony Hopkins. My line, which we dreaded, was: 'How do you feel yourself?'

Below left: As the Prince of Morocco in *The Merchant of Venice*. Laurence Olivier supervised my make-up, so naturally I look like Othello. *Below right*: Derek Jacobi working up a temper, or working on his Northern accent, upstage from me in *A Woman Killed with Kindness*.

A still from *The Author of Beltraffio*, adapted from the story by Henry James, directed by Tony Scott. Georgina Hale seated, played the wife.

With Kate Fitzgerald in
Educating Rita by Willy
Russell, Royal Shakespeare
Company, 1985.

*Centre: She Stoops to
Conquer*, as Mr Hardcastle,
with Julia Watson as Kate
in 1984.

With Julie T. Wallace in
*The Life and Loves of a
She-Devil* for BBC TV, 1986.

In Liverpool, on a return visit, 1992.

Auckland, New Zealand, 1997, with my son Piers.

Planting a tree at Dickens's house, Gadshill Place, Kent in 1987. Dr Michael Slater, the great Dickens scholar, stands smiling next to me. His book, *Dickens and Women*, really got me going as a Dickensian.

Off duty from Sherlock Holmes in
Dublin, 1985.

As Sherlock Holmes in
The Mask of Moriarty by
Hugh Leonard, with
Alan Stanford as Watson,
Dublin, 1985.

Inset: As Holmes with
Ingrid Craigie as the
villain, Dublin, 1985.

With my wife, Sue, who encouraged me by laughing a lot.

Above: Among my beloved neighbours in 1986.

Left: Chez nous.

at five thirty and went to Mass at the Brompton Oratory. This salved my conscience a bit and I hoped that God would forgive my betrayal.

There was the problem of what to do after work was over. I was far too nervous to go to the cinema or the theatre. And then the landlord at Courtfield Gardens asked me if I was interested in a little evening job as a barman in a nearby pub called the Bolton Arms. I was taken on straightaway and my enthusiasm aroused great interest. No training was given, you just watched the others and copied them. In a few days I was reasonably competent and my fear of inactivity led me to rush about serving like a mad thing and this endeared me to the barmaids who were benevolently baffled by the pleasure I took in pulling pints. 'If he likes it that much, let him do it then,' a girl called Maureen said.

There was some sort of gaming machine in one of the bars and people were often asking me for change to put into the machine. So if somebody gave me a pound and asked me for the change in sixpences I used to ring up a pound on the till and pass over the change. Immediately the till was out. This went on for several days and there was considerable tension behind the bar as the grey-faced governor scratched his head and looked frantic. His relief when he saw me commit this act of idiocy was palpable.

So I was quite busy and very happy at all this activity. The job at the Research Council started at eight thirty and finished at five thirty. So I had time to go home and get a wash before my shift at the Bolton Arms. I was so full of energy that I thought of getting a little job in my lunch hour as well, but I couldn't find anything suitable. So I began to go into bookshops and sometimes I would strike up a conversation with one of the assistants. In Foyle's I got to know a girl called June Judge. After a few little chats I asked her if she would come and have a sandwich with me some lunchtime. When she said yes I nearly fainted with happiness and promptly fell in love with her. She was a keen amateur singer and her heroine was Kathleen Ferrier. She took me to a concert at the Albert Hall but the crush of people scared me and made me very tense and not good company.

I liked the smell of June so much that I used to stand as close to her as I could. This bothered her a little and she asked me not to stand so near to her. I then stood so far away from her that she was embarrassed because people thought she was alone until I started talking to her from across the room. She tried to teach me to smoke but I didn't like it at all as it got in the way of inhaling the smell of people, especially girls. I bought her a Kathleen Ferrier record, 'Northumbrian Folk Songs', I think, and a box of chocolates as big as a bread tray. Poor June. She must have been so bored with me. I became so obsessed with her that I forgot to gobble God one morning at the Oratory; it was the first time for at least two thousand days. It gave me a great jolt. And then my call-up papers arrived. Destination: Royal Army Medical Corps.

TEN

THE TRAIN FROM WATERLOO was packed with pale-faced young men all trying to be cheerful. We had all heard distorted stories of army life and most of us were dreading it. I tried to strike up some sort of conversation with a chap but he just told me to 'Fuck off'. I kept my head down after this and waited patiently for the train. There was a very amiable sergeant at the platform barrier who urged us all on to the train and smiled a lot. I got into my seat and said to the man next to me, 'Well, if all the sergeants are as agreeable as that one we should all have a jolly time, eh?' He said: 'I thought I just told you to fuck off.' It was the same fellow I'd tried to talk to earlier. I crept away and sat in a corner and practised the cutting phrase.

I have often noticed that in a theatre bar during the interval there will be somebody who very evidently wants to start a conversation with someone, with anyone. And everybody suspects this and avoids the would-be chatterer. It's sometimes the same in a doctor's waiting room where the trier gives you the impression he is doomed. He smells, often quite subtly, of hopelessness. I was a bit like that on the journey to the training camp. Frightened and depressed, I looked at the others. Most of these conscripts were eighteen, I suppose, but they seemed older than I was although I was twenty-one. Tradesmen, professional people and religious people were allowed to defer their stint in the services. They seemed to be resentful at being taken away from home and their mothers. My secret was that I was running from God and looking for the devil. But I couldn't use that as a conversation opener.

On arrival at Aldershot station we were met by three or four more sergeants, all of them very friendly, who herded us on to some waiting lorries. And then as soon as we were aboard the lorries all the sergeants went mad and started to scream at us. Nothing could have prepared us for the brutality of this appalling verbal abuse. They kept screeching at us: 'You're in the army now, you're in the army now.'

On arrival at Boyce Barracks we were rushed to the stores to be kitted out with our new identities. And all the time the dreadful yelling went on from everyone around us. Even people without any obvious stripes of rank seemed to think they should scream at us. Everybody kept shouting, 'Move it, move it.' Once or twice I glanced about to see if there was something I should be moving but this only intensified the fury of the screamers. One of them, his nose suddenly glued to mine and his eyes on stalks shrieked at me: 'Are you taking the piss, soldier? Are you taking the piss?' I tried to lean back and disengage my nose from his but he wouldn't have it. He was a lissom fellow, that sergeant, and the further back I leaned the further forward he leaned until I could feel the sergeant's privates rubbing up against my own shrivelled parts. So I straightened up and surrendered to his nose instead. 'No, sergeant, no,' I cried, 'I will never take the piss.' 'Well don't, just don't, that's all,' screamed Popeye as he recalled his nose and looked about for another victim who might be taking the piss. It was the new expression of my life. Everybody was always asking everybody if he was taking the piss. It is a phrase that has lasted as long as the fashion for denim.

As we were prodded on towards our company office and then to our billets hundreds of other young men gathered about us demanding to know where we came from. 'Anyone from Manchester? Anyone from Catford? Anyone from Barnstable? Anyone from Birmingham?' They were looking to be friendly with fellow townsmen. Contacts were made to the great joy of those concerned as the young men sought out their own. As far as I could see there were no wide-eyed ex-monks looking for company. Nobody shouted out: 'Any old Benedictines? Any old Carthusians?'

There was one powerful-looking young fellow standing slightly apart from the others. He glanced at me and I mistook the glance for interest. Quick as a flash I judged him to be an ex-Trappist and I smiled and called out: 'Dominus Vobiscum', which means 'The Lord be with you'. But he just shrugged and said: 'Get fucked ye great big nancy boy.' So I guessed he was probably an ex-Jesuit and, lowering my head, I plodded on towards my next station of the cross.

I found I was in F company and billeted in hut F 10, the Roman Catholic squad. It was army policy in the first few weeks of training to keep the Catholics on their own. 'No talk of religion or politics' was the rule. Strange that the army thought that young men would talk of anything other than food and girls. We were hungry all the time. All day long we marched and marched. It was quite surprising how quickly we learned to do it. I found myself enjoying it all. I grew to like the complicated movements and I was made right marker for the squad. At first I thought it was because of my skill but it was only because I was the tallest man in the group. All day long the drill corporals called out the time: 'Left, left, left right left'. All day came the accompanying growls: 'Fuck, fuck, fuck fuck fuck'. And when we stopped for a smoke break the only thing that changed was the tempo of the swearing. For a few days it was hell. And then, just like any word that is repeated constantly, it all became just noise – noise noise noise – and soon drained of all meaning. And in the evenings we polished our boots and scrubbed and blancoed our webbing. We learned to fold our blankets the way the army liked them folded, and to look after our possessions for fear of thieves. And we were always hungry.

In the dining halls of the great cookhouses we ate at tables that sat perhaps twenty men. As we stood in the queue for our food all dignity was abandoned in the scramble for a good helping of swill. The cooks with their unassailable power despised us and did things to test our hunger. In the mornings, especially, like shameless gulls we would gather around the huge trays in which a hundred eggs could easily be fried and we would hope for two. What a ceremony the breakfast was. The cook would sometimes be slow in the cracking of the eggs and might ask us, as if we were his equals, 'Do you think the fat is hot enough for frying eggs?' And then he would pretend to hold his hand close to the fat to test the heat. And then, shaking his head as if in dreadful doubt, and making sure by his conviction that we were all watching him attentively, he would spit into the smoking fat. The spit would sizzle and skip across the tray. And glancing at us casually to see if our squeamishness was greater than our hunger he would start cracking the eggs at great speed. The sight of the egg whites frilling in the molten fat, and the yolks misting over and the smell of fried bread erased the memory of the spitting and we all held out our plates for as much as we could get. Sausages like old cartridge cases and mashed potato the colour of abandoned plimsolls could not deaden our lust for something to eat. Once a man next to me found the handle of a radiator in his mashed potato; he said nothing, merely moving it to the side of his plate after sucking the mashed potato off it first. Nobody else said anything either. If the truth was known several of us were probably jealous.

And so the first weeks fled by. And new words arrived as well. Not just the swear words of the barrack room but mysterious words of foreign origin. We had to learn the names of all the bones in the body, all the major arteries and organs, too. Femur, patella, thorax and aorta. They seem a bit tame now but they refreshed me then. Of course the new words couldn't crowd out the old swear words so beloved of the chaps. They simply talked of 'your fucking cerebellum, mate, a bullet in that and Bob's your fucking uncle'.

We were taught how to make beds in the approved army fashion which was a bit like creating a huge starched envelope into which a sick person would not have had the strength to climb. We were shown how to bed-bath people and do it without hurting them or embarrassing them either. It was all a very intense rehearsal for our brief careers in the Royal Army Medical Corps. I remained very enthusiastic and I was quite a quick learner because I was fascinated by it all. Often my keenness grated on the nerves of the others and they were then cruelly sarcastic to me. I was rather eager to have a mate like all the others had – you were nowhere without a mate – but I didn't have the skill.

Once a week we had a kit inspection by the company commander. I was not too good at the laying out of buckles and belts, and it showed. But my desire to get it right and my willingness to learn slightly disarmed the CO. Once as I stood to attention by my bed knowing that my lay-out was not all that good, I saw the CO frown and then glance towards the duty corporal. The corporal made a little gesture as if he was scratching the side of his head which he changed into a tapping of his temple. The CO spotted the reference to a half-wit and his frown became a beaming smile. 'Good lay-out, soldier,' he said, and went on with the inspection. Afterwards the word went about that I was some sort of hypnotist. 'Good lay-out?' they roared incredulously, 'Good lay-out? It's a fucking dog's breakfast.' But there was nothing they could do about the way the CO saw things though they looked at me with more suspicion than usual.

During this training at Boyce Barracks, Aldershot, the Roman Catholic crowd was separated from the rest because we were a bit suspect. By that I mean the army felt we actually believed in something – God, for instance. Not that we were the only ones to believe, but our faith showed and we were likely to be touchy about it. We were marched to church every Sunday and on Holy Days of Obligation, I think. Our corporal was called Pavey, a decent fellow who found church and religious parades mysterious. But he was keen that the regulations were observed and he was full of respect for the Padre. We would be hustled into the chapel in good order and crammed together according to Pavey's idea of respect for the Lord, which is how he talked of God on church parade days. There was a fellow in our squad called Manning who was a 'dog's breakfast' of a soldier according to Pavey, and he was a bit dozey. At penning-in time one Sunday poor old Manning forgot to take his beret off in chapel. The corporal, in his fervour to get us all huddled in, hugger-mugger, didn't notice until he was leaving the chapel to go and have a smoke with the other little corporals outside. In an instant fury, he strode up to the end of the row where Manning was dozing, leaned in and, with the driven whisper of the actor, hissed very audibly, 'Oi! You! Take your hat off in the house of the Lord, cunt!' Which Manning did as meekly as Stan Laurel, not seeming to notice Pavey's lack of affection.

In those days I still thought I believed in God and these outbursts of rage filled me with terror. I couldn't understand how the NCOs could be reasonable one moment and demented with rage the next. I wasn't quick to spot the wonderful theatricality of army life.

After the basic training was over came the postings. Everybody wanted to go overseas and see the world a bit. There was the bait of overseas rates of pay but, more than that, there was the desire for excitement. We had been shown a terrifying film of what VD did for you if you dipped your wick in the wrong place. There were rules about prophylactics, another new word for us. After pollution, prophylactics, or your nob fell off. It all boiled down to washing your tackle in carbolic soap when you signed in after sin. Even if you hadn't parked your prong it was wise to cleanse the gear if only to save face. I never saw an audience so utterly attentive as during those films. Later, when I played Macbeth, I tried to recall the sensation of horror I felt at the rotting-nob shots in the scene where he sees Banquo's ghost but it only sparked off roars of laughter in the audience. Sometimes I suspected that Sheila Allan, who played Lady Macbeth, had a hard time keeping a straight face.

The National Servicemen who were shipped back to Boyce Barracks to be demobbed treated us with the contempt that old soldiers reserve for 'sprogs'*. They told us terrible stories of men who had gone mad or missing in Singapore and Benghazi. And the reason was always sex. Stories of how young men got up in the night for a pee and discovered that their dicks had disappeared. And how they had screamed and screamed and then rushed back to town to find

* A sprog is a term to describe young inexperienced soldiers. It is a term of contempt and dreaded by the sprogs.

the brothel where they thought they might find their best part and never did. It was the style of old soldiers to tell terrifying stories to the young ones. They laid it on as thick as they thought it would stick. And there were tales of other lads who thought they would be safe as 'rimmers'* but whose noses fell off. These poor sods who were supposed to have lost their noses were said to be stored in some section in Netley hospital, the army nut house, where they were issued with masks so as not to frighten the nurses. But these stories didn't seem to frighten most of the Catholics I knew. How could they scare them? They had heard wilder stories than of noses falling off: of devils in pigs and eternal fires. They were not afraid of God or the devil. They would chance their noses as they would chance their arm. They chatted and laughed rather nervously but defiantly, too. I was still very quiet and the company of dirty-talking cunt-struck papists aroused powerful feelings in me. The hell of it drew me as heaven once had but I was too afraid to join in.

And so at the interviews with the company sergeant-major, who had heard about my bent for God, it was decided that I should become the curator of the camp museum. This was quite a small building near the guardhouse and contained all sorts of nostalgia from the old days. The Medical Corps was very proud of the number of VCs it had won and one of these was on show. There were also souvenirs from old wars, like samples of long-forgotten brands of cigarettes and blood-stained field bandages from former campaigns. All this stuff was in glass cases and the heavy-duty linoleum was highly polished and this reminded me of church. There were no chairs and no books either; and, unfortunately for me, there were no visitors. I might as well have been a lighthouse keeper. The hours were from 9.30 a.m. till 8 p.m. with two hours off in the afternoon.

The keys of this museum were kept in the guardhouse and had to be signed in and out by the curator once a day. The Regimental

---

* Rimmers were fellows or girls who thought that all problems could be avoided if they stuck to oral sex.

Police who held the keys and supervised discipline around the entrance to the camp were notoriously keen.

The word keen in the army had a deeply pejorative meaning in the 1950s, especially when applied to regimental policemen. They had a wonderful job; all they had to do was look us over at every minute of the day and if they didn't like what they saw then they were authorized to give us hell. They were the sort of men who were so keen that they never sat down on duty in case they spoiled the creases in their trousers. They were a picture of lunatic smartness. As for posture, the word clockwork comes to mind. They used so much starch when they ironed their trousers that even their fly buttons were inaccessible. This meant that bladders pleading to be emptied and bowels squeaking for release were ruthlessly snubbed. This refusal to recognize the legitimate demands of nature led to them feeling very uncomfortable. And the pain led the policemen to feel very angry. And this meant that any innocent young soldier coming into the guardroom was likely to be shredded by furious Redcaps who were bursting for a piss. Their movements were very jerky. The policemen's movements, I mean.

The whole aim of the average regimental policeman was to instil terror into any passing soldier by his fiercesome aspect. He would give the impression he had an iron railing up his arse and that it was giving him gip. His cap – no beret for him, far too friendly – was pulled over his eyes so that he had to look up to the sky to see whom he was talking to. They also had a vile habit of standing very close to you, nose to nose, and asking daft questions, 'What are you doing in Singapore, soldier?'

To which you might say: 'But I'm not in Singapore, Corporal.'

To which he would say, 'Oh, we've got a right one here, I can see. Good at geography, are we? Got a keen sense of direction, have we?'

I'd say: 'No, Corporal, I've got no sense of direction at all.'

'Then how do you know you're not in Singapore, then?'

'I don't know whether I'm in Singapore or not, Corporal.'

'But you just told me that you weren't in Singapore,' would snarl the red-capped Jesuit, tilting his head and slyly smirking at his victim. 'What do you know, soldier?'

'Nothing, Corporal.'

And so it would go on till he was bored or spotted another victim over my shoulder. He would nod and I'd be able to enter the guardhouse to ask for the key to the museum that nobody came to. As I went in, I saw at a glance and with a gaping anus that there were five Redcaps standing about the place. For the merest split second there was quiet as they saw me. And then they all started to scream at me at once:

'Come here.' 'Get out.' 'Mark time.' 'About turn.' 'Where's your brown paybook?' And then all together, 'Get out, get out, you horrible man.' And another one, 'Come here, come here.'

With my highly developed longing to be a martyr I tried to obey all these orders as they came at me. This was what they wanted and their pleasure grew as I pirouetted, came forward, went backwards and about turned, all at the same time. Even when they called me back, I realized they were enjoying it and I tried to anticipate their orders; like a frantic, crazed dervish, I spun and retreated, fumbling in my pocket at the same time to produce my brown paybook. They were appalled at the intensity of my co-operation. As perfectly common sadists and gobshites they found my performance just too much to bear. 'Stand still,' they screamed, 'stand still.' But I couldn't stand still. I whirled and hopped and grappled with my top-left pocket which gave them the idea I might be on the verge of an infarction. Swiftly they seized me and shook me out of my ecstasy. 'What d'you want?' came the coarse voices from far away. I looked at my tormentors and seeing concern in their faces, I piled on the agony. 'I'm so sorry, Sergeant,' I muttered to the corporal, who seemed pleased at his sudden promotion from me. 'It must be nerves, did I disturb you?' And it worked. Instead of kicking me all the way back to the billet, they calmed down, gave me the key and said: 'Off you go soldier. Off you go soldier!' It was positively affectionate. So off I went.

*　　　*　　　*

As National Servicemen our pay was four shillings a day. So that if a lad fancied a few pints and a packet of cigarettes and maybe egg and chips in the NAAFI he would find it hard to manage on twenty-eight shillings a week. As I didn't smoke or drink at that time I was able to supplement the army rations with chocolate or chips. Most evenings we lay on our beds and listened to Radio Luxembourg. The freedom to chat was still a novelty for me. I just could not get enough of it. Of course, after all the silence of the previous six years I was not good at chat between chaps. After all I was out of practice. I couldn't time things properly at first and often jumped in when it wasn't my turn. And then when it was my turn I missed it. Some of the men in the billet found it quite funny. One fellow asked me if English was my first language. I suppose I was a bit like a young Harry Worth.

The talk was often of girls and reduced me to paralysed silence. The others knew that 'girl talk' made me uneasy and they never missed an opportunity to try and embarrass me.

'What? Never seen a fanny then, Baker?' they would ask. And the sight of my terror would make them chortle with malicious joy. If the truth were known there were others there who hadn't seen a fanny either but they knew the chat, and like people who can't read they were often very clever at concealing their ignorance. A fellow called Wagstaff always got a big laugh with his knowing description of the mysterious fanny as: 'Like a cat with its throat cut.'

Sometimes, before the lights were put out, the lonely young soldiers would sit around in small groups on somebody's bed and chat quietly. The Christians would gather on a bed near the door and witness to each other as Christians always seem to do. And the Fantasy Shaggers would sit somewhere else and spin their tales of girls they hadn't had. I never quite knew which group was which as I was too nervous to join in. I remember seeing a small group of three or four chaps sitting on somebody's bed who all seemed to be kissing each others hands. And then by straining my ears it dawned on me that they were the lads who had been out with some of the local girls that evening and were now exchanging sacred smells. A small brotherhood of treacherous gropers had returned to the billet carrying the gorgeous smell of willing fanny on their fingers to share with their pals. Their outrageous reactions to each other's smells sometimes had the entire billet in uproar especially if the Christians showed that they were upset. Once I was held down while several grotto-gropers covered my nose and mouth with their fish fingers.

It was deeply humiliating at first but I soon began to learn how to play my part in this hideous cabaret and even to get some laughs on my own account. And when things became quiet and the lights were out we would lie there in the darkness and the talk would turn from fanny to food. There was a man called Wainwright who could describe the smell of fresh scones that his Auntie Jean made on Sunday afternoons. He would do this in such detail that we would lie there completely spellbound. The silence would be absolute as he described the sultanas in the thin, hot pastry and the butter running on to the side of the plate as he spooned on the blackcurrant jam. 'With mugs of fresh tea, of course, and two sugars.' There would be a pause, a long pause while we all savoured the picture of those Sunday teas at Wainwright's Auntie Jean's. We would lie there salivating and wishing we, too, had an Auntie who could perform the miracle that Wainwright was describing. And after a silence of perhaps two minutes some greedy bugger would say thickly: 'Tell us again, Wainwright.' And the rest of us would moan in agreement. And Wainwright would pretend to be asleep. And just as we accepted that it was all over, he would start the tale again and renew our pleasure.

The only regular visitor to the museum where I was imprisoned for most of the time was an elderly major-general. He was a nice old boy who was always asking me if I was happy in his museum. It wasn't really his but he thought of it as his own property. I always said I was very happy there but the old boy had reported that I was talking to myself whenever he went in. It was, in fact, the worst place I could possibly have found. It was too like the religious house that I had escaped from with the help of Fr. Bernal. The only advantage was that I was able to read a great deal. I had got through all the plays of G. B. Shaw and that kept me amused for a while. But I was restless and uneasy and the old general suspected it and must have spoken to the company office about me. One day I was called in and told I was to be posted to British Army Headquarters in Northag, Germany. I was to be a hospital orderly there. This was a lucky break for me as I didn't have all that long to do before my demob. So off I went.

Suddenly I was working in a very busy military hospital called BMH Hostert among thousands of people. For a while I loved it all. I began to get on much better with people and my timing improved in casual conversation. I found I could sometimes get good laughs, too. My basic training had to be put into practice. I really did make beds and bathed real patients.

Perhaps I had a gentle touch or perhaps they thought I was sycophantic but I was soon moved to the officer's ward in the rather more luxurious part of the hospital. Here I was used as an occupational therapist as well as a bed-bather.

A very senior officer asked me to read to him in the afternoons. He liked it so much that the word spread around the section and while the rest of the orderlies were scrubbing and polishing I was often reading to the top brass. It was a doddle really and the books were sometimes quite interesting. The wife of a brigadier became a bit jealous of me after her husband said I was a better reader than she was. She smiled at me, arsenically.

All the officers were in private rooms which meant that we were very busy most of the time. This was because they had no idea how busy any one of us was. I suppose they thought they were doing us a favour by pressing the bell; orderlies were there to answer the bells and do what they asked us to do. I found most of the officers to be very nice. It would not have been a good idea to get difficult with the private who oiled your piles or polished your nuts and they knew it. But there were a few exceptions. One of these reckless old buffers was called Egerton, Major Egerton, the Joey Blagstock* of

* The bull-shitting major in *Dombey & Son*.

92

the officers' ward. He had a highly developed sense of bad timing. He was a heart case as well as a head case and, curiously, for a chap with the MC, he was very nervous of dying. One of my colleagues had told me about Egerton's fear of dying during NAAFI break. We always betrayed confidences during the break which was one of the reasons we hated missing the mid-morning treachery session. Armed with this bit of secret knowledge I decided to crank up the tension in room 101.

'Would you say you were nervous of dying, sir?' I asked him one morning as I was tidying up his room. He looked at me with a slight expression of anxiety in his little milky-blue eyes. He had been told by his consultant not to exert himself for fear of provoking a heart attack and he had taken the advice very seriously – to the point that he even blinked carefully.

He said, 'Why do you ask, Baker, do you know something that I don't?'

'Oh no, sir, it's just that as I was doing up my shoelaces this morning I thought about what happened to you yesterday week when you were doing up your shoelaces, sir.'

'Why, what did happen to me yesterday week while I was doing up my shoelaces, Baker?'

I looked at him with the innocence of the born torturer. 'Well, I suppose you suffered a big attack, sir. Heart attack, that is, sir.' Egerton's face went pink and then it went burgundy. In an effort to stop changing colour which he suspected might bring on another skirmish with death he began to growl softly. Then there was a silence as I carried on making the room ready for the Recording Angel. I stooped behind a chair in case the pleasure I was feeling leaked out of my eyes. The static in the room was palpable.

'Would you say you were a tactful sort of fellow, Baker?' whispered old blue eyes, sarcastically.

'Oh yes, sir,' I answered, pretending he'd used the wrong word. 'You have to be tactile in my job. I mean where would I be if I didn't like touching people? Yes, sir, I'd say I was very tactile.' I peered around the side of his armchair to see his reaction. His face was the colour of very well-hung steak, nearly matt burgundy. Just then Sister McHale came in, a very tall woman with immense bosoms and a tiny bottom, as though she had been built the wrong way round or, perhaps, had never been hugged as a child. She was the nursing officer in charge of the officers' ward that shift.

'Everything all right, Major?' she asked with the rising inflection that means, please say yes or I'll be bored.

'Everything's perfect, thank you, sister,' said Egerton MC, with very heavy irony. I pretended I hadn't picked it up and gurgled like a fan which only added to his fury.

'Private Baker not making you laugh too much, I hope,' burbled Tits McHale. 'He's something of a jester, you know, according to Captain Aitkin next door, aren't you, Baker?' she said and laughed very loudly. A tooth mug rattled above the wash basin about fifteen feet away. Major Egerton stirred in his bed and seemed to be checking his pulse as if he suspected he'd already died and landed in a Jean Paul Sartre play.

He said, 'No, sister, Private Baker isn't making me laugh too much.' And lobbing in the heavy sarcasm again, 'He's not making me laugh at all,' he added, with one eye on me and the other on Tits McHale.

'Good, good,' whooped Tits, missing everything. 'Then he can come and give me a hand with Lieutenant Finn's enema. He's been here nine days and hasn't gone yet and the doctor insists he goes before he leaves.' And she swept out with such turbulence that I was sucked out after her.

From then on old Egerton had it in for me. He knew that the morning tea break was from ten until ten thirty; and he knew very well that I was usually on duty along his section of corridor. So every day at exactly nine fifty-nine and a few seconds he would ring for a bed pan. It was a fairly trivial inconvenience really but, as I explained, it meant missing the early morning gossip and malice which nourished us for the rest of the shift. The gossip in a hospital is much more interesting than in a theatre green room. People in green rooms and television studios may bitch a bit but in hospitals people die every day and the reports of this process can be astonishing, giving a marvellous edge to thirty-minute theatre or tea break as it was known officially. To be fifteen minutes late was to be out of it. And I didn't like to be out of things. But old Egerton's bowels seemed as if they might keep me out of the NAAFI for the rest of his life or the rest of my service, whichever was the longer. I didn't want to be deprived of my daily ration of detraction and I became rather irrational about it to the great pleasure of my fellow pan handlers. So there I was every morning all ready for calumny when the buzzer of postponement would go.

When an officer called for a bed pan there was a special procedure. On each corridor on our wing there was a sluice. This was a small room where unsterile instruments like bed pans were kept and things disposed of. As a courtesy towards Her Majesty's Commission we not only saluted officers, we also warmed their bed pans. Isn't that a nice touch? The warming process took about ten seconds under the powerful jet of hot water in the sluice. The bed pans were made of chrome and were very pretty, like giant's slippers in a panto. You would place the pan in the sluice shelf and when it was warm you would pick it up with a lovely thick and well-ironed napkin, shake the pan, and go sailing into your patient's room as if you were bringing him a takeaway from Fortnum & Mason. As you arrived at the side of your man's bed he would smile with joy and, licking his lips in anticipation, he would put his arm around your neck, which he used as a lever, and raise himself up as, with exquisite tact, you slipped his pan under him and lowered his buttocks into place on his warm pan. Then you disappeared leaving the patient to his pleasure. Quite often when you came back to mop up, so to speak, the stool pigeon would ask to see his jobby and sometimes would cry out with pride at the sight of his depth charge. If it was heroic, I'd often shake hands with the young stoolies and congratulate them. 'Well done, sir,' I'd say to some young signaller, 'a fine specimen.' And the young fellow might sob with happiness and say, 'Do you mean that, Baker? Is it really a goodie?' And I would reply, 'Sir, in my job I see a great deal of movement and this is easily par

95

for the course.' And then we'd shake hands. I didn't always mean it but it cheered up the patient and gave him something to write home about. And that's important in a hospital. Generally it was a pleasure to perform. But Major Egerton was a different kettle of fish altogether.

I grew to resent deeply his daily call. He impinged on me. His heavy sarcasm and petulance suffocated my feelings of sympathy. He diminished my humanity. But he was ill and knew he should not risk too much movement even when he was at stool. He was even forbidden to shave himself. So fed up was I one particular morning that I started to prepare Eggy's pan about five minutes to the hour. I turned on the hot tap and sulked for several minutes as tea break was called and the others went off to the NAAFI. As usual, as the clock started to strike, so Egerton's buzzer squawked. All prepared but with no love at all, I icily picked up the hot pan with a fresh napkin and went into Eggy's room to do the business. He sighed heavily as I entered. I stood next to him in silence and with another sigh he put his arm round my neck and I raised him up, hitched his night shirt, slid the pan into place and lowered his pink buttocks on to the scalding hot chromium-plated bed pan. What a fuss. Egerton roared in agony and jack-knifed to avoid the hot pot. He did a triple salchow and then remembered that the slightest exertion might kill him. As he was convinced that I wanted to kill him his blood pressure rose like a Harrier jump jet and instantly reached bursting point.

'Stay calm, sir,' I cried. 'Don't excite yourself, it could mean death.' He took me at my word and instantly fell inert. I didn't know whether he was obeying me or had died. He fell away from me on to his left side and I noticed with relief that there were no burn marks on his arse. By now, of course, the pan was cold, dead cold. It went through my mind that with a bit of deep concern and a tear or two I might be able to persuade the cantankerous old bugger that he had imagined the whole incident. But it was not to be. Gradually the seizure passed and his fear was replaced by the cold need for revenge. I ran to the other side of the bed and crouched close to his mouth in case he had a last wish or some piece of advice for me. He was whispering something.

'What is it, sir?' I urged. 'Is there anything I can do?'

His little eyes opened and he looked at me without affection.

'Baker,' he whispered, 'I'm going to have you charged with the attempted murder of a senior officer.'

'Oh no, sir,' I said, 'No, sir, there's been a misunderstanding, sir. Trying to help you towards a nice warm bowel movement, sir, I inadvertently overheated the pan.'

Egerton closed his eyes and, for one wonderful moment, remembering that there were no arse scars I thought he'd died. But no.

'Get me the ward sister,' he hissed at me. 'Get me the ward sister and call reception for the duty officer. Tell them it's urgent, very urgent, and tell them that you're a murderer.'

'Yes, sir,' I said as I went to the door with the now-cold murder weapon in my hand. And in the hope that I could roll back time I said, 'Would you like a cup of tea, sir?' The ungrateful bugger didn't answer me. As I went towards the sister's office, pan in hand and brain in tumult I saw her coming towards me in company with Captain Abraham Goss, the senior physician. He knew me well and always asked for me when broken-hearted old majors were brought in for their cardiogram tests. He saw that I looked miserable and assumed that I had an empty pan and that was why I looked depressed. He knew I had a tendency to blame myself for the costiveness of others.

'No movement from Major Egerton?' enquired the Captain.

'No, sir,' I replied. 'I'm afraid the bed pan was too hot for the Major and he's very angry, sir, very agitated, sir.' I followed the doctor and the sister to the door of Egerton's room.

As they paused at the door I said, 'He thinks I tried to kill him, sir.'

To my astonishment they both laughed as they went in. I crossed the corridor to garage the Major's pan and wait. My own heart felt close to infarction as I loitered near the sluice expecting to see a grim sister emerge at any moment. But nothing. After several minutes I nipped to the kitchen to prepare tea and biscuits for the Captain and the sister. He loved his Garibaldis did Captain Goss and I was relieved to find the barrel nearly full of them. I set up the tray and covered it with a napkin – Goss was fussy about things like that and simply hated dusty biscuits. Then I returned to my loitering outside the sluice. Still no sign of Goss or sister. I crept nearer to the Major's door and was amazed to hear the sound of laughter from within. It sounded slightly maniacal but it was laughter and it nourished me a bit, and my vision of being locked up in the army nut house at Netley faded a little. After a few more minutes the door opened and a very cheerful Captain Goss came out, followed by a cheerful pink sister. Goss winked at me. I loved him instantly. I still do.

'How is the Major, sir?' I asked with deep, deep concern.

Goss replied: 'Well, as I've just told him that he's going to be all right he's very cheerful, Baker.' I clapped my hands together like a happy old nun. Goss laughed.

'I'll fetch your Garibaldis, sir,' I said. 'I've done your tray the way you like it, sir,' Goss smiled and I left him to flirt with the sister while I returned to Egerton's room to congratulate him. I glided in as if on Nivea cream and materialized as if by magic at his bedside.

'Captain Goss has just told me the good news, sir,' I said. 'I'm so glad you're going to be all right.' I must have sounded sincere or perhaps the relief of the good news had wiped Egerton's memory clean.

'Thank you, Baker,' said the strawberry-faced old boy, 'thank you very much, you're very kind.' And I never heard anything more of his threat to have me charged with attempted murder. Another amazing side effect of the good news was that the old boy's bowels changed their opening time. But my work on the wards was cut short when the matron, a lath of a woman, sent for me and said that she had recommended me for other duties.

I reported to the company officer and was told that I was to take over looking after the Commanding Officer's pigs. This promotion from people to pigs filled me with foreboding. What did I know about pigs? What did the duties involve? Not much, I found out. I had to feed them twice a day and close them down each night at seven o'clock. This meant that I had plenty of time for the hospital Christmas celebration and Hop. This was the big theatrical event of the year. It would also be my last chance to perform as I was about to be demobbed not long after.

I was cast to play the part of the Padre and that of the Matron. The doctor in charge of the whole operation was called Creakle, I remember. Or was it Jekyll? Anyhow he thought it would be a good idea if we all tried to write our own material. As the Padre I wrote up a piece about the incarnation and delivered it as a sermon to a bunch of squaddies. At the first rehearsal, I plunged in with my carefully written bit.

'I've heard what some of you chappies think about how it all came about. There was Mary, a little spanking new virgin doing her petit point one night and thinking happily about Joseph and his joints – girls took a bigger interest in their boyfriend's work in those days – when, all of a sudden, there was a fluttering of wings and . . . Good Lord! Standing there in front of her was an angel. Yes, an angel. Actually his name was Gabriel and for your information he was an Archangel. Naturally Mary was terrified. Who wouldn't be? And she dived into a cupboard which stood wide open just behind her and slammed the door closed and cowered in the corner under a pile of Joseph's spare smocks. But God will not be mocked. The angel hammered at the cupboard door and called out: "Fear not, Mary." Fear not! The poor girl was scared out of her skin. She was even more surprised when old Gabriel called out: "You're going to have a babby, Mary. God's babby."'

It was then that Creakle interrupted me.

'Okay, Baker that'll go down a treat I can see.'

I didn't spot the irony and I felt deeply hurt when he told me I was sacked. 'But it gets quite funny a bit further on, sir,' I told him. No go, I was cut.

The part of Matron was quite small and there were no lines, just a lot of eye rolling and fierce pointing at beds and bandages.

My awfulness was just slightly less apparent. But in the unit there was a fellow called Killen who had done some theatre work as a stand-up comic. He talked to me afterwards and said he thought I had something as a performer. I was very grateful. 'Don't get me wrong,' he said, 'you're terrible at the moment, absolutely bloody terrible, but there's something about you that might make it work if you can find anyone to give you a chance.'

After the army I came back to Liverpool convinced that I could be an actor. But how? I found out the names of various London drama schools and wrote away for details of how to get in and learn to be a star. Back came the replies double quick. Would I like to fill in the forms and wait for an invitation to do an audition? I thought I'd try a place called the Rose Bruford College, Lamorbey Park, Sidcup, Kent. When I went down to see them I was astounded at the sight of beautiful girls sitting on the grass at the lakeside, feeding the swans and learning sonnets. There and then I decided I would like to be there too. The audition took place in a beautiful library. There were about five elderly ladies sitting behind a long table and smiling; it was a frosty day and there was a distinct nip of Karvol in the air. In those days older ladies often splashed on the decongestants. Two of the ladies, a Miss Scorer and, I think, a Miss Scott were also sucking Fisherman's Friends; and with the radiators going at full blast the vapours of the cinnamon and pine oils were released into the atmosphere of the library with such intensity that they caught at my throat and brought tears to my eyes as I recited 'Dover Beach'. By the time I reached the line about 'The long melancholy withdrawing roar', I was sobbing for lack of pure oxygen. The five ladies were deeply moved by my emotional power and so on the strength, the overpowering strength, of Karvol decongestant, I was accepted into the Rose Bruford College of Speech and Drama where I met Laurie Taylor and shared his jockstrap.

Over the next few years this sharing process bonded us closely; in the winter it's very comforting to have a warm jockstrap, and as Laurie's class always preceded mine my balls were cosy for nearly two years. We both found drama school ideas quaint. In mime and modern dance sessions we were always divided into two groups, Good and Evil. I was driven into terrible tantrums in the Evil group because we were never allowed to win. I was never allowed to be in the Good group either which meant that I was always on the losing side. If it hadn't been for the comfort of Laurie Taylor's hot jockstrap I think I might have despaired.

Again, the rules of this little institution seemed crazy. On the first day Miss Bruford, with perfect seriousness, stressed the value of obedience to superiors and then ordered us to run about outside for three minutes screaming the while like banshees. Naturally, while I ran about with the screamers I remained silent. When the whistle went and we all trooped inside Miss Bruford asked us questions. Nobody had any voice left to answer the queries of our Principal, who then smiled sweetly and said, 'Now you know what not to do when you're on stage.'

All the tutors, without exception, talked about the dead all the time: dead actors, dead writers and dead teachers. We were always being told how Gerald du Maurier played scenes. We were always being told about upstage knees and how Stanislavski was the oracle of actors. Articulation exercises, deep-breathing exercises and 'raise your diaphragm, dears, and clench your buttocks' were the slogans that swamped us every moment of every day. But the secret of everything at this little seminary of Dramatic Art was unquestioned belief that freedom of movement led to freedom of speech. When I mentioned that if it were so then the best speakers would be the dancers I was shouted down. 'Oh, don't try to be smart, Tom, just do as you're told or you'll never be a star, dear.'

And so for the next three years we went about with raised diaphragms and clenched buttocks. This may explain why the actors who were trained in the early 1950s walked so peculiarly. Lots of them were tempted by ambitious young policemen when they went down into the public loos. I found it very difficult to put up with and very tiring, too. It is exhausting walking about for twelve hours with clenched buttocks. To endure this discomfort most people took to clenching their teeth as well as their buttocks and this triple tension played havoc with their articulation.

In the spring of the second year, Laurie Taylor and I went to a meeting in the Black Horse pub nearby. There were just the two of us so there was no disorder. We decided that as the course was not consuming all our energies we could, perhaps, do something else as well. We could open a little business, Laurie suggested. But what? We didn't have very much money between us, about twenty pounds. At the most. We adjourned the meeting and went to the Station Hotel for a drink. After a few pints Laurie remembered that he'd seen an ad in some magazine or other for cheap peanuts. Naturally we were familiar with the sight of roasted chestnut peddlers near Cambridge Circus and Villiers Street. 'Got it,' hissed Laurie in a driven whisper, 'got it.' He had to pause for a few moments as several people passed our table. He didn't want his idea to be hijacked. 'Got what?' I asked, out of the corner of my mouth. 'Got what? Got what?' echoed Laurie, 'got our future that's what I've got, cock, our whole bloody future.' Naturally, I stayed quiet but showed intense interest. 'Tell me,' I implored. And he did.

'Hot roasted peanuts,' he said, urgently and with great discretion. And he added, 'In bags, sold at the side of the road or delivered to your own home, to your own very fireside.'

I whistled softly at the brilliance of the idea. It was so simple, so beautiful, so pure. 'Yes,' I murmured, 'yes, it's a marvellous idea.' Laurie smiled enigmatically as if that wasn't the end of his invention. It wasn't.

'And,' he continued, 'and I've got a name for the company.' Company? That made me jump. Company?

'Steady, steady,' I warned, 'not too fast'. With an angular gesture he dismissed my caution.

'And the name of the company will be . . .' and here he looked about in case we should be surrounded by industrial spies. Seeing none, he lay back and said triumphantly, 'Fireside Foods Ltd'. The name hit me with great force. Of course! How could we fail? Fireside

Foods, Fireside Foods, Fireside Foods and each time I said it Laurie nodded with delight.

And so was born our first enterprise which would keep us distracted as we waited for stardom. It wasn't an easy birth. We had to get a handcart that would also carry the brazier that would heat the nuts that would sell like hot cakes. And we found all the necessary stuff, firewood and anthracite coal so that we wouldn't have to haul great sacks of coke or any other type of fuel about with us on our travels all over south-east London; for by now we were passed the vision stage and were hallucinating on our new ambition.

We started trading on May Day 1957. It was quiet to begin with that morning at seven thirty. And it was quite warm, too. By nine o'clock the temperature was pretty high and still not a customer in sight. As it got hotter it went through my mind that ice cream might have been a better product for us. I kept this thought to myself. And then I realized that if we did go into ice cream because of this sudden act of God, we would also have to change the name of the company. You can't call yourself Fireside Foods and then sell ice cream. By eleven o'clock we were parched with thirst and hadn't sold a nut. The nuts themselves were hopping in the heat and splitting open. Fortunately there was a pub nearby called the Woodman. We were so dehydrated and hot we began to hear strange noises. It was when we both saw an oasis and a line of camels that we realized that we had to get our throats wet or die. The noise we had heard was the sound of the bolts being drawn on the doors of the Woodman. Dousing down the anthracite we dragged ourselves to the pub and ordered pints.

As the sun blazed down without pity that day we realized that it was too hot to go out in it, indeed it would have been reckless. So we sheltered in the pub. From where we were sitting we could hear our nuts cracking and we could see them jumping in protest off our hot plate and down to the relative coolness of the pavement below.

Deep down I think we both knew that we were seeing the beginning of the end of Fireside Foods Ltd. The death of our beautiful idea. It was deeply distressing I remember as we both sat there in contemplation of our pints.

That Christmas at Laurie's house in Liverpool several of his friends were staying with him. Among this little group was a girl who was a couple of years behind us in the seminary. Her name was Anna Wheatcroft.

ELEVEN

BEING POOR IS a little like having an earache over a Bank Holiday. All you can think about is the pain and how long it will be before a healing hand can be found to take away the anguish. So it is with poverty. You lie in bed and the refrain throbs on: 'I'm poor. Oh God, I'm poor.' If you wake up in the night for a pee – and the poor always do – the refrain knocks on again: 'I'm poor. How long, oh Lord, am I going to be poor for?' And you go back to sleep, exhausted by thoughts of poverty and the bloody alarm goes off and the chorus is picked up. It's morning time again. 'Another day and I'm still poor.' Even in the evening it's mourning time. I have no doubt that poverty spoils everything. It impinges on the imagination, spontaneity vanishes. All you can think about is the condition of being poor. Poverty can curdle the libido and corrode civilized thoughts. One's sense of humour vanishes, to be replaced by a curry-spoiling sarcasm as one's Mr Hyde emerges from the swamp of the subconscious. And you go to church and pray for a touch on the National Lottery. It has to be St Jude, of course, the patron saint of hopeless cases. 'Hey Jude, don't let me down.' And suddenly, the local priest, an oblate of Mary Immaculate intones a Beatitude: 'Blessed are the poor . . . .' And you think, 'Oh, bollocks to the poor.' But follow this with a stifled apology: 'Sorry, Jesus, but it's not on.' There's the paradox: it's the poor who provide the colossal jackpot. Oh, I see, that's why they say, 'Blessed are the poor.' But it's not true. It should read: 'Cursed are the poor.' The poor don't really like that ticket. They are desperate to get away and join the rich, and have glossy hair, bright eyes and white teeth. The rich live longer and can afford to be charming. Do you remember that daft saying: 'Civility costs nothing.' What? It's almost impossible to be charming and polite when you're skint for, above all, there's nothing like a few bob for raising your spirits. And your dick. All of a sudden, he'll change from being a shrivelled and abandoned chicken liver into a lovely, bright, shining pulsing skittle, his one eye blinking with the milky tears of anticipation.

So having elbowed the Lord and his spin doctor St Jude, I married a girl called Anna Wheatcroft. She was very pretty and had shiny hair and white teeth and wonderful, soft honey-coloured skin. I so admired that skin. When I think back I realize that I just wanted to be near her skin. She was a nice girl, too, but above all she had that ring of confidence that comes from possessing a few bob. I was never at ease with poor girls. Most of the time I couldn't even perform for them; they made me feel insecure; that is their poverty made me feel insecure. Yes, I had always found it hard to be hard for the poor ones. No one is willing for a shilling, as they say, but with a pound you're on safe ground*.

I have always been afraid of being poor. Of course, I am looking at it from the point of view of a man who has been professionally poor, and professionally chaste as well. And what with the obedience, I hadn't liked it at all. But that was because I was weak. After I jacked in the chastity and the obedience, I discovered that my will (poor blind faculty that he was) wouldn't move in any direction at all except towards self-loathing and destruction. There's always a catch, isn't there? And so I got married to a nice girl from a family with a few bob and my poverty made me despair because what the Wheatcrofts felt towards me was what I felt towards the poor. They found that I made them uneasy. They found me disgusting. They would really have preferred that I hadn't come into their lives at all. And so I was unhappy and resentful. I was poor and I couldn't do much about it. Most of the poor feel like this according to the ones I've asked.

I found out that to be near one Wheatcroft could create a

* Paraphrase of Asdak in the *Caucasian Chalk Circle* by Bertolt Brecht.

saddening feeling, but to be near a coven of them was to embrace utter despair. Skint, jobless and the wife pregnant, I got a job in a pottery, John Sadler and Sons, Burslem, Stoke-on-Trent. Entirely thanks to the wife's family we had a flat near the factory. I felt marvellously inadequate and I was. The boss at the factory was Mr John Sadler himself, the wife's uncle. He was kind to me and I worked like a maniac to prove something. So did he, though I couldn't see what it was that he had to prove. Maybe he just wanted to get away from his wife. In the factory he couldn't wait for the automatic conveyor belts to reach him. He used to rush ahead and go faster than the machine. Some people thought he was trying to kill himself. They were right and he did. His heart went odd and wouldn't do the business. No Magdi Yacoub then*. Still, I suppose it kept him out of the house, and that's something.

For a while he was impressed by my capacity for work. He liked us to get on our hands and knees and crawl down the long ovens and pull through the trucks of hot pots a bit faster than the machine wanted. Grappling irons were supplied. It was so hot in there, you couldn't stand or breathe deeply and sometimes my gloves would burst into flames. But it passed the time and kept me from thinking too much. At last I was in hell. And it got me out of the house and I loved it. The other workers knew I was married into the family; they probably guessed as much when they saw Mr John and me going down the ovens on our hands and knees. And they watched my frenzy with the good-humoured contempt that it deserved. The thought that this torture might go on forever, and that perhaps, like Krook in *Bleak House*, I too would one day spontaneously and entirely combust, kept me going. It's a mark of self-pity or self-hatred that one hopes a crisis can be forced that will resolve one's problems. You hope that a fire will break out and eat you. A hell fire. The more that Mr Sadler smiled at my efforts – and he could smile, he had a really lovely smile – the more I went at it.

It didn't break me, of course. I was young and strong and didn't

* World-famous heart surgeon.

quite realize how very much I was enjoying it all. Conjugality simply couldn't compete with the drama on the pot bank. It was a good part. I was the Hairy Ape. This was better than a small part in a Royal Court production of *The Fire Raisers*, directed by Lindsey Anderson. I had been interviewed for the play. Anderson was very considerate and really wanted me and the title drew me irresistibly. And then suddenly a song was added and they went off me as a singing fire raiser. I couldn't understand why a pyromaniac had to be able to sing in tune. So I went back to bursting into flames in Stoke-on-Trent. At least it was a bigger part and Mr John, my very own director, liked my howling as my finger nails fell off in the heat. 'Don't kill your pig, Tom,' he used to say, which meant, don't overdo it. And he meant it, too.

The only way I could cope with my feelings of anxiety was to attack the work like a madman. The voluntary hyperactivity removed the need to think clearly about anything. I couldn't even enjoy the consolation of alcohol because my stomach was so jumpy. I would often be explosively sick and couldn't eat. Unable to get a job in the theatre, I was simply acting in a one-man show called *The Confusion and Self-pity of Tom Baker*.

One day Mr John asked me if I'd like to go and have a day out at the Great Yorkshire Show where the wife's family were mounting a large exhibition of roses, for they were famous forcers of flowers and, as I was to find out and never forget, even more famous forcers of labour. I said yes, not realizing that this was a heaven-sent opportunity to descend into the next layer of hell. I didn't know it but my fire-eating days in the potteries were over as the next stage of punishment beckoned. It smelt sweet and would have seemed to an outsider to promise a good way of life.

I went to the Great Yorkshire Show and met a squad of flower-arranging salesmen headed by a monster called Harry Wheatcroft. He was a man of firm opinions and often talked of his hard upbringing. The name Bounderby* leapt to mind after five minutes. He was

* World-famous hypocrite in Charles Dickens's *Hard Times*.

a thrifty man, too; I once saw him sell a handful of rose petals to a partially sighted flower lover so you see he wasn't entirely without feelings. Men who worked for him were kept going by their hatred of him. Back at the nursery he would creep along the hedge bottoms in the hope of catching a man leaning on his hoe. He would play hell with any poor student who was hungry and holding his hoe too tightly. And as he loped away from us all, there would be murderous mutters and several men would deliberately knock out the newly emerging rose eyes.

Silly hairy Harry seemed not to grasp how much his outbursts cost him. When he was well out of earshot we would all begin to fantasize some ghastly end to him. We dreamed of kicking him head first into a swamp. But of course we never did anything at all except kowtow to him. Working long days in a mood of hatred is extremely tiring and very depressing. We all need the nourishment of a cheerful thought and the benefit of a kind word. Our loathing of the name Wheatcroft and our daily contact with them diminished us as human beings. And the sight of Harry Wheatcroft striding across a field with his thumb up his arse bellowing at someone on the horizon shrank our spirits. Like a perverse Mark Tapley I accepted what I considered my lot, and wallowed in the misery of it all.

At the end of every day I went home to Harry Wheatcroft's brother, Alfred Wheatcroft, my father-in-law. He was a tall, slim, interesting-looking man with a very sensitive face. He looked rather scholarly, and wore glasses for his very bad eyes. The frames of his spectacles were real tortoiseshell. He hated his brother and wore an ill-fitting truss which he was constantly adjusting. It was said that he had procured the truss from an old relative as he lay dying and had got it for a good price. But it's a dodgy business buying a secondhand truss even at a keen price; you only get what you pay for, as they say, and Alfred's truss was obviously a very approximate fit. After his death it was buried with him and legend has it in Nottingham that the grave was broken open later by a mean trussless neighbour with a severe rupture. But I give no credence to such a story. In Spinney Hill, as his house was named (Castle Dracula would have been more appropriate), he kept his wife, Constance, his daughter Anna, his dog Julie and, as he kept reminding me, he kept me.

All my life I have felt myself to be on the edge of things. All my life I have suffered from bad dreams. All my life I have had difficulty in knowing whether I am awake or in a nightmare. All my life I have had learning difficulties and been unable to grasp the point of what everybody else sees clearly. All my life I have entirely missed the point; and the turning, as I also have no sense of direction. This long period of uncertainty in the twilight land of the fuddled (it is now more than sixty years) has taken its toll. It is only in the enclosed asylum of a play that I have any assurance at all, and then not much. So, naturally, I have evolved a strategy of always being in a play. That way pain and humiliation are the responsibility of the writer. But more importantly, I can pretend it isn't really happening; it's just something that one feels passionately and then goes away.

This method of pretending that something doesn't exist applies only to pain or sadness. Pleasure, joy and ecstasy are embraced with fervour and are sensations to die for. And quite right, too. There isn't nearly enough pleasure in the world. As soon as people start getting some more pleasure and a bit more cash the world will be a better place.

When my son Daniel was born in Nottingham I was at the nursing home. It was in 1961. Like most new fathers I was taking care of my wife as her contractions began to come. We were together in the nursing home in down-town Nottingham. It was in the month of November. Anna was put to bed and the waiting game went on. And I waited and waited, sitting there making conversation with Anna. I don't remember us being very good at the talk. I had brought her a small box of chocolates as a gesture towards the special occasion. No, it was a medium-sized box. I can see it very clearly still, Terry's All Gold chocolates. And so I sat by the fire in this very nice, comfortable room and thought how well Anna looked sitting up there in bed. I remember I was talking about the weather while Anna sat in bed and tried to seem interested. While we were waiting, a doctor in evening dress came in smoking and smelling comfortingly of whisky. I don't mean he was drunk. He had a loud voice and said to me, 'Bartlett.'

I shook my head and said, 'Baker.'

He laughed. 'No, I'm Bartlett,' he said. 'That's my name.' And he crossed to Anna who was beginning to have contractions more frequently and disappeared under the sheet and between her legs without as much as a by-your-leave. He didn't even remove his cigarette. I felt my eyes dilate as he vanished. 'Two fingers,' came his muffled voice and he emerged for a pull on his cigarette. He said, 'Not to worry, Anna, I'm not far away,' and off he sauntered.

What confidence I thought, and with a ciggie in his mouth, too. I opened the chocolates and offered my wife one. She shook her head so I had one myself; it was a chocolate nougat as I recall, not a favourite. As the time went by and contractions came quicker a nurse came in and took Anna away, saying as she went that Mr Bartlett had been called. As soon as I was alone I felt hungry and started in on the Terry's chocolates. There was nothing to read except the fire which was very red and eased my panic at being left alone without a book. So I sat there wondering how I'd manage as a father and wishing I didn't have to. I can't say I was happy at the thought of children. But I didn't feel resentful either. I just felt I'd rather not. And I had another chocolate and dozed off. When I woke up, I was sweating a lot and felt very sticky being so near to the fire. By the clock I'd been asleep for nearly an hour. Reaching for the chocolates I noticed that there were only three left and I felt guilty. I took out the lucky three and put them on the arm of my chair and threw the box into the fire. Now I couldn't see the box, it had never existed and I felt better. The surviving three looked at me and I looked back at them. And then without giving them any warning I snatched them up, all three of them, and popped them into my mouth. Cor. What a mouthful. As soon as I'd done it part of me said, 'Spit them out', but I didn't. I carried on trying to grind them into a malleable ball that I could control – not easy – and I felt my face all contorted in my efforts to master the three hard centres. This went on for about five minutes, and just as I'd got a grip on the sticky buggers in my mouth and reduced them to the size of an above-average golf ball the door burst open and in bounded Bartlett carrying a bloody big baby. 'What do think of that, then?' he said. 'What do you think of that? Ten pounds and nine ounces, biggest baby I've ever delivered in this place.' I looked at the child and for a split second I saw a resemblance to my brother John and I felt the deep love for a child, for my son. I will love him, I thought.

'Well?' asked Bartlett. He looked at me expectantly. But I had three hard-centred Terry's chocolates in my mouth and could only gurgle like a puzzled sea lion. 'I understand,' said Bartlett, 'I understand, most fathers are speechless at a time like this.'

But he didn't understand. Every time I see a box of Terry's All Gold, this scene comes back to me and I resolve to call my brother John and Daniel my son, and tell them how much I love them; but I don't. I finished the chewing and my jaws ached and I felt suddenly sleepy. The hospital bed was yawning and I was very tempted to climb in. But they brought Anna back and the nurse fussed around her, telling her with great glee how her bikini days were over. Anna ignored their malice. I smiled at Anna and she looked very happy and full of love for Daniel.

Alfred and Constance adored Daniel, they lionized him. They were both concerned that he must have perfect sight and perfect hearing. Alfred was always making passes in front of the baby's eyes to test the baby's sight, while at the same time Constance would creep up behind the child and clap loudly to see if he could hear. The sight of Daniel leaping in shock brought a version of a smile to her thin lips. But they did care for the baby. Perhaps it was because he looked like them. He certainly didn't look like me. He had golden honey-coloured skin for one thing.

On Sundays, when other members of the family would turn up to endure a couple of hours of parental love, I would seize the opportunity of turning myself into a dumb waiter as I served them drinks. I thought my self-abnegation was complete, but I was wrong. And having poured large gins and Italian for them all, I would retreat to the edge of the circle and watch them. 'Oh, the horror, the horror,' as Mr Kurtz said. How they all made each other suffer. Their eldest son, Philip, seemed reluctant to even start a sentence in the presence of his loving mother and father such was the power of their affection.

Like a lot of bullies, Alfred the father was devoted to little babies. He would dandle Daniel on his knee. He would bob him up and down with many loving noises and smile his ghastly smile. 'Hello, my baby,' he would say, again and again. 'You're my baby, aren't you? You're my lovely baby, my baby, my own lovely boy, aren't you?' And the baby, seeming to know which side his bread was buttered, would gurgle his agreement. And this would delight the old boy and the same insufferable refrain would be resumed. 'My baby, who's my baby then?' as he waited ominously for the child to call out, 'I'm your baby.' And then Daniel would gurgle with terrific energy and smile in agreement. And Alfred would cry out in triumph: 'You see, he said yes. Did you hear that, he said yes?' And we would all attempt a smile. But the Wheatcrofts, clever at business though they were, were lousy smilers among themselves. They simply couldn't do it. But Daniel's mother, Anna, the Cordelia to this Nottingham Lear, used her favoured status to say, quite lightly: 'He's not your baby, Father, he's Tom's baby.' I was touched by this kindness for about one-thousandth of a second. For in that brief time the temperature dropped to zero as Lear snarled: 'What did you say?'

His instant rage was terrifying.

'What did you say?'

And Anna, a little shakily, repeated: 'I just said he was Tom's baby, that's all.'

And Lear burst out: 'Tom's? Tom's? He's mine. He's mine.' And he held my child close and asked: 'Who paid for the best nursing home in Nottingham? Eh? Tell me that. I did, I paid. Me. Who paid for the finest gynaecologist in the whole bloody county? I did.

Doctor Bartlett. And he didn't come cheap. Cheap? Have you got any idea what the Bartlett bill was?'

He was by now very close to apoplexy.

Constance tried to intervene: 'Dad, Dad, now Dad.'

He turned on her, 'Shut up.' And to Anna, as he hit frenzy, 'Who pays for all the baby's clothes, eh? Who pays for everything you've got? I do. Not him,' and he pointed to me, 'he's got nothing,' he roared as he eyed me. 'He's got nothing. I paid for it all so he's mine, the baby's mine.'

For a moment I wondered if I should just pick up an antique and strike the cruel old bugger across the head. But I did nothing. I just shrank into utter freezing self-loathing as I realized I was not even going to protest. The thought came again that I should kill him. And then I sensed that I didn't even have the strength of character to avow my love for my only child. Even the family was impressed by Alf's volcanic convulsions. Nobody stirred. I faded in my own sight and I couldn't even weep. This is the end, I thought; but it was not the end. Yet. And so I was caught up in the violence that only two old pacifists could practise on their own families.

There was one exception among the Wheatcrofts, one sweet, funny and adorable member of that nest of vipers who always tried to comfort me in my misery. His name was Jonathan Wheatcroft, Harry's youngest son. He was so unlike the others that it was spooky. Not a trace of their malice and his tongue unforked. He was strong and kind and he knew of my hopes and he hoped along with me. I don't know whether he ever escaped from that family, but if he did I never heard from him again.

Gradually I got used to the abuse and the terror. Constance, the fishwife (all the ghastly lot of them had terrible voices), was always on to me about how invulnerable they all were. 'I can see you looking at us and wishing us harm,' she'd say (she had guessed), 'but nothing can hurt us, nothing.' And then she'd pause and reflect and add: 'Except maybe an atomic bomb.' I love the arrogance of that 'maybe'.

She and Alf would row so loudly that men working in a field

near the house would hide and tremble and toy with murderous thoughts. One of the astounding qualities of that family was their capacity to fill innocent passers-by with thoughts of murder. Once when she screamed at Alf the Terrible and then fled the house to her car, we all watched as she continued to shriek abuse at her beloved as she drove off. Going down the drive she leaned out of the window to fire the last insult; the car careered over a rockery and crashed to a hopeless halt among the heathers and stones. There was a terrible silence after the bang; and then from among the rose trees came a feeble cheer of joy from several hidden slaves who assumed from the silence that Connie the Viper had been catapulted into Arthur's bosom and was even then biting his nipples. But no. After the crash and the silence came the shrieked abuse of the indestructible she-devil.

'I'll put you in a home for this,' she screeched at her old sweet-heart who must once have thought it a good idea to share his life with her.

And then came another son for Anna and me. Piers, nine pounds and ten ounces I think. Like his mother's lot he was blond and had the usual honey-coloured skin. They all had such great skin. I was the only one there who didn't have golden skin. 'What a pity you've got such working-class skin,' Anna remarked. That really hurt me. It still hurts me. It's not my fault that my surface is rashy and working class. But Piers was one of the sacred line all right and they were pleased with another golden boy and they practised their smiles. I wanted to call him Solomon but Constance looked askance and my suggestion was overlooked. And so my misery deepened and I was content.

Once a short break was proposed for Anna and me and we went to Honiton in Devon for three days, that being about the maximum time I could be with anyone. We drove there and tried some conversation along the way but we were neither of us too immense at that sort of thing. Fortunately we met up with some friends who were actors and that helped a lot. We saw a play and attempted a couple more conversations, but to no avail; so we headed back for bedlam. There was a message waiting for us to call Castle Dracula. Obediently we rushed up to the dragon's lair, also known as Spinney Hill.

'Alfred's had a stroke,' crowed Connie the Triumphant as she conducted us towards the sick room. I wondered what a stroke might have done to the big fellow. We kissed the children and were led into the chamber by Constance. What a sight. It had drawn big Alf's venom all right. He was tame at last. He lay there in terror and acute discomfort, humiliated to be steaming in his own urine and feeling the onset of bed sores. Some hired Sairey Gamp knitted at his bedside and I felt a flicker of pleasure as I sensed that the click of Sairey's knitting was needling him. She was just going off duty and so we were left standing there looking at the ruins of the great monster. And there he lay, the man who never stopped reminding us that he owned us, like a huge, abandoned, whimpering old Guy Fawkes, not at all frightening now. And I remembered my few skills from the Army Medical Corps where I had been a common nursing orderly.

I was strong and suddenly I knew what to do. I bed-bathed the old rip and with a little spirit and talcum powder got his arse dry. The skin was not yet broken. With clean sheets and pillowcases his lot was improved. The relief he felt caused him to recognize me and suddenly he was muttering: 'Tom Baker. Get Tom Baker, keep Tom Baker. Don't let him go.' And he clung to me in terror of being left alone to his fate. The irony was not lost on me. The man he hated most in the world was the only one who could comfort him. The cruel bastard was in my hands. And I did comfort him. It is possible to nurse someone you hate. All at once things began to look up for me. The family did not want to look after their poleaxed father and were glad to leave it to me for the moment. The monster could not move his limbs but he could move his bowels. This filled his wife and children with disgust. Not only could the Wheatcrofts not smile, they couldn't wipe bottoms either and I knew as I wiped his arse that I had them by the balls.

When the doctor was there, Alfred refused to believe that he'd had a stroke. 'I can't have had a stroke,' he grated, in a terrible rage, 'I've got £93,000 in my current account.' The doctor coughed politely, for Alfred was a private patient and, as we all know, private patients can talk any old bollocks they like and get away with it. The doctor urged them to find a full-time professional nurse and promised to arrange for Sir Russell Braine to come and see Alfred. Phone calls were made and a male nurse arrived. He was very experienced and very well qualified. He settled in and within two weeks was close to nervous collapse and fled.

Money being no object, another male nurse was located, interviewed and hired. This man also had a wonderful record as a nurse. He had seen serious action in the army and had a medal or two. Within two weeks he left nursing as a profession to become a lighthouse keeper.

A third man was procured who, amazingly, had actually been a lighthouse keeper before becoming a nurse. And so he came to take on the impossible task of nursing the source of all ingratitude. He lasted eleven days and then went to join the Trappist monks at their place in Charnwood Forest, Leicestershire, where, after the rules were eased, it was said that he electrified the monks with his tales of lamping. As Alfred wanted only me, I was able to get rid of the entire family at one go. They were delighted to hand over the raging carcass to me. So for nine months I tended Alfie the Ungrateful and he swallowed all my energy and wore me out. Not the tiniest effort would he make to walk or talk or be nice. I wiped the hen shit off his eggs every morning before soft boiling them to perfection. His toast was fresh and generously buttered with the crusts off. I spoon-fed him and afterwards scrubbed his dentures. And when I popped them into his mouth he used to tut. Yes, he actually used to tut, and loudly. And then he would growl, 'Lavatory,' and I'd fix that, too. And after a great Rabelaisian movement he seemed nearly to enjoy my servitude. Never once did he say, 'Thanks, cock. You might be a lousy son-in-law, but you wipe good arse.' No, he never said it.

To relieve his self-pity Alfred was prescribed an anti-depressant pill called Tufrinol, I think. The doctor said it might cheer him up. The dose was one, three times a day. As he was often asleep in the afternoon, I managed to hoard a good number of these pills. A plan was forming in what passed for my brain. I was sinking into sadness myself. Alfred used up so much of my energy and time I had no opportunity to refresh myself elsewhere. The selfish old sod had killed my pig. I had become impotent at home, a condition that swiftly leads to misery. Having ditched Almighty God in favour of a hard on and now having lost it, my will to live slackened, too. And so I started to work out how I might end it. Life, I mean. I counted up all the Tufrinol pills I had saved. How potent were they, I wondered? There seemed to be a lot, though I'm not good on pharmaceuticals. So I resolved to take all of the Tufrinol pills and die of happiness. I thought that the ecstasy of more than two dozen pills might outweigh the misery of a blank future and a dead dick.

Constance the Unspeakable was away in London at a meeting of the National Rose Society. She was a great one for Peace. The rose I mean. Bundles of Peace for sale but crowns of thorns at home. I decided to die in the late afternoon of a day when I knew that nobody would come to the house for at least four or five hours. I gave Alfred a large tea of smoked salmon and thinly cut brown bread, followed by raspberries well soused in sugar and cream over the top. After that he had a medium-sized custard from Burtons of Nottingham and two cups of tea, three sugars in each. I thought that would keep him going while I got out laughing.

I sat in the kitchen and swallowed all of the pills I had saved. I wanted so much to die of happiness. I wrote no note. I sat there and waited for oblivion. 'Let the buggers try to decipher my smile,' I thought as the last three beans sailed down my throat in a stream of Jersey milk. I became drowsy and then, blackness. I woke up about half an hour later to the noise of the old devil banging his stick on the floor. He was very agitated and wanted to go to the lavatory. I leapt to my feet feeling miserable on discovering I was still alive.

'Quick, quick,' growled Alfred, 'I think it's a big one, get a move on.' A big one? The movement was heroic, the wind gale force, tumultuous, the stool like a shillelagh. I mention this detail because within a few days I realized that the Tufrinol which had failed to help me to die happy had cemented my bowels. Costive was not the word. I grew frantic. Was I never again to know the pleasure of a normal bowel movement? Impotent and constipated, too? I strained so hard in between wiping the big fella's arse that I nearly lost the sight of my left eye. And the harder I set, the looser bully boy became. I grew distraught and ate lots of any fibre I could. I was saved finally by Senekot, the natural laxative. If anyone who is reading this needs any reassurance, take it from me, SENEKOT. If Henry the Eighth had known about it he would have used it to dissolve the monasteries. Senekot moves the immovable. And gives pleasure, too.

The advantage of Big Alf's stroke was that it protected me for a lot of the time from the attentions of the rest of his family. Once it became accepted that there was not a single male nurse in Nottingham, Leicester or Derbyshire who would look after the cantankerous old dog, they were glad for me to relieve them of the duty. So, bad as it was to be trapped with him from morning till late evening, it was better than being in the hands of three or four of the rest of them from moment to moment during the day. Most Wheatcrofts had a curious mistrust of anybody who wasn't bending to his work. The sight of someone simply sitting still goaded them into inventing things that needed doing. Constance would ask you where you were going, and no matter what your destination, she would have something for you to do on the way. She could have kept a battalion of Welsh Guards busy. And now at the end of their lives only one friend came to see them, a Mr Billy Boot, a very amiable little man who couldn't cross his legs. He drove a Humber Super Snipe, a big car for a chap who couldn't cross his legs. He was the only person from all that great catchment area who came in the evenings. He could sometimes even get Alfred to smile.

The woman who came to help in the house was a Mrs Farmer. She was a lovely, hard-working and very sweet lady. I sometimes had conversations with her – in a whisper, of course, for talking was forbidden at Castle Dracula. The grunting of stricken Alfred and the creaking of Connie's corsets were the daily sounds that gladdened our working hours and warned us that they were both still alive. The distant noise of Connie's threats to have her husband put away would cause Mrs Farmer and me to lower our heads and think of our last ends. We would smile furtively to each other and that helped to alleviate our fears. Mrs Farmer had a wonderful smile. I used to think about her smile when she wasn't there. This struck me as odd. And then I began to notice that I was losing the knack of smiling. I actually began to forget how to do it. And my fear of them all grew. I longed to be bursting into flames back in Stoke-on-Trent.

If I was reading in the kitchen when Mr Wheatcroft was asleep, I always kept a bucket of water, a scrubbing brush and floorcloth in the middle of the room and the kitchen table drawer open. If I heard the click of the front door, I would sling the book in the drawer and throw myself on the floor and scrub away as if it was my vocation. At home I discovered that I couldn't look at my wife because she looked like her mother. I couldn't look at her brothers because they looked like their father; and finally I couldn't look at my children because they looked like my wife. I began to feel very isolated. The only little change in these drab days was that the my patient seemed to be somewhat quieter and rather glazed in the eye. This caused me some anxiety as I realized I was afraid he was going to die. 'Don't die, Alfred,' I prayed. 'Don't die, and leave me to the rest of the pack.' The monster had become my protector. But he didn't hear my prayer. He slipped into a coma, and we waited and waited. Constance was the model of a loving and caring wife for hours together, but her patience wore thin and I suspect that like a lot of married women she was yearning to be a widow.

The coma drew him down deeper and we that were to go on stood by and watched. No soft-boiled eggs were required now. No more bullying to look forward to. I washed him carefully, and kept his hair neatly combed. He was very proud of his fine hair. As his breathing grew more rapid and erratic we knew that Alfred was ready to go. His two sons, Philip and Roger, clung together in terror as the moment came. I stood back in case they wanted to be close to their father. My last act of deference in Alfred's life. But the sons were afraid and gripped each other. Constance was in the kitchen about ten feet away and I went to the door to signal to her that she was nearly free. Before she could reach the bedside Alfred gave one last great sigh and died. Constance was so self-controlled that a passer-by might have thought she didn't care. A half sob nearly escaped her but she stifled it and solemnly kissed the dead man's forehead. I wrapped a box of tissues in the top sheet and pushed it up under his chin to keep his mouth shut. The sons left the room with their mother and went to the kitchen to drink tea. I remained, watching the changes that take place a few minutes after the last sigh. And I thought of all the Wheatcrofts on my side of the family and of what sort of a future lay before me; and I envied Alfred.

Constance in the part of a new widow asked me if I'd like to lay the old sod out. When he was alive I often wanted to lay him out, but now that he was gone the passion had passed. How often when he was so unkind to me I had wanted to cork his arse or sever his jugular vein. So I settled for giving him his last wash before a professional layer-outer came in for the nitty-gritty. I bathed him with all due respect and tidied him up for the man who was to cork and knot him. Not all of you will know that orifices have to be bunged and willies tied off – but they do. Alfred the Cruel had an immense organ. I had been washing it for nearly a year now and so was used to it. But death seemed to have added to its enormity. Usually a four-inch bandage will do to tie off an organ. In Alf's case I could have used his length and done a granny knot, a reef knot or, perhaps, a tangled Turk's head eye-splice. But I did none of these, I merely washed him.

The funeral was fascinating to me, as I watched the family in their grief. They all kept their heads down and held their noses in hankies. And so we buried the old bugger in his secondhand truss. Everybody was very pleasant after the funeral, and phrases like

'Blessed relief' were heard as the ham sandwiches were passed around.

The change in my life was noticeable. So busy had I been with the father that the rest of the family had become used to me being invisible in the sick room. Now what was to happen? Alfred was dead, my dick was dead and so was my alibi.

Nobody said what I should do. So I took a day off which was far too long a time to be with the daughter of the dead man. The next day I reported to the treadmill shed where Philip Wheatcroft through the mouth of the foreman, Jock Murdock, issued the orders for the daily round of work at the rim of madness. There must have been thirty men working there in those days. Each morning little Jock invented a strategy and groups were posted in all directions to maintain the lovely roses, Wheatcroft Selected Roses as they were known throughout the world.

I was assigned to a tractor driver who was to harrow the plants as the growing season started. The tractor had special wheels and the harrow straddled five or six rows of young trees. My job was to steady the harrow from behind. This involved being bent very low and struggling to make sure that the harrow didn't veer left or right and damage the new plants. It was extremely arduous work which really should have been shared between five or six men during the day. But that was not how things worked in the world that Alfred had bequeathed to his heirs. For two weeks I went through the pain of working from seven thirty till ten and then from ten thirty till one o'clock. After lunch the shift was from two till five thirty. It was a wretched two weeks. I could scarcely prepare anything to eat when I got home. After the usual bathing of children I fell into my sack and died until six thirty the next morning, when the torture would start all over again. By now I was part of this family that I rarely heard speak two sentences to each other. How did they think I was feeling all those hours as they watched me from the headlands of the fields?

Why didn't I just stop? Why didn't I just tell them I couldn't bear it any longer? I cannot answer those questions. Somehow I got through it. But the harshness of the experience left me very disturbed.

The next job was to help clear up the great shed and prepare for the showing season, when big firms like Wheatcrofts competed against other rose growers from all over the country for the lucrative trade in retail plants to the ordinary gardeners everywhere. After the anguish of the harrowing, I was enjoying working with a kind fellow called George Sycamore. He carried me to a large extent for I wasn't really very good at anything. And he certainly didn't drive me like the Wheatcroft man did. Anyway, one day we were painting some squalid little caravan and washing labels in preparation for the flower shows when George noticed we were getting short of paint. So off I went to Nottingham, a distance of about five miles. It gave me the opportunity to get off the place for perhaps an hour.

'What's going on here, and where is Tom Baker?' asked Constance Wheatcroft of dear old gentle George about five minutes after I'd gone to town.

'Gone for paint,' explained George, who was a nice man whom I shall never forget.

He could not know that Constance the Cruel was having a turn. But when she stayed near the shed and kept asking questions and being very sarcastic it dawned on him that death was sometimes very desirable when a Wheatcroft with power was on the loose. She suddenly started to give George and a young student very sharp orders. She started to behave like a mad fatigue sergeant in the pioneer corps. And quite innocently I returned and found my pal George and the student being bullied mercilessly. She didn't notice me for a minute or two so I was able to assess the scene. There was nothing novel about it. I had seen and accepted such a happening scores of times. My usual reaction was to be conciliatory and very busy. But that day my hearing was sharper than usual. Her dreadful voice was more grating than usual. Then she saw me.

'Come on, there's work for you, too,' she cawed as I got out of the car. I began to lift out three or four large cans of paint which were on the back seat of the car which was also crammed with perhaps ten newly sharpened hoes that I had collected while down in the town.

'Never mind the paint, there's clearing up to do first,' screeched the old witch. Slowly, I went to the other side of the car and just messed about for a moment or two with the tools that filled the entire rear of it. 'Never mind playing about at nothing,' came the voice, 'you've had it easy enough for too long as it is, it's time for real work again.'

I was honestly very nervous of Constance Wheatcroft. And I wasn't the only one. Her entire family was afraid of her. Dogs were afraid of her. Bindweed in the hedge would wither as she passed; birds would forget their nesting instincts and fly back to north Africa at the sound of her hideous cries. Suddenly I could not bear it. The sight of George's pale face and the student trying to hide anywhere he could and birds abandoning their half-built nests seemed to me to be unfair.

'Why don't you just fuck off and leave us alone,' I said. As the words came out of my mouth my legs began to shake and my sight became strange. George and the boy became slightly distorted and seemed to me to need protection. Protection? From me? From me with a rampaging Wheatcroft there, a ghastly old bag who would have frightened the hound of the Baskervilles.

'What did you say?' she yelped.

I repeated what I'd just said.

'You dare to speak to me like that after what we've all done for you?' she screamed.

I turned away from her and went to the front of the car and began to get in. It wasn't easy with my legs out of control and my eyes seeming to fail me. Of course, they were trying to save me from seeing her. But I could see her, and she could see my fear of her.

Her voice suddenly seemed strong and confident. I was so frightened I put my right leg into the car first. I was in a terrible tangle. I heard her snort; and as I clutched hold of the steering wheel to stop myself from falling down, she laughed. 'Don't you dare get into that car when I'm talking to you, you kept man, you. That's all you are, a kept man, You couldn't eat if it wasn't for us.'

I tried to straighten up and turn towards her. But my right leg was even more afraid of Constance than the rest of me. It didn't want to come out of the car at all. I wrenched him too hard and fell between the car door and the running board. She laughed again. She seemed suddenly very large and ugly. Beyond her George and the young student were watching this grotesque little happening. George seemed to be making patting movements with his right hand as if that might allow us to go back in time to just a few moments ago before I'd told her to fuck off. But George could not take back what I had said. I struggled to my feet and heard myself trying to clear my throat. I opened the back of the car and tried to climb in there. And she laughed again.

But I wasn't trying to get into the back of the car because I had lost my bearings but because the sharp hoes were there. I reached the bundle and fell out of the back of the car and drawing one hoe I took aim at the screeching old bat and hurled it straight and hard towards her face. She was only about fifteen feet away and my aim was excellent. But old she-devils don't die that easily. She ducked and turned to look where the hoe had landed and scurried towards it to pick it and defend herself.

'Who bought that shirt you're wearing?' she wailed as she stooped to pick up the hoe. And as she did so with more speed than I could have expected, she ripped off a tremendous fart. That should have eased the tension and perhaps saved my mind, but no. She straightened up and turning towards me she said: 'You're common and disgusting, too,' as if it was me who'd farted. That did it. Hoe after hoe flew towards her. I was utterly frantic. But not one got to her. She ducked and weaved and skipped and panted, all the while shrieking, 'Take that shirt off, you kept man. Kept man.' And like a banshee I fled screaming across the fields towards a main road. The house where I lived was about a mile away. There was a man called Bob standing by his tractor as I screamed past him. He looked at me helplessly, as if he wanted to help. I was past him in a flash and near the main road. Several motorists seemed able to hear me and looked beyond me for a sign of the terror that had reduced me to a wreck.

I lay on the bathroom floor and was sick into the bath. I suddenly remembered it was their house and I stumbled down and locked and bolted the door. I got back to the bathroom and was sick again. I was trying to be sensible and not make too much mess. My thoughts kept yanking me back to her trying to blame the fart on me. I tried to drink some warm water but then had to gargle to unlock my throat. As I struggled to swallow and to stop shaking, I remembered a girl I had treated badly and I suddenly got a terrific trembling erection. I was very mixed up and in the tumult I was sick again and my stalk vanished. After a while I was able to brush my teeth and try to think a bit. Anna, my wife, was in London doing some shopping. And then it hit me: the children were up at Castle Dracula. That meant I would have to face Constance yet again to get my little boys.

After a while I managed to clean up the mess. And then I thought I'd have a bath and tidy myself up a bit. It wasn't easy. I was so tense I couldn't stand properly. I had to crawl over the side of the bath and I lay in it heaving with anger and fear. The hot water soothed me a bit and I kept adding more hot water to calm me. After a while I tried to get out of the bath but I discovered I still could not stand properly. It passed through my head that perhaps I had broken some part of myself. But there was no pain anywhere. So I crawled out of the bath and into the bedroom to dry myself in the dark. The bedroom walls were painted deep tapestry blue – a good colour for someone on the edge of total collapse.

I lay there for a while and then tried to stand again. This time I was more successful. I realized that the crouching position I wanted to adopt was something to do with my desire to be sick. Lots of people tended to stoop or crouch when they were near Constance Wheatcroft, and if the truth were known most of them probably felt very sick, too.

I managed to get dressed and go downstairs. Nothing in the

house seemed familiar anymore. My books seemed to me to be someone else's books. I remembered that the house was called Lark Hall, and that the name of the village was Bunny, and that my next-door neighbour was called Blood. I found myself saying over and over again, Lark Hall, Bunny, Blood. It made me giggle a bit so I changed the order: Blood, Bunny, Lark Hall. Because nothing in the room seemed to be mine anymore, the name of the house and village comforted me a bit.

The thought of the children being up at Constance's house filled me with fear. How was I going to get them back? Suppose she insulted me again? And pretty calmly I thought of having to kill her in order to shut her up. But there was nobody to help me with the children. I had no close friend I could call. Never have had one, even to this very day. I wondered if Anna's car was in the garage. I couldn't remember if someone else had driven her to the station or not. Maybe her brother Roger had taken her to Nottingham? He was very fond of his sister and was quite capable of doing a good deed.

Her car was there. Good. Strangely my stooping was eased when I got into the little car and drove towards Constance. I couldn't go very fast as the road also seemed strange. I found it helped to keep repeating Blood, Bunny, Lark Hall. In the forecourt of Spinney Hill, Constance's lair, I carefully turned the car round for a neat escape. I walked into the house muttering Blood, Bunny, Lark Hall, Blood, Bunny, Lark Hall.

'What did you say?' called the old witch as I crossed the hall. Her voice was slightly lower than usual. I guessed it was because the children were with her. They were so pleased to see me. They loved me. And I loved them. I picked up their toys and other bits and pieces and tried to usher them out of the house without speaking to Constance. The car key was safely in my pocket. I wasn't going to let her suddenly get to the car before me and steal the key. But she didn't try it. She just said: 'Well, haven't you got anything to say to me?' I looked her right in the eye and said: 'Blood, Bunny, Lark Hall.'

As I got the boys out she tried to speak to me again and again I repeated, 'Blood, Bunny, Lark Hall.'

'What time will Anna be back?' she asked, and I told her: 'Blood, Bunny, Lark Hall.'

The children thought this was very funny and they began to repeat it. As I bundled them into the motor they said: 'Blood, Bunny, Lark Hall.' I kept smiling at them and laughed as I struggled into the driving seat. As we drove off we all said in unison: 'Blood, Bunny, Lark Hall.' And all the way home we laughed and sang the same old silly refrain with me tooting on the horn in time. It was only a few miles back to Lark Hall but we laughed and laughed and laughed.

Back at Blood, Bunny, Lark Hall I prepared the children for bed. Anna told me once that I was very good at it. Certainly the children seemed to enjoy it. Their night things were always kept immaculately clean and I adored that marvellous moment of holding happy clean children before putting them to bed. They had kept on with the silly Blood, Bunny, Lark Hall in the bath and as I said goodnight they burst out with it again and we all laughed together. It was to be the last time.

TWELVE

WAITING FOR A 136 BUS from Highgate station to Muswell Hill Broadway on a misty evening in February is a bit like lurking outside the gates of purgatory. I stood there once; at the bus stop I mean, one nineteenth of a grey-faced crocodile of the depressed, all anxious to get away from each other and find comfort in their homes. The feeling in the queue was that the next 136 might come in about a fortnight's time. Resignation tinged with despair was in the air. Nobody spoke, a few shuffled and one man caused a near-ecstasy of excitement when he had a fit of coughing; but it soon passed and apathy returned as we all took root again. About a quarter of an hour passed, during which time several of the rooted queue glanced furtively at the man who'd coughed, as if in the desperate hope that he might cough again and thus suggest we were still alive. As these sly glances darted about the Trappist line, something happened; an event took place. This event changed my life.

The fence to Highgate Woods lay to our right at a distance of about six feet. It was a beaten fence, a fence that looked as if it was made up of former queue members for the 136 bus who had waited in vain and finally weathered into knot-holed palings. Through a hole in this fence came an angel of change in the shape of a mongrel dog. No best in show this little fellow, oh no. He might have got his coat from an Oxfam shop, for it was without a hint of lustre and had a whiff of other long-dead dogs. He gave me the impression of having once belonged to a taxidermist. What I mean is that there was something odd about him. His ears didn't seem to match and might have been won in a raffle in, say, Kentish Town.

They seemed unacquainted with each other. One stood up quite boldly and the other one was obviously a bit shy. But in his eyes there glowed the life force. Greyish brown and twinkling bright, speckled and flecked, and full of unquenchable optimism. A bit like Sir Ian McKellen, I suppose. Be that as it may, he wriggled through the broken palings and stopped short at the sight of us undead all in a line. But he wasn't daunted. He trotted down one side of the queue and up the other, wagging his tail and whimpering quietly to himself as if to say: 'He must be here somewhere.' He repeated this journey around the queue about three times, stopping here and there and sniffing at a shoe or a trouser turn-up. As he came near to me I looked down at him and smiled beseechingly, hoping he would sniff at me and approve of my bouquet. But he didn't. He continued his quest elsewhere among us.

About four zombies along from me stood a pale, grey man with a tinge of blue to him. He could have passed for a ghost anywhere. There was not a single feature in him that leapt at you. Born to be in the Special Branch but as though even they had overlooked him, he was instantly appalled when the tail-wagging mongrel chose him. With a yelp of sudden adoration the dog looked up at the near-invisible man he had chosen, this revenant, and with a quite goatish leap he butted spy man just below the knee. Then he raced away and round the queue and back to grey face and butted him again. The excitement caused the queue to tremble into life and people began to look towards the chosen one in curiosity. I was drowning in jealousy. Malice rose in me and I began to loathe the pale, blue-grey figure who had been preferred to me. Again the dog tore around the slightly trembling queue and again he stopped at shadow man, rose a little on his hind legs and butted him below the knee. Shadow man didn't want to be noticed. He shifted slightly, ignoring the giggles of delight that ran among us. Giggles of delight. We had been brought back from the dead by a mongrel dog. One of us had been chosen for God knows what mysterious reason and it wasn't me. Twice more the ceremony was repeated and the giggles turned to laughter, healthy laughter; a girl smiled at the man next to her.

Our saviour seemed to sense our rebirth and did another circuit. As he arrived at the feet of the drab bastard he'd selected, a huge truck roared towards our bus stop. The darling dog arched his back and attempted his knee-butting act of homage. The grey man shifted again and more nimbly than you'd have thought possible, he kicked sideways and caught our life-giving little dog on the side of his mouth. With a yelp of amazement he leapt away from his kicker and back into the road right in the path of the great truck and disappeared between the wheels of an Ernest Roderick Foden. A gasp of horror burst from us all as our miracle maker disappeared under the truck. In a second the lorry was past us and there, looking quite amazed, but still smiling, was our God. I mean our Dog. And do you know what? He rushed with delight to the swivel-eyed git who'd kicked him, and arching his back he butted him affectionately again as if to say: 'You didn't mean that did you?' And he circled us one more time before dashing through the hole in the fence and disappearing back into Highgate Woods as the 136 came to carry us all away.

I didn't get on the bus with the others. I decided to walk down to the Broadway. Some of my meanness evaporated and I felt at one with that dog. 'I don't care who kicks me in the lip,' I thought, 'I'll go on and do what is necessary.'

At the time of the dog incident I was living in a wonderful house off Muswell Hill with an actor friend, Richard Ainley, his wife Rowena Woolfe and their three children. Richard had been very badly wounded at the very end of the war and his career as a handsome young leading man had ended. He taught in various drama schools and when I'd found myself guttered he and Rowena took me in. In return for shelter I got the children off to school and met the little one, Rosa, from her school and took her to piano lessons. I was very happy with the Ainleys and they encouraged me more than anyone else. Rowena was a doctor and a wise one, too, and lots of warm and generous people came to the house. When the children were off to school Richard and I would read together and he would make me laugh with tales from the old days. His father was the great Henry Ainley and Richard adored talking of Harry and his adventures. There was always plenty of Guinness in the house and always a few bottles on various radiators, for Richard liked his stout with the chill off. I told Richard about the dog and he responded as I had. 'That's it, Prince,' he said, 'be a mongrel, fuck the thoroughbreds but be a mongrel.'

Living with the Ainley family was a great stroke of good fortune for me. I was in an awful mess and state of confusion being away from my own children. And being away from Anna, too. And then she met a man who came from Leighton Buzzard. What's in a name? Her preference for a fellow from Leighton Buzzard helped me to come to terms with the break in family life. Of course the Ainley children were in a way a substitute for my own children who, in my imagination, and to my horror, were calling a man from Leighton Buzzard Daddy.

A couple of mornings later I had the house to myself. About ten thirty, waiting for the second post, I made myself a pot of tea and sliced a couple of rounds of bread for toast. I folded back the paper and thought I'd enjoy an hour at the crossword. While the tea was drawing I went to the front door and looked out for the postman. There was no sign of him, but just outside of the gate was the regular roadsweeper leaning on his brush, which served him as a third leg and helped keep him upright in quite a swirling wind. Christ, he was an ugly old bugger. He was ageing very badly and might be said to have let himself go a bit, not to say entirely. Perhaps he was at the Dr Collis Brown* mixed with rum, blackcurrant and Jeyes fluid. I'd noticed him before on my way to Rosa's school or while waiting for the bus up to Highgate station. He generated a terrible smell, so bad that even cab drivers raised their windows as they passed him. But I'd never spoken to him. This was unusual since when I'm out of work I'll talk to anybody. He was often muttering to himself as he went about his tasks and for a while I suspected that

* An Imperial medicine which helped regularize bowel movements wherever the Union Jack was raised.

he might not have been a career roadsweeper at all, but perhaps an opportunist of some kind, maybe a novelist; you never know, do you?

When I'm on my way to Soho during the week, I often give a beggar or two the chance to make a pound. By that I mean I like a chap who's on the make to have a pitch of sorts, you know, a story of some kind. Years ago beggars always said things like, 'Jesus, you're a great handsome lad, I wonder could you help us to a bottle?' And if one felt charitable that morning a coin would change hands and the fellow would be on the way to his bottle while I was on my way to tap some agent or other for a job. Nowadays when I stop and talk to *Big Issue* lads or semi-sleepers I'm often struck by their resonant voices and swift articulacy. Sometimes I recognize them as actors from the RSC or the National Theatre and discover that they're researching a production of say *The Lower Depths* or maybe a script for Mike Leigh. Or, if they're not actors, they're journalists from the *Guardian* or researchers from Channel Four. This is around the Strand, especially on the corner of Villiers Street or John Adam Street, which is quite handy for the Green Room Club. I've never noticed a Garrick Club member on the game, which is not to say they don't do it; I wouldn't put anything beyond a Garrick Club loiterer.

But back to my sweeper outside Richard Ainley's house that morning when I was looking for the postman in 1966. As I looked at my sweeper clinging on to his great big brush and being buffeted by a freezing February swirler I suddenly wanted to talk to him. I wanted him to be a brief listener. When I'm in that sort of mood anyone will do. 'Hello there, boss,' I called out to him. He lurched a bit at my shout and looked at me over his left shoulder in a furtive manner. It had to be his left shoulder because we were an odd number and he was facing west. When he saw me properly one of his eyes widened more than the other. I smiled as winningly as I could in such a cutting wind and enlarged on my greeting. 'Do you fancy a mug of tea and a bit of toast?' I called out to him.

'What? What did you say?' he called back. I repeated my invitation, coming down the steps to reassure him.

'Do you fancy a bit of toast and a tea?'

He stiffened in the wind and said, with the appalling certainty of a Roman Catholic, ''Ere, are you after my bottom?' Curiously, I went hot at the squalor of the thought.

'I just wondered if . . . ,' I began, but he cut me off and in a louder voice he shouted out, 'I've heard about you theatrical buggers, trapping innocent . . .' I didn't hear the last bit as I slammed the front door shut. But my rage mounted as the warmth of the house hit me. I stood there in the little hallway panting with temper. The gall of the bugger. After his bottom? Christ, you couldn't have persuaded a termite near his mouldy arse. And yet, just two minutes before I'd wanted to use him as a listener. I've been pretty wary of street sweepers since, though it is true that since we left the European Exchange Rate Mechanism some sweepers are really quite dashing to glance at. Even so, you can't be too careful, can you? Nowadays I am reconciled to being solitary when at my early morning pot of tea. It's very sad really, but I suppose it's a sign of these awful times we live in. Even the Latter Day Saints won't come in for a mug. They prefer to trade secrets on the doorstep for the first few dates. So now I sup alone and watch the cartoons on the telly.

It was Miss Egan who said don't look back. She was the headmistress of my elementary school. But she wasn't the only one to say it. Don't hark back all the time said Mr Harte, the headmaster of the new secondary modern. The reason that Catholics said don't look back was to do with their obsession with death. 'Let us think of our last ends' someone was always intoning. And it was supposed to comfort us! 'At any moment we may die and enter into our eternity.' It was as if the past reminded the church of the fall from grace in the garden of Eden.

But we can't escape into the future like we can escape into the past. So those of us who are not certain of things, and there are an awful lot of us, often rush back to the past. And each one has a particular past he prefers to the present. Sometimes I feel that any past is preferable to the present.

Today I saw the two men who would be our leaders. God, dear God (oh, of course, You don't exist, sorry), they made me realize how frail we are. We must believe in something and so they take advantage of us. And what do we do? We believe them. To repeat the old adage from G. K. Chesterton, 'Men cannot believe in nothing. When they stop believing in God, they will believe in anything.' And I think that is true. It is the only explanation I have for my own uncertainty. It is the only way I can begin to explain why it is that so often I feel dead when I know I'm alive. And why it is that I feel so alive when I know I'm being entirely fictional. It's rather like the ecstasy so many of us feel at a great football match, or sometimes a great production of a fine play. We watch other people being heroes and we are nourished by their heroism in the struggle.

I thought back to my mother today, remembering that it is more than sixty years since she delivered me into a world that has always baffled me. I can still remember her so well. She was slightly tall, had brown hair and brown eyes and a lovely smile. She had beautiful hands, hard but beautiful. And her fingernails were curved and lined very noticeably though her thumbnails were flat, which was useful when she picked the lice out of my head for the practice was to crack them between the thumbnails. She always showed me the louse before the slaughter. But she crushed them too hard and I could never separate the bodies and take them to school, all counted up and in a matchbox like a boy called Raymond Monaghan did. I think his mother killed his lice with a look.

How to be invisible was what my mother was always teaching us – what to do to not be noticed. It was part of a servant mentality; thanking God for the station in life that He has called us to. Her willingness to say, 'Know your place' and to mean it amazes me. I suppose it goes back to the permanent state of fear everybody lived in. At school we were told the same, 'Never forget that you are nothing. What are you?'

'Nothing, Miss, I'm nothing at all, Miss.'

In my house of religion it was the same. Annihilate the self. In the army we were always advised never to think only obey. Never to volunteer for anything.

'Just keep your head down and don't get noticed.' My poor mother said things as silly as that.

'Listen,' she'd say, 'Just say your prayers, keep your bowels open and always polish your shoes.'

'Is that all?' I'd ask. And she would add:

'Know your place, tell the truth and keep your nose clean.'

Her mother must have told her that because I once heard my Auntie Chrissie say exactly the same thing to someone else. So my Mam was just passing on the old claptrap she got from her Mam, a fierce old bag who punched anything she didn't understand. Christ, she punched an awful lot of people in her time. Why should I be surprised that it's always the same script? For after that came Miss Egan, Miss Reynolds, Miss O'Leary, Mr Ryan and Mrs Fogarty, Miss Sharkey and Miss Deegan and more. Come to think of it, they were also obsessed with bowels. Chastity and bowels and do as you're told. Keep your nose clean; keep your shoes clean; wash behind your ears; and only speak when you are spoken to. We sought approval in every glance that an adult might aim our way. And if instead of a nod there was a frown, we would shrivel up and want to die.

The priests were our biggest fear; if you couldn't please a priest then you couldn't please Our Lord, for the priests were the embodiment of the Saviour on earth. They would appear from nowhere to make you uncertain of yourself. Where are you now, blessed Fathers Dougan, Molloy, Heenan, McCormack, Nugent and Flanagan and Moriarty himself; the line stretches out to the crack of doom. They were powerful teachers who knew the party line. We were worthless and evil. We were. So evil were we that our mothers had to be purified after our birth. There was nothing to do save despair and die.

'Any questions?' asked Fr. McQuaid (there, I knew there was another of the buggers) as he counselled us on empty stomachs

136

one morning. 'Tommy Ryan, I believe you are going to ask me something?'

Tommy Ryan didn't know of the existence of Bogotá at that time. Did he have a question! 'Do you mean, Father, that there is hope for us all if we are sorry for our sins?' We didn't know that the question was a plant.

'Well, now I'm glad that one of you can see the light,' replied Fr. McQuaid, the Edward Carson of the parish, so silky he was. 'When Our Blessed Lord died on the cross for us – and do I need to remind you of the rusty nails through His hands and feet? And let us not forget the vinegar sponge – He made heaven possible [pause] even for the likes of you.' He seemed to be looking at me as he said that and my anus squeaked. Tommy Ryan raised his hand.

'Do you mean, Father, that we needn't be afraid?' McQuaid the Terrible looked at Tommy as if that wasn't the way he'd have put the question.

'I wouldn't go that far,' he growled. And then he gave us the line on the ten big ones, the Commandments, I mean. He laid special emphasis on the Sixth and Ninth; the terrors of fornication and coveting your neighbour's ass were imposed early, we were about eight years old.

Pier Paolo Pasolini was seeing people at some hotel in Knightsbridge for his film *The Canterbury Tales*. So, along with lots of other fantasists who didn't fancy the real world, I trotted down to see the famous Marxist director. Of course, I knew nothing about him and cared even less; it was just another trip towards another rejection.

Well, I was sitting in the outer office when in sauntered himself, wonderfully relaxed and very gentle. He was a small man, full of easy grace and especially full of natural authority. He glanced at me and smiled, and then he stopped and looked at me more carefully. Then he called into the other room and out tumbled one of his assistants who spoke English. Paolo hadn't taken his eyes off me during this brief moment. He exchanged a few words with his man and seemed pleased with what the man told him. Then he smiled at me again, shook my hand, and told me through his interpreter that he would like me to play the husband of the Wife of Bath. He asked if that was all right with me. He had such a lovely way of looking at an out-of-work actor (we are not always a very pleasant sight) that I could have embraced him. I said I would be delighted to play the part. 'What sort of a part is it?' I asked. He said, 'Your sort of part.' When people are out of work they are very impressionable and I was very out of work and I thought his answer was magic. He asked me if I had read the story and when I said no it was his turn to beam.

'That's wonderful. He thinks that's wonderful,' said the interpreter.

'The character is very unspoiled,' said Paolo, 'are you unspoiled?' I looked at him wondering what the answer was. Should I tell him, yes, that I'd led a very sheltered life? That I still lived with my sister and collected butterflies?

'Do you mean he's not corrupt?' I asked.

'That's it, he's not corrupt,' said Paolo. 'Are you corrupt?'

'Yes,' I said, 'I'm afraid that I'm very corrupt.'

Pasolini smiled and said, 'How interesting, but you don't look corrupt and that's all that matters.' Then he asked me if I had seen his film *Theorem*, with Terry Stamp. I told him yes. 'Do you remember the scene where Sylvana Mangano took her clothes off at the station?' I nodded. 'When I put that together it was artistic, don't you think?' I nodded. Even if I hadn't agreed I would have nodded.

'Then we are agreed,' he said.

'Oh, absolutely,' I said, 'absolutely,' wondering what it was that I absolutely agreed with.

'Good,' said Paolo, shook hands again and off he went.

The production assistant said, 'So you've nothing against nudity?'

'Do you want me to be nude?' I asked, reaching to undo my shirt.

'Not now,' he said quickly. 'Later, later. In the film.' Suddenly I was gripped with anxiety. Nudity? On camera? I wanted to tell him that self-loathing was my speciality. I must have looked a bit baffled. 'Look,' he said, 'there's a scene where you offer the Wife of Bath a strawberry, okay?'

'Oh, absolutely,' I told him, my fears diminishing at the mention of strawberries. 'Got you, don't worry about me, I'll offer her a strawberry all right.' I must have said this in an odd way because the man looked at me in an odd way.

'But she doesn't accept the strawberry, she knocks it away and without more ado tears open your flies, hauls out your skittle and starts to play with him.' The man was English but he had obviously spent a long time in the sun and he pronounced the word skeetle. This made me feel unsophisticated.

'How do mean, skeetle?' I asked him. He said impatiently,

'You know, your skeetle,' and after a second, 'your prong'. And seeing my poor face he asked in a low voice, 'You have got a prong?'

The background office went faintly out of focus. Prong? Skeetle? I looked at him for help and he hissed through a chink in his top set, 'Your dick, for Christ sake, your mutton dagger.' That rang a bell from my army days; even the vegetarians said mutton dagger. Then pulling himself together he told me what was required. He told me that the scene was very rural, very summery and lyrical, very hot.

I was to offer the Wife of Bath a strawberry from my punnet, she was to knock it out of my hand and dive into my flies. Then she was to haul out my skittle, say hello to him, and, in shot, pay him some attention. 'Off the wrist, you know,' said the assistant as he mimed the action of relief to me. 'It'll look terrific, the audiences will love it.' And then he said, 'Maybe you'll love it too, it's up to you.' My heart sank, my skittle shrank and tears came to my eyes. 'Don't cry,' ordered the assistant. 'Stay there and don't cry.' He disappeared into the office. After what seemed a long time he came back and said, 'Don't worry, Paolo likes you so we can shoot round your skittle.' And so I kept the job.

And a couple of weeks later we went off to Sussex for the filming. On the night before we were to shoot the scene between the Wife of Bath and me I met the production assistant who'd ordered me not to cry.

'Can I get you a drink?' I asked him.

'Sure,' he said, 'as long as you promise me not to cry.' And so, dry-eyed, I bought him a drink and he told me what they planned to do.

'Lucky for you,' he said, 'we've got a man on the unit who can get it up just like that,' and he clicked his fingers with astonishing force. I looked at him neutrally as if to say, 'Could you explain that to me, please?' The assistant cocked his empty glass as if to say, 'Don't forget, you owe this job to me.' Swiftly, I fetched him another large G and T. 'Make sure it's High and Dry,' he called out as the barmaid approached me.

'Large High and Dry, kiss of lime and a ton of ice,' I said, marvelling at how quickly a sycophant can pick up a catchphrase.

'Yes,' he said, pulling hard on his High and Dry, 'it was one of the sparks that told me about this bloke.' And then he told me about how at a session at the hotel 'this bloke' had casually remarked that he could raise his skittle to order. The claim had been met with fog horns of derision and disbelief.

'Bollocks,' said the set dresser. 'Bollocks, a fiver you can't. No, a tenner.' In the uproar that followed a hundred and sixty quid was thrown into the kitty against the promise of a drink each and eternal shame for bragging. 'It was a late session,' the assistant told me, 'and only the lads were there and the old night porter who was in charge.'

'And, of course, he did it,' I said, knowing that otherwise I'd have lost the job. The expression on the assistant's face was astonishing as he told me the story. He was obviously describing a miracle. Imagine the faces of the people who saw the feeding of the five thousand. Imagine the faces of the people at the marriage feast at Canaan when the water was turned into wine. Okay? Now try and imagine the faces of the people who saw Lazarus raised from the dead. Got it? Well, it was nothing compared to the look of amazement on the face of the third assistant as he said in a voice that was hardly of this world: 'Yes, yes, right there and then, in front of us all, in front of the old night porter as well he opened his flies thumbed out his dong, looked everyone in the face, looked down at his dick as if he was going to hypnotize it and said, "Come on old cock, up you get."'

I found myself leaning in and whispering, 'And it arose?' I didn't mean to sound biblical, it just slipped out.

The third assistant nodded, and picking up my Easter reference said, 'Yes, it slowly became engorged and stood up to attention.'

Curiously, I felt a little empathy in my loins, but I wouldn't swear to it.

'Yes,' said the assistant with a kind of grating whisper, 'it stood up. Veins as well.'

I found myself echoing the words of the true witness: 'Veins as well?'

'Veins as well,' he murmured.

And then he said, as if he felt sorry for me, 'Which is just as well for you, eh? As it's his dick we're going to show in close up. All you have to do is look blissed when we do the close up on your face, okay?'

I looked at him in humble silence, and after a moment he whispered, with a very faint smile: 'It might make you a star.'

'Don't move,' I said, 'I'll get them.' And I glided to the bar and fetched him another.

'Well?' he demanded, when I had returned with his third large High and Dry. 'What do you think of that?'

And then I heard myself say: 'Did he go to RADA?'

The assistant lowered his glass, looked at me with pity, and said: 'RADA? RADA? Fuck RADA, cock, this fellow's an ex-Trappist monk, mate, seven years of chastity and silence, seven years, with nothing else to think about, and no chance to talk about it either. He's an American,' and he paused before he added, 'from Gethsemane in Tennessee.'

The next morning at about six we were on location and shot the first part of the scene with me and the Wife of Bath. It was April, bright and clear. All went well as the lecherous Wife of Bath looked at me with such intense desire that my blood ran thin. Meantime I was acting as if I had no idea what was going on. Apparently I was utterly convincing and Paolo ordered us to move on to the next bit of the piece.

It was now nearly eight o'clock. The little scene near the corner of a field had been dressed and lit for the Wife and me. 'Action,' called the first assistant, and with an innocence to make St Francis weep, I held out my strawberries to the Wife of Bath. The whole punnet exploded with the force of her lust-fuelled blow. She grabbed me with amazing strength. I felt I was being sucked into jet engine as she pulled me to the ground ripped open my flies and scrabbled in vain to find my cock who, having more sense than I, appeared to have done a runner. He may have gone, but my balls were still there, shrivelled as they might have been, and who could blame them? I screamed with fright and felt my anus gape in sympathy. 'Cut,' shrieked the first assistant but the Wife of Bath hadn't heard. Like Mike Tyson ignoring the bell she kept after my member. Easier to have found a needle in a haystack. Eventually, two dressers and her agent pulled her off me to a round of applause from the Italian crew. The scene was reset while three people from wardrobe stitched my medieval trousers together.

Paolo talked to us and emphasized how we must have a sense of sequence or the scene would appear blurred. And so we started again. 'Action,' yelled the assistant. I offered my strawberries and wham, I felt my wrist snap as I offered myself up to her as the South Sea islanders give themselves up to a king octopus. I was embraced by the storm, sucked in, snatched and pulled to the ground. With a tremendous flourish, as if she was opening the curtains of her apartment to admit Count Dracula she parted the seams of my flies and tried to enter. 'Cut,' bawled the assistant and the rescue squad piled in to save me from her. I felt as I'd been rescued from the inside of a very active volcano. The crew was convulsed with laughter and they kept showing each other cigarette stubs and winking as they did so as if to say that was the size of my skittle. Camera crews are notorious for their unkindness in these matters.

To my astonishment, Paolo liked the take and I was brought some coffee, a cigarette about three times the size of my dick and two blankets to keep me alive; it can be very chilly on a Winchelsea hillside in April. And so I sat there waiting for my stand in. About halfway through my fag I became aware of a certain atmosphere, as they say. Everybody seemed to know something that I didn't. It's always been like that with me.

Then the assistant arrived, looking very much older than half an hour ago, pale and, I thought, a little stooped. He whispered hoarsely in my ear: 'He can't get it up.' It was lovely having his warm breath on my ear.

'Who?' I asked rather unhelpfully. This archness on my part sent the assistant into a frenzy.

'The fucking Trappist, that's who. He can't raise his dick.'

'Well, I'm not surprised,' I said, 'I can hardly raise my eyes in this weather.'

'That's not helpful,' he said. 'That's not helpful. We're going to have to shoot the scene again and use yours.'

That revved me up a bit. 'Mine?' I shrieked at the poor pasty-faced git. 'Mine?' It suddenly became like a scene in some Victorian lunatic asylum with two frantic inmates screeching at each other. 'Mine?' I bellowed. 'Mine? You mean you want to use my prong at this time of the morning and in this weather? You daft bugger, you wouldn't find him with a macro lens. You'd better get down to Winchelsea and find a watchmaker. And tell him not to forget his eyeglass.' We stood there, the assistant and I, panting like two old swimmers on the verge of serious heart trouble.

Erect against the hedge stood the ex-Trappist whose dick had gone shy. Seven years of chastity and silence – what a preparation – and no dice. The props department were called over and with the wonderful flair of the Italians, they found a screwdriver, wrapped some tape around it, stained it a bit to make it look broken down and offered it up to Paolo as a substitute for my invisible tool. With the sort of sublime calm that Buddha might have envied, Paolo shrugged and smiled at me. Somehow or other we got it done. Somehow or other I managed to smile beatifically as the Wife of Bath caressed a screwdriver; and we moved on to the next scene. I never did see the film, and I never met anyone else who had ever seen it either. But I would not have missed it for anything. Just to be near Paolo Pasolini was great.

THIRTEEN

PETER CROUCH, my agent, called me and told me I was wanted by York Rep for a part in a Northern comedy by William Stanley Houghton called *Hindle Wakes*. I was to play some windy old Manchester businessman. 'You're too young,' Peter said, 'But it'll pass the time, and you can do something with it even if it's only fucking it up.' He was right, of course, it would pass the time and I could do something with it. So off I went to York to try my luck. But my luck was out, I was a disaster. That was what the other actors thought but the audience seemed to like me and that's the main thing isn't it? They particularly liked it when I shook my head and disappeared in a shower of talcum powder. So you can guess what sort of a performance I gave: a real headshaker. When you can't act, shake the talc. Many a performance has been saved by talc or a slipping toupee. I once did the talc and wore squeaky shoes.

When I look over my shoulder into my past, I mostly see flops or even disasters. I have seen plays that were so bad I would have paid a small sum to be in them. There was a production of *Henry V* given by out-of-work professional actors on a Sunday night in a little theatre near Paddington Green. The Duke of Exeter was so drunk and so wonderfully brave that I felt he should have been knighted. When it came to his speech about the harmony of the spheres in the heavens he just could not get started. While the court looked on in horror, Exeter, not admitting defeat, started to improvise.

'My Liege.' He got that out okay and went on, 'You know how

in the sky there are lots of er, er . . . balls. Planets! And they're just all whizzing about all over the show?'

The audience was shaking with pleasure. This was a good way to spend a Sunday night. Exeter, looking at the others who were looking back at him in amazement, tried to be more helpful. He seemed to suspect that they hadn't noticed the planets whizzing about in the sky.

'You must have noticed them?' he declaimed.

The audience roared and Exeter, glancing in surprise at them, I suppose because the speech hadn't got any laughs last week, emphasized the point.

'And the amazing thing is that they never collide. And that's because of God and the power of music.'

At that point the King, being unable to bear the laughter any longer, cried out – guess what? He was so into the part of the King, he shouted, 'Let's away!' And all the actors buggered off leaving Exeter on his own. And he, suddenly feeling that the others knew something that he didn't, tried to exit too. Suddenly, he remembered that he had to strike the tennis balls. It was that sort of production, the actors did everything; out-of-work stage hands never work for nothing on a Sunday night. Now in this production the tennis balls were oranges; there was a stage-struck greengrocer nearby. And as Exeter stooped down to pick up the oranges/tennis balls, he went arse over tit and landed on his back. The audience was in a state of hysteria. Some were standing and stamping their feet, others were holding on to each other and all were weeping with pleasure. Some wanted to step forward to affirm that they loved the Duke of Exeter, and all were applauding madly. Meanwhile, the Duke was on his back like an overturned tortoise, unable to get a purchase anywhere to get up. In this production the Archbishop of Canterbury was played by an actor called Oliver Barton. So here we have the Duke of Exeter on his back, oranges everywhere and pandemonium in the stalls. Suddenly, like a thunderbolt, somebody threw the Archbishop of Canterbury on to the stage to rescue the stranded Exeter. Now Barton is not a big man and Exeter is. Further comedy as he struggled to raise the mighty Duke. In the audience, St John's ambulancemen and women were treating people who were overdosed on pleasure, as the struggle went on. At last, to a mighty cheer, the Archbishop raised the Duke. As the cheer died down a little and the audience watched them together, Exeter looked at the Archbishop, smiled sweetly, and said, with marvellous clarity:

'Thanks, Olly, you're a real pal.'

The tumult in the theatre cannot be described. But in the Bunch of Grapes opposite, the actors drank free that evening courtesy of the ecstatic audience.

York was not quite that jolly for me but Peter Crouch had been right to encourage me to go there. The Houghton play was well attended; he's a very popular writer up there, his great humanity and high old commonsense endears him to Yorkshire people, who feel he is reflecting them – and he is.

My next play was *Stop it, Nurse* by Sam Cree. What a hoot. It contained everything a bunch of actors could wish for. Sex, drink, operations going wrong and plenty of chances for very broad visual comedy. In one scene four characters in a line drink a tumbler of vodka each. The audiences in Yorkshire are pretty generous and they liked our efforts to play drunk. Well, one night a member of the cast, a professional wrestler, thought it would be a good wheeze to put real vodka in the bottle. So we blithely poured it out and with our usual lack of subtlety toasted each other and swigged it down. Boom. Our reaction was, of course, real. We were exploded with spirit. We fell about coughing and spluttering and rolling our eyes and making noises like booming bitterns in a heavy fog. But the audience wasn't very taken with our efforts and thought we were overdoing it.

There was one terrible joke somebody put in during a scene when the patients were supposed to be reading out to each other bits from magazines. 'Hey, listen to this,' called the joker, 'Dear Marge Proops, can I find happiness with a man twice my age, I am fifty-one. Yours Hopeful.' (Big laugh from the audience.) Answer: 'Dear Hopeful, grab it while you can!' This got a terrific laugh and we all enjoyed it. There is no doubt that British audiences adore terrible jokes. And there is no doubt that a lot of actors like cracking them.

It was approaching the time of the York Festival, a heavily cultural affair in the 1960s. In between our broad comedy at the Theatre Royal I had been seeing a good deal of Laurie Taylor, my old friend from my student days. He and I had started out as actors and he got off to a fine start at Stratford East in a new play by Alan Owen. But he soon got tired of acting and, by a terrific effort of teaching during the day and studying at London University in the evenings, he got a first-class degree and changed careers. By the time I met him in York, he was a professor and becoming very well known. Seeing me revived old interests and we decided to write and present a fringe comedy show. And so it was that Professor Laurie Taylor and I put on *Late Night Lowther* starring Laurie Taylor and Tom Baker with Jazz Quintessence. All the good ideas came from Laurie, and most of the jokes, too. He encouraged the musicians and persuaded a technician from the university to rig a light for us. But the real big idea was this: York was a bit dull in those days after hours so Laurie, with his standing as a professor, got us a late-night drinking licence for the Lowther and, here's the sweet bit, you could only drink late at the Lowther if you had a ticket for our show! We were a sell-out. There was no opposition. And with two lamps and a hundred candles we set about preparing the material. We needn't have worried, the audience was so drunk and so grateful to us for the late drinks, they simply adored us. But Laurie left nothing to chance, cod reviews were written up in which we gave ourselves stupendous notices and were distributed by students eager to break the monotony of being honest. What a scam. We made a fortune. And Laurie was clever enough to make sure we had a fair number of awful jokes. We did sketches about the Pope's underwear and talking dogs and jokes about the Theatre Royal and crazy appeals on behalf of the daft in our society.

The talking-dog sketch in which I played the dog Clint and Laurie my brutal Bill-Sykes-type trainer, caused a great stir. Behind my back Laurie would hold up three fingers and ask me how many he was showing the audience. He would then kick me three times and elicit three very pathetic yelps from me which was, of course, the answer. People wept when Laurie kicked me and some threatened him. I went along with the audience, of course, and overdid the beaten-dog stuff. People offered me saucers of Guinness and drags at their fags and yelled abuse at cruel Laurie. Laurie later retrieved the affection of the audience by a great impression of Malcolm Muggeridge demonstrating the existence of God.

I remember all this because in the audience one night there was someone from the National Theatre. He thought my dog was a masterpiece and on the assumption that Laurence Olivier needed a dog down at the Waterloo Road, he quickly arranged for me to come down and audition for the National Theatre at the Old Vic. About ten days later, it being the time of the year when the National collected down and outs to walk on and understudy I arrived at the head office of the National Theatre in Aquinas Street in Waterloo. I was all revved up at the thought of spinning a line to Laurence Olivier and it so happened (isn't the theatre wonderful?) that Lord Olivier was working late at some studio or other, Pinewood, I think, where he was dubbing some film and the auditions had been cancelled. As I was travelling overnight from York, the message missed me. And so when I turned up everybody was dumbfounded. Gillian Diamond, the casting director, and Ann Robinson, her assistant, could not have been kinder. But what to do? The great man wasn't there. And then came a small miracle. Olivier happened to telephone the office and somebody told him that a poor shagged-out dreamer had come all the way from York by mistake. And Sir Laurence said that if I could wait till he got back to the office he would see me. If I could wait! And I did wait and other people on the staff gathered around: Kate Fleming, the voice coach, and Michael Halifax, the head of planning, and Donald McIntyre and Donald McKechnie, too. And I was presented to the Lord. And he was great. He was just marvellous. He thought I was funny and strange and hopeless and he invited me to join the National Theatre. And I said yes. And he said he was pleased. And I was pleased. And there you are. It's not so simple nowadays. Peter Crouch, my agent, thought I'd do well there so he was pleased, too.

A contract arrived and in it I was to play and understudy as required. The only play mentioned was *Rosencrantz and Guildenstern are Dead*. I was to understudy the players. I missed that plural and read 'The Player', a wonderful part at that time being played by Graham Crowden with almost supernatural aplomb. I was in heaven. For the next three weeks before the first rehearsal I worked on the part and learned it, dead letter perfect. The play was coming back into the repertoire and new people were being rehearsed in. On the first day Claude Chagrin, our resident mime teacher, and Edward Petherbridge, the leading man, were in charge. The stage-management team was led by the incomparable Diana Boddington, a woman who feared nobody, was the world's greatest authority on Catherine Cookson, and a wonderful knitter and very good to me. Those of us who were new, Michael Edgar, Malcolm Reid and a few others, were terribly self-conscious as we tried to fit in unobtrusively. The time dragged as we were placed as courtiers and learned a few shouts-off for the storm scene at the beginning of act two. We all bellowed 'Splice the mainbrace' and 'Land ho', stuff like that. I rather spoiled it a bit and added, 'Whales off the starboard bow.' Some wag asked very loudly how I could see whales in the dark. This led to me being asked to cut the reference to whales. Those who had been in *Treasure Island* at the Mermaid found this very undemanding. We new fellows were all sizing each other up. Nobody knew our names and the principal actors seemed brilliant, and that lowered our spirits.

On the second or third day, we got to the entrance of the players and for some reason Graham Crowden wasn't there. 'Who'll read in?' asked Edward Petherbridge, glancing around the company. Claude Chagrin said she would and there was a move to get on.

'Excuse me,' I called out.

Honestly, I really only meant to call out. Why was everybody looking at me so amazed? I must have said it too loudly.

'I'll do it,' I said, standing up and walking towards Edward Petheridge in a fierce way. He looked astonished, but he smiled thinly and held out the script to me.

'I don't need that,' I said, 'I know it.' And I walked to where the players were gathered. The whole room went quiet and everybody looked at me and then at Diana Boddington.

'What's your name?' she asked me, not unkindly.

'Tom Baker,' I whispered. Why did some people cover their ears?

'Are you the understudy?' she asked me.

Again I whispered, 'Yes.' And again several people blinked.

'Don't shout, dear. We're not deaf,' she said.

'Sorry,' I whispered. 'But it's in my contract, you see.'

One quick phone call to the office cleared up the confusion. I was not the understudy. I had misread the contract. And so the whole trivial misunderstanding was unravelled and explained gently to me. I felt very unwell. Everybody knew my name, but I felt very unwell.

In the pub next door at the lunch break, Edward Petherbridge came over and shook my hand and said how glad he was to see me and he bought me a pint. I shall never forget his kindness to me. Years later in a Manchester hotel I tried to tell him, but he couldn't remember and anyway I was by then a children's hero and Edward wanted my autograph for his son who lived in New Zealand. But it still makes me weep to think of that incident. He could have so easily crushed me; but he didn't, he spared me. And so *Rosencrantz and Guildenstern* went on and continued to be a great success.

The next play was *The National Health*, by Peter Nichols directed by Michael Blakemore. I read the board extremely carefully to find out what my parts were before we went into rehearsal. I was to play various doctors and ward orderlies as well as a hospital visitor during the interval. So that kept me out of the pub. I was also to understudy Jim Dale who was the comic lead. My army service in the hospital came in handy.

Michael Blakemore is the most fastidious of directors and he was pleased with my enthusiasm. I admired, from across that big ugly rehearsal room, the expertise of the leads and how Michael worked with them. Robert Lang, Brian Oulton and Charles Kay, Harry Lomax, Ken MacIntosh and John Nightingale as the biker. Poor John was not to live much longer, and neither was Brian Oulton and Ken MacIntosh was soon to lose a leg. None of these sad events could be blamed on me but I felt that, perhaps, I could have done more to cheer them up. But it was good fun and I felt really alive. It was only when the rehearsals were over that I died.

The only imperfection in life then was that we didn't really have much money. We used to get thirty shillings a performance. I was not unhappy with this; indeed, I would have worked for nothing if it had been necessary. Later on, when I knew the ropes a bit better, I worked as a builder's labourer to help make the eating more regular. And I wasn't the only one. Some poor fellow who had three children to support worked nights at a filling station to get some more money. He had a breakdown during *Volpone* and was led away. The shortage of money was only really felt from Wednesday afternoon into Thursday midday, when we were paid. Treasury, it was called then. In the army it was called 'the day the golden eagle shits'. Anyhow, one Wednesday Jim Dale, who wore very smart gear and had a Gucci briefcase, was sitting next to me at rehearsal. As I was his understudy he was very good at passing on any notes I might have missed. Suddenly this particular Wednesday afternoon he said, 'Eh Tom, look at this,' and he opened his Gucci. It contained £2000 in one-pound notes. I was thinking about egg and chips as he opened his case and the sight made me salivate. I was sorely tempted to ask him for one and I'm sure he would have given me one, he's a nice fellow. But I didn't dare and Jim didn't read my face or sense my appetite for chips. 'I sold my car this morning,' he explained. I have never forgotten that little moment. Later when I began to earn some money, I developed an anxiety that actors might be hungry and always offered them sandwiches. I still do, but quite discreetly. Usually I take in biscuits and leave them near the tea table. Jaffa cakes are a great favourite among actors and so are chocolate digestives.

Once when I was at an audition for some American series, the American producers kept me waiting for a couple of hours in the lobby of the Royal Garden Hotel. I got very fretful and murderous and Maud Spector, the casting lady* calmed me down and said I'd probably get the part. When I was shown up to the producer's room, a really nasty, rather small place for such a grand hotel, I was tense. We got off to a bad start, 'Well then, tell us what you've done,' said some bonehead, trying to put me at my ease.

'Why don't you read the list that Maud Spector has written out for you?' I asked him, looking straight at him and thinking 'God rot your bollocks'. This unkindness in my thoughts may have reached the hulk for he seemed suddenly uneasy. Maud Spector's head went down a bit. Knucklehead cleared his throat and pushed out his tits.

'Well,' he said, 'we're about to make a motion picture based on a book by Albert Speer, called *Inside the Third Reich*.'

I'd like to cut your dick off, I thought. I kept looking at him. He looked at me. Silence. And then he said, 'Have you heard about the Third Reich?'

I put on the look which suggested doubt and said, 'No, would you like to tell me about it?' And he started to tell me!

'Well,' he said, reflating his tits. 'In the beer halls of Munich just after the First World War . . .' And he saw I was shaking with unmerry mirth.

'Are you really interested in my motion . . . ?'

'No,' said I. 'And the way you explain it nobody in the whole world could possibly be interested.' And I strolled out, giving him a little Buddy Hackett wave. In the gents down the corridor I nearly choked with nerves and tears and resolved to jack it in. But I didn't.

The word was out that we were to do a Christmas show called *The Travails of Sancho Panza* by James Saunders, from the Cervantes book. It was announced that Joan Plowright would direct assisted

* One of the most important in London, possibly the world.

by Donald McKechnie. The designer was to be Tony Walton and the music was to be composed by Marc Wilkinson. On the internal phone next to No.16 dressing room I got a call from Aquinas Street, our headquarters, the Vatican of the National Theatre. It was the two Donalds, McKechnie and McIntyre. They sounded mysterious, each on his separate receiver. 'We'll see you in the pub in ten minutes,' was the message.

The two Donalds arrived breathless and worked me towards the corner of the saloon bar. They were really excited and both looked at me the way good-news carriers look at their targets, with a sense of power.

'We've got news,' said the Donalds in unison. 'You know about the Cervantes piece?' I nodded, the pain was exquisite and I became breathless, too.

'Well, you're in,' they said. I nearly swooned at the thought of Don Quixote.

'Dons,' I said, 'I was born to play the Don, I really was, I am Quixote.' The two Donalds looked at me in amazement.

'The Don?' Don said. 'Are you mad? Derek Godfrey's the Don, isn't he, Don?' Don agreed.

'Well, what's the news, then?' I asked.

'The news?' said McKechnie, 'The news is that you're the horse, you're Rosinante, you're to be the most famous shagged-out old jade in all literature and Tony Walton's going to design you. He used to be married to Julie Andrews.'

The news sank in like a dagger. I was not going to play Don Quixote, I was to play his horse. His horse? The National had spotted me playing Clint the dog to Laurie Taylor's Bill Sykes and now they wanted me to be a horse. Was this progress? I asked myself.

I remembered how in Venice I had played the Bear in *A Winter's Tale* – my first job, which first ran at the Cambridge Theatre. At the very moment when I was towering over Alan Foss who played Antigonus he turned too quickly for me and banged my left paw. The costume was so large and so high that I was looking through a little grill in the chest of the bear skin. As Alan knocked my arm the grill shifted and I was in the dark. It was just like real life. But it is a scene where the stage direction famously states: 'Exit Antigonus, pursued by a bear.' Alan didn't know that I was now blind and off he went as we had rehearsed. The problem was I could not pursue him because I didn't know which way the bugger had gone. I turned this way and that, desperately trying to remember the way off. The audience sensed something was wrong and they laughed as they saw I was lost. They also knew the play and when they spotted Antigonus coming back on stage they realized that he'd come back for the bear. Meantime, utterly lost, I guessed wrongly about the way off and, so they told me, I began to walk towards the orchestra pit. The Italian audience shrieked in pleasure and then alarm as I neared the edge. But Alan Foss raced downstage to rescue me from the huge drop into the pit that might have killed me. As he caught me by the paw the Italians cheered with relief and delight and they simply screamed as I was led off by Alan. Thus, for perhaps the first time since Shakespeare wrote the play, the stage direction was altered and became: 'Exit a bear, led by Antigonus.'

And now I was to play a shagged old mare. For a moment I was anxious, but then I told myself that this was the National Theatre of Great Britain and anyway the British loved animals, especially horses. My fears fled and I began to wonder what Tony Walton's designs would be like.

'And Marc Wilkinson's to do the music,' whispered Donald, looking at me in a very odd way. 'Isn't he, Don?' And the other Don agreed, and that strange look made me hope desperately that there would be a number for my horse. My life was on the turn. But then my life has always been on the turn even when it was going well. Especially when it was going well.

So we started in on the Saunder's script. Derek Godfrey was the Don and Sancho Panza was played by Roy Kinnear. Anna Carteret was the love interest and Freddy Pine was Sancho's mule. Tony Walton had designed me a wonderful trolley with eccentric wheels that made the back end sway in the manner of a Derby favourite. Well, I thought it did. Joan Plowright could not have been more encouraging and, as time went by, I became more and more certain that the play was about this clapped out old mare that was me. Laurence Olivier, supporting his beloved Joan, often came to the rehearsals. Don Quixote was not really Sir Laurence's sort of character so he took more notice of the grotesques and oddities. And as I was the pushiest old jade you ever saw, he noticed me. People told me that when I wasn't in the rehearsal room he tried out my trolley. Lord Olivier had a go on my trolley! The horse masks were astonishing, with great detail but space enough for the audience see our faces. Years later I thought that John Dexter had been inspired to have similar masks in *Equus*.

So we rehearsed and rehearsed, and Marc Wilkinson, the musical director, was always there encouraging us; and Joan and Donald McKechnie worked themselves to a standstill. It was marvellous. Roy Kinnear was terrific as the wiseacre Sancho Panza; Derek Godfrey was quite charmingly mystical as the Don. Anna Carteret looked amazing. The music was lively and the movement and special effects were excellent but the audience was completely indifferent. It was a hard show and lots of performances were scheduled and we grew very despondent. My efforts as Rosinante got more desperate by the minute. Roy Kinnear started to improvise and I took to stamping on his foot if he came near me; the actors played with redoubled energy and still the audiences would not come in. I was told that I had got a tepid review in *Horse and Hound*, but that may just have been malice. Compared to my Dog, my Horse was a flop.

Some good did come out of it. Sir Laurence and Joan Plowright were very generous hosts and often had the cast back to their flat in Stag Place, Victoria. And that's how I began to get to know Sir Laurence. He once asked me if I had ever played humans and I told him not often. He laughed and I nearly fainted with pleasure. And so we dragged our way through the remainder of the performances. The audiences didn't see me but Sir Laurence had and that was more important to me.

A tour to America was announced. The productions of the *Three Sisters*, starring Maggie Smith and Robert Stephens, and *The Beaux*

Stratagem, again with Maggie and Bob and with Ronald Pickup as Archer, were booked to go to Los Angeles for a season. Supporting actors and understudies were invited as well. Michael Halifax came round to all the dressing rooms to find out who wanted to go. We all wanted to go. I suddenly had an idea that with half the company away in the States for a while my chances of a decent part might be improved, so I turned down the trip and hoped that something might turn up while the other half was away.

Something did turn up. The two Donalds remained loyal to me and were always on the look-out to recommend me to some innocent director. *The Merchant of Venice* was announced with Sir Laurence to play Shylock and Jonathan Miller to direct; the sets were to be designed by Julia Trevelyan Oman. Once again a Donald encouraged me. Naturally I had read the play and thought I could play Gratiano. I had more chance of playing Portia. I had no real idea how things worked there. Joan Plowright was to be Portia and Jeremy Brett Bassanio, Charles Kay was to be Aragon and Ben Whitrow the Duke of Venice. The whole play was sewn up. Perhaps I should have gone to America? Anyway Donald McKechnie found me in the pub talking to a down and out I'd mistaken for a journalist. I thought he was making notes and certainly he seemed impressed and amused by my delusions. As Donald joined us I realized my 'journalist' was trying discreetly to open an abandoned sandwich he'd probably found in Aldwych. Donald, no snob most of the time, muttered, 'Who's your friend?'

Leaning left I whispered, 'I think he's from the *Guardian*.'

'A word,' said Donald, and to my guardian, 'Excuse us for a moment, please.' In the corner where staff directors (that was Donald's title) plotted with actors for a line, any line so they could stop miming, Donald hissed, 'Jonathan Miller's over at Aquinas Street.'

'Can I audition for Gratiano?' said I to my Donald.

'Gratiano?' Donald gaped at me. 'Gratiano? Pull yourself together, that's for Derek Jacobi.'

'What's left that speaks?' I asked him.

'Just hold it a second,' he said, 'and I'll tell you. There's only one part left, the Prince of Morocco, and Jonathan likes the idea of a dwarf for the part.' I mulled it over for a moment.

'But Donald, I'm standing next to you, towering over you and you are five foot ten tall. How can I get the part of a dwarf? Jonathan Miller is a doctor, he's clever, he'll notice straightaway that I'm not a fucking dwarf. As I walk in he'll say to himself or to his assistant, "Hello, this fellow's a bit tall for a dwarf, wouldn't you say? He's the size of two dwarfs, one on top of the other, what are they up to these staff directors?" And then you'll be in trouble for trying to pass off a chap who was too tall for the Grenadier Guards as a dwarf in *The Merchant of Venice*.'

Donald looked up at me and said: 'Tell him he doesn't want a dwarf.'

And off I went to Aquinas Street on Mission Impossible. The girl at the door with the short list looked at me carefully and said: 'You're a bit on the tall side, aren't you?' I smiled shortly and strolled in. The rehearsal room at Aquinas Street was very large. It wasn't tall, but it was large. As I closed the door and tried to lean nonchalantly back on it I realized with horror that I'd stepped in too far to lean back. As I fell away from Jonathan Miller, who was about sixty feet away, he seemed to grow towards the ceiling. In a flash, I pretended to be a cowboy and with my right hand hovering over an imaginary holster I approached Jonathan as if for a shoot out. Hiding his disappointment at my size, he also swung his shooting hand into the area of his National Theatre holster and we approached each other in pale imitation of Alan Ladd and Jack Palance. As we met in the middle I said: 'Hi, sorry about the height I was brought up a Roman Catholic.' Jonathan was instantly appeased by this confession and asked me to sit down. 'I'd like to play Morocco with a tall hairdo and a bone through my nose and have a small boy to carry my scimitar,' I said.

Jonathan looked at me and smiled and said: 'Yes, and you could talk like George Sanders and gimbal all the way through the scene.' He explained that a gimbal was a continuous side-to-side nod. He showed me and then I said the opening line, 'Mislike me not for my complexion,' and I gimballed.

Jonathan laughed and seemed to have forgotten about the dwarf and an hour later little Donald gave the news that I was the Prince of Morocco and that Jonathan thought it should be funny. I should mention for the sake of anyone who doesn't know the piece that Morocco in our version had only one scene. Anyway, after my efforts as a horse and having made Sir Laurence laugh, I was well on the way to being funny at the National Theatre with the help of Sir and Jonathan.

There are lots of people who can tell horror stories of being an actor, me too, but in that production it was roses all the way. From Jonathan and Sir Laurence to Charles Kay and Jeremy Brett I was encouraged to be extravagant. There is a wonderful line when Morocco opens the wrong casket, 'Oh hell, what have we here?'

'Break it,' Sir Laurence said. 'Break it and there'll be a big laugh.'

On the first night there was a woman in the audience who used to haunt Sir Laurence. She was near the front, watching and listening carefully. I didn't know about this until afterwards. The scene was going well, Joan Plowright being very generous in her reactions to my alien naturalism. I approached the casket and remembered Sir Laurence's advice – the audience was very attentive – I opened the casket and said, 'Oh hell!' The laugh was terrific. As it eased, the mad woman in the front called out, 'That's not Shakespeare.' This caused another big laugh, and as that one eased, I looked towards the lady at the front and said, 'What have we here?' There was uproar. It was the only great laugh I have ever had. Forgive me dwelling on it but as I turned back towards Joan and Anna Carteret I saw Sir Laurence in the assembly watching me. He looked delighted. As the scene ended and there was a big round, I wanted to die.

All I have ever wanted to do is to make someone laugh. In between performances I was as inert as Count Dracula in his coffin. And so it went on for more than a hundred performances. Years later Mike Ockrent told me he saw the production when he was on his way to Perth Rep to play Morocco. 'I nicked your performance, Tom,' he told me. I glowed with contentment.

Between performances I was cheating on two lovely girls who were both devoted to me. I had a bedsitting room on the Blackfriars Road, only two minutes from the theatre. It was known as Baker's Shagging Cabin. Quite a few of the usherettes were out-of-work young actresses and I used to try to lure them back to the neat little grotto which was my coffin between performances.

My difficulty in existing outside the plays became extreme. I used to go into the theatre with the cleaners at about five thirty in the morning. Not long after, I'd hear Anthony Hopkins rapping out some speech or other. Sometimes he and I would go for breakfast in some cafe in The Cut opposite. We became quite friendly for a while, and then quite inseparable. I absolutely adored him. I would listen, rapt, to the tales of his demons.

At the time he was going out with a wonderful girl called Jenny. She was utterly committed to him in the lightest possible way. She was a girl to die for. One night Hopkins and Jenny and I were in Luigi's in Tavistock Street, Covent Garden. Lots of actors went there. It was a good restaurant, more like being in a play, really. If you were really down in spirits you could sit near your own picture and be reassured that perhaps you did exist if only in a photograph. And if nobody was looking you could smear zabaglione on the picture of someone you envied – John Wood, for example. So Hopkins and I were there, full of conviction and red wine. Jenny was, as usual, completely self-assured and patient towards us. Suddenly something unusual occurred. Hopkins said: 'Well, Jenny, it's all over, love. I'm off with Tom, to live the way he does.'

Drunk as I was this jolted me a bit. I couldn't remember discussing this with Tony. Besides, I only had a single bed, and what would the landlord say? Pushing money towards Jenny, we tottered out hissing at Norman Rodway and Alan Howard who were sitting quietly at a nearby table. So, on the boil with house red, we rolled out into the night to start a new adventure. Outside the restaurant we turned left and walked towards the Theatre Royal, Drury Lane.

We crossed Catherine Street and passed one side of the theatre and then turned left along the other wall. The Fortune Theatre loomed up and we tuned left again along the third wall of the Theatre Royal. Still we didn't speak. We turned left again and walked down past the front of the theatre and noticed the Opera Tavern on our right. We eased across the street in silence and found we were back in Tavistock Street. This time, dizzy from going left, we turned right. Outside the restaurant Jenny was sitting in her car. As we approached she leaned over, opened the door, and Tony got in and slammed the door. Jenny waved kindly to me and drove off.

He could be quite fickle, that Tony Hopkins. I consoled myself by thinking that he would not have been happy living in the Black-friars Road in a small room with no piano. I lay there on my bed and within a few minutes I passed through the grieving process into a coma.

FOURTEEN

LIVING IN AN INSTITUTION, rumours of change can make life more bearable, and starting rumours can be a wonderful pleasure for those without much hope. The National Theatre was like that. We used to watch each other with eagle eyes to make sure that nobody had strange powers, to make sure that, give or take a patron, the degree of suffering through uncertainty was more or less equal. I am talking, of course, of the other ranks. The leading actors were consulted by the directors. Below decks we had to guess what was going on and we guessed like mad and mostly got it wrong.

As love affairs broke up we watched girls alone in the canteen reading *The Pursuit of Happiness*, or *Small Is Beautiful* or sometimes *Henderson the Rain King* – but that was rare. Grief would be resisted by taking counsel from some kind soul who was sometimes only the next seducer. What pleasure these scenes of real drama gave us. For those of us who were not used up by the casting directors, these personal dramas were our substitute for lack of parts. Such dramas were mostly two handers, of course, but no less intense for all that.

The lunches in the pub next door were just as good as the food in the canteen in the Old Vic basement, and going to the alehouse got us out of the theatre for a while. I was sitting in there one day with the wardrobe girls and a couple of actors when the mighty John Dexter, who at that time was one of the most famous directors in the world, wandered over to us. I'd never met him before, but I knew of his fiercesome reputation. He didn't really know anyone in our little group except Vera Martin, the head of wardrobe. I was to discover later that Dexter was not at home in pubs. The crowded and noisy atmosphere diluted his authority and that didn't go down well with him, as he was very keen on discipline and self-control in other people, not subjects that get you much attention in a bar. But sometimes, because nearly everybody else was in the pub, he'd stroll in and spoil it for one or two poor souls. It passed the time and made a few of his victims long for death. Even the great Dexter had to relax.

So he came over and first asked Vera Martin what she would like to drink, then Michael Edgar, and Malcolm Reid and the two girls. I remember it was an easy round, most people were fairly abstemious; looking back, you didn't know if an offer of a drink from Dexter was a trap or not.

We were very aware of him as we knew that he was preparing his production of *A Woman Killed with Kindness*. As he took the round of drinks his eye fell on me and I noticed a slight change in him; he became almost interested in a sinister way. 'And the good doctor?' he asked. 'What's the good doctor's pleasure?' I didn't know what he was talking about until Vera Martin, a kind lady, tried to resolve the enigma by pointing out to John Dexter that he was mistaking me for Jonathan Miller, a very good doctor, indeed. Dexter changed mood slightly, shrugged and went off to get the drinks. He came back with the first three drinks and then, after a little pause, he arrived back with two more drinks. But there were three of us left. Vera got hers and Michael Edgar got his and I got nowt. In pub life it's a very hostile act to deliberately exclude someone in a group after taking on the round but Dexter didn't care about pub-life conventions. The whole group was deeply upset at the maestro's cruel snub and the remaining quarter of an hour was spoiled. 'Well, cheers everyone,' said Dexter as he strolled off to viper someone else. For people who don't use pubs it may seem a small matter but John's attitude diminished that little group.

This insult of Dexter's was talked about a good deal that season, as we laughed and swapped stories about the tyrants in our lives. We marvelled that after the way they treated us we were still capable of enjoying them. Dexter's brutality often brought to mind the army tyrants most of us had experienced on our national service. Our monsters in the army were theatre, too; theatre of the absurd, perhaps, but then most theatre is, which must be because life itself is absurd a lot of the time.

Our vivid gutter language was sometimes poetical and always vital. Ben Whitrow at the National once told that when he was in the army he fell foul of a company sergeant-major who didn't like his turn out and made life hard for him. As a soldier your most prized possession was not your gun or ammunition but your brown paybook. This was called your AB64. Without it you ceased to exist; the army could hardly cope with you if you lost your AB64. It contained all the basic information the army needed to know about you. Anyway, Ben Whitrow's sergeant-major was taking duty parade one morning and was particularly irked by Ben's appearance. Leaning in to rub noses and shaking with instant passion, he roared at Ben: 'Whitrow, if you don't pull yourself together I'm going to stick my prick in your brown paybook and fuck your next of kin.' The sergeant-major was staggered by the look of admiration on Ben's face.

Tony Hopkins went as far as to trace his company sergeant-major and call him up to ask him out to dinner. He actually got through to the now-retired Sergeant-Major Hackett. 'Yes? Hackett here.'

'Sergeant-Major Hackett, this is Hopkins here, 23260976 Private Anthony Hopkins, sir. I was a clerk in the company office at Second Battalion headquarters, sir.'

'Hopkins? Hopkins? Haven't you become some sort of film star, Hopkins?'

'Yes, sir, and I was wondering if you and your wife would like to come to the National Theatre and maybe have dinner with me, sir?'

'Have dinner with you, Hopkins? With you? You were a shambles at headquarters office, a shambles, Hopkins. Why should I want to have dinner with you?'

'Well, sir, I was thinking . . .'

'Don't think, Hopkins, it doesn't suit you. It didn't suit when you were in the army and I don't suppose it's changed now. Get off the line, I'm going to New Zealand, tomorrow.'

This ferocious rejection from his old sergeant-major gave Hopkins a lot of pleasure and he told the story very well, even with affection.

Suddenly, it went up on the board that Derek Jacobi was to play his first title role, Myshkin, in *The Idiot*. The piece was to be adapted for him by Simon Gray. Rhogozen was to be played be Tony Hopkins, the narrator by David Ryall and the female leads by Louise Purnell and Diane Cilento. The director was to be Anthony Quayle, that master of dullness. I was in the crowd. At the read through Anthony Quayle held forth for ever on Russia and Russians and told us all about the Russian characters, how they wept more than we did and generally felt things more profoundly than the rest of us. All balls, of course, but par for the course in Quayle's mind. His opening talk went on for so long and was so dull that Tony Hopkins suddenly developed a gumboil and had to withdraw from the production. There was some consternation about this and for a day or so a lot of talk about who would get the part. If Quayle had stopped talking for a while Hopkins's gums might have got better but he wouldn't stop, and Hopkins's absence was announced as eternal. Simon Gray, who was spending a good deal of time with Quayle, looked shattered. There were quite a few changes in the script and Simon looked even more clapped out. This, of course, may have had something to do with having to work at London University where he was a teacher as well as a playwright. It may also have had something to do with malnutrition because Tony Quayle shared his lunch with no-one.

Eventually Quayle asked me to audition for Hopkins's part. Major Quayle had a habit of calling actors 'amigo'. I was just about to say he called us 'hombres'. But that might not be true. He kept putting his arm around my shoulder and saying duff stuff like: 'I can see there is a fine actor deep down in that old hulk, amigo.'

And his eyes would fill with what seemed to be tears. I never met a man who could move himself so swiftly.

So I took over from Hopkins. The cast was huge and the blocking was very difficult. Poor old Tony Quayle had eight performances a week of *Sleuth* to do at the Garrick as well as constant planning meetings and rehearsals. Why on earth did he accept to direct *The Idiot*? Was it, perhaps, that nobody else wanted to do it? Fairly soon he ran short of energy. The designer had the idea that if boat trucks were used we could speed up the scenes. As one scene finished, there would be a cross fade of the lights and trucks would come cruising in to push the narrative along faster. It was a great idea.

When we reached the technical rehearsals the stage looked a bit like Clapham Junction. But all worked well as trucks quietly disappeared upstage while other trucks came in at quite lick downstage. Then came the dress rehearsal. The scene change was from an orchard to a banquet. The orchard scene ended and the cast sailed away on it's truck. From dark upstage came the banquet truck carrying about twenty Russian toffs all loaded with champagne and no sense of direction. The audience, made up of heads of department and other staff, gasped at the brilliance of the idea as on sailed the banquet gang, looking like a piss up on the top deck of the *Titanic*. The truck reached its mark and stopped, and all the actors fell down. It was a scream. Nothing in the theatre has ever surpassed the pleasure I felt at the sight of twenty National Theatre actors in a heap as a result of this idea. It was plain that there was an imperfection in the arrangements. What to do? Well, I'll tell you what we did: the upstage trucks were kept in service and entered empty behind the actors who ran on at the beginning of a scene. At the end of the scene the actors boarded the ship and were carried upstage into the darkness and all fell down at the upstage wall. The downstage trucks were taken out of service. And as the upstagers disappeared, the downstagers ran on across the train lines which inexplicably criss-crossed the banquet hall. Nobody dared to ask why we were doing the play in a railway yard. Nobody seemed to be surprised that in the ballroom there were railway tracks every-where. It didn't make any difference to the piece.

As the murderer Rhogozin I didn't make much impression on the audience. I just had to stand around and look menacing. This bored me as well as them. At one performance I tried to make it more energetic than usual and as I folded my terrifying knife away I caught my fingers and nearly cut them off. Blood flew everywhere. Luckily it was my upstage hand so only the cast saw the blood. I felt no pain, though the sensation of blood dripping from my hand was quite interesting. More interesting were the faces of the some of the girls who obviously did not like blood. I clearly remember Anna Carteret swaying about a bit and looking ill. Someone in the wings also spotted the blood and as we came off stage the St John's first-aid people were waiting for me. The more they fussed the more I pretended to be indifferent.

In the late 1960s a book about the Russian royal family had been published, called *Nicholas and Alexandra*, by an American writer, Robert Massie. Beautifully written, it told the story of the last of the tsars and his family, and the fall of the Romanovs. This book had been bought by Sam Spiegel and was being made into a movie at exactly the time that Tony Quayle was telling us at the Old Vic about how sensitive the Russians were. Everybody who was anybody was in this movie including Lord Olivier, who was playing the Rus-sian prime minister. Sam Spiegel loved to be with the leading actors and therefore saw something of Sir Laurence during the filming. It so happened that the part of Rasputin remained uncast. The pro-duction was moving along quite smoothly apart from this one detail of the mad monk. Spiegel was a very opinionated fellow and could not accept any of the suggestions for Rasputin that were offered by the casting people. He told Laurence Olivier of his dilemma and Sir Laurence remarked that he had just such a character as Rasputin in his company back at the Old Vic.

With a sore finger as a result of being an incompetent murderer, and always skint by Wednesday, I was waiting for something to happen. Anything would have been welcome. I received a call from my agent, Peter Crouch. He told me that Maud Spector wanted to see me. 'Go and talk to her,' said Peter. 'There may be something in the wind.' He often said things like that. So off I went to Upper Brook Street, Mayfair, to see little Maud.

'Darling, do come in, sit down and have a drink.' I was dumbfounded. On the several occasions that I'd met her she hadn't taken much notice of me and I hadn't blamed her for that. 'Take your coat off, here, I'll take it, sit down, and I'll get you a drink.' Bemused is the word I'd use, bloody bemused. 'Darling, have you got any pictures of yourself?' I said yes. She kept peering at me as though she'd never seen a tall, bearded fellow who might be said to be a bit vague. 'Please, please can I have one or two?' I told her that I'd send her a couple when I got home. 'No,' said Maud, emphatically, 'I'll send you home in a taxi, dear, and you can give the driver the pictures, I must have them today.'

'What's this all about, Maud,' I asked. 'Never mind, darling, don't ask, but I've had an idea.' And I did as I was told.

That night I told Derek Jacobi about this little event as we sat in the railway carriage on stage at the Old Vic, waiting for curtain up. He seemed interested, but then Derek has lovely manners. I told Edward Hardwicke about it and for some reason I felt he knew something. Later he mentioned that Sir Laurence was in Spain on a film about Russia. Then Peter Crouch told me that Sam Spiegel was coming to the play to see me. And he did, and he was not impressed, and I couldn't blame him. The play was going well mostly on the performance of Derek and the name of Simon Gray as the writer; Anthony Quayle appeared to disappear after the first night. It may have been on a Tuesday that Spiegel came because the next day, there being two shows, a message came that I should go to Grosvenor House, Park Lane, between the shows, to be seen by Sam Spiegel. There wasn't much time between the shows so Diana Boddington, our stage manager, lent her Mini to my friend Lionel Guyett and he drove me to see the great film producer. There was so little time that I went in full Russian costume minus my padding. Sam looked at me and I looked at him and he said, 'Don't look at me like that.' So I stopped looking at him like that. It then came out that Sir Laurence had mentioned my name and that was why I was now in the presence of his greatness. He told me that I was to come to Spain as soon as possible and be tested for the part of Rasputin.

Back to the theatre I went and among my lot there was great excitement and I was touched by their kindness. So it was fixed that I should go to Madrid very soon and be tested for the part and that the director of the test would be John Dexter. This caused me a second's anxiety. My old skill at self-delusion overrode my doubts as I told myself that Dexter probably believed in me. I could believe anything then. I still can as long as it is improbable. And so a date was fixed for me to fly to Spain (first class) for make-up tests and costume fittings in preparation for a film test. The excitement nearly suffocated me. There were three trips, all fairly short, and then, when a gap in the schedule allowed, I was taken back to Madrid to await John Dexter who was coming up from his home in France.

I was picked up at the theatre by a big car. Later I would casually call it the limo.

'Mr Baker?' enquired the driver.

'Yes,' I said.

"Passport, please, sir.' I passed it over and he looked at it and gave it back with a reassuringly thick envelope. 'Ticket, sir,' he said, and I was on the way, first class to Madrid.

The head of security at the airport met me off the plane and whisked me through the formalities. Dexter met me at the smartest hotel I could imagine and I was given a few pages of script to learn and another envelope which held a wad of exotic-looking dosh. John was very kind, and over the next three days we met about three times a day and worked on the pages. At night he arranged that I could see a few of the actors he knew for dinner or drinks. Michael Jayston, star of the film, was one of the first and was certainly the funniest and most encouraging. His kindness was all the more surprising as he was totally and supernaturally in love with Heather Sneddon. Just the sight of her nourished him. Later I saw that he could scarcely drag himself on set to film he loved her so much. And, indeed, she was a beautiful girl and obviously returned Michael's madness. The day of the test came and I was put into the hands of Tony Sanchez for make-up. Janet Suzman was friendly but cool, too. Dexter cosseted me all afternoon and did his part. It was like a dream, with all the heightened actuality that dreams can have. I floated through it and, on Dexter's advice, never wasted a single second looking at anyone but Janet. I had to rush back to London for a performance and then wait.

A few days later my agent rang and told me I'd got the part. I rushed to Aquinas Street, the head office of the National Theatre, about half a mile away, to find John Dexter and thank him. He was in one of the offices making a phone call. I caught his eye and made gestures of happiness, thumbs up and silly, bowing efforts. John seemed not to understand why I was doing this which made me feel embarrassed as he turned his back on me. For a moment I was baffled at what to do. Should I creep off and speak to him later, or had he misunderstood my mime? I waited a split second too long. As he turned again and found me still there and still smiling fatuously, he muttered into the mouthpiece, covered it up and snarled: 'What do want, Baker, can't you see I'm talking?'

I was astounded at his anger and said lamely, 'Sorry, John, it's just that Sam Spiegel has offered me Rasputin and I just wanted to say thank you. Thanks, John, I'm very grateful.' Too late, I realized I was talking too much. That marvellous head turned away and then back towards me and I could see that he was furious about something. It hadn't entered my head that his conversation was more important than my delight over getting a part.

'Baker,' he said tightly. 'You are so fucking boring that there's nothing else for you to do except to be a movie star. Of course, you got the part, I showed you how to do it, didn't I?' I raised a hand in surrender as if to say I understood. It didn't placate Dexter. With a sigh of infinite weariness he said, 'Just go away, will you, go away,' and he turned his back and resumed his phone conversation. I got the message and I crept away feeling baffled. I was filled with disgust at my lack of anger. Was there no limit to what I'd put up with to hold on to a job? No. There was no limit that I could think of. That's how it is with incomplete personalities.

Back at the Vic I brushed my teeth and my memory and putting on a tie went off to meet Maud Spector at the White Elephant restaurant in Curzon Street. I had never been in such a place as a guest. I was led to Maud's table, she had a permanent place there, and the waiter laid me out for her, covering me with a napkin as big as a sheet. For a moment I thought he was going to shave me. He merely offered me a menu as big as a Monopoly board. And the wine! The smoked salmon! The quality of the glassware! I glanced around me and saw all those famous faces. I was the only one there I'd never heard of. Such posing, such loud talk, such vulgarity. I was completely at home.

I think that to be a good actor you have to prefer strangers. After all to act you have only to be able to fake the truth. And it's much easier to convince strangers than it is to persuade those who know you. If the audience believes your story, you're home and dry.

I have always liked the rehearsal period as much as the performance itself. If the cast is interesting and friendly then you are assured of a fascinating time. If the director is sympathetic and helpful then things often go well. And if the director is very special, like Michael Blakemore or Jonathan Miller, the work becomes much more fascinating. I shall never forget the pleasure of working for Jonathan Miller. I have never heard anyone say otherwise. Of course, I'm hopelessly biased; Jonathan's production of *The Merchant of Venice* did me so much good at the National Theatre. I was never able to exploit it but Jonathan gave me the chance.

Before the days of read-throughs and speeches – 'Rodney will now say a few words' – lots of supporting actors didn't know what the play was about. They just knew their scenes and played them. And even today there are plenty of leading actors who don't take much notice of what the supporting people are up to. They just get on with their own scenes and hope for the best.

I don't think I care to know what a character has been up to in another room or another country. But the style these days is for investigation of the text. This can lead to an acceptance by the cast that the director knows best. This is not always easy to take.

Once when I was asked to be in *Hedda Gabler* I arrived knowing Hedda pretty well only to discover that Donald McWinnie had promised Hedda to Susannah York. I was deeply hurt and as Susannah insisted she was to play Hedda Gabler, I had to settle for the part of Judge Brack. I played Brack the way I would have played Hedda and it was a great success for me, one of only three that I've had.

In a production of *The White Devil* at the Old Vic, Anthony Nicholls, an actor whom I admired immensely, had no time to black up for the scene in which he meets Zanche the Moor, played by Jane Lapotaire. When he met her he had to say: 'I never loved my complexion until now.' Nobody noticed he was white and the play did about a hundred performances. And Beatrix Lehmann once told me that when she was acting in a play at the Queen's Theatre, a drunken actor who was in a play next door at the Lyric walked into her theatre by mistake and right into her solo scene. He looked at Bea, looked again, as if to say 'What are you doing here?', said 'Ah!' in a very meaningful way and nipped next door to his own play.

'Were you angry, Bea?' I asked her.

'Not until I heard the round of applause he got,' she told me.

So off I flew to Madrid for what I thought was stardom. A large apartment in Calle Doctor Fleming, instant intimacy with famous actors, and a driver by the name of Jesus – I was in heaven. Late evenings with Harry Andrews and sometimes Jack Hawkins and Michael Redgrave; I never wanted it to stop. When Harry asked me out, 'Would you like to come to supper with Irene [Worth] and me, Tom?'

'Yes, Harry, yes,' I said.

Sam Spiegel had an apartment that seemed to me like another universe. He had a valet called James who read me real quick and liked the empty spaces he detected. Caviar with chopped egg whites and little lozenges of toast and chopped onions. Fish jam some people call it. Not I. The vodka bottle encased in ice and carried in a gleaming napkin. Janet Suzman was there, I think. It was as though the Oracle from Delphi had dropped in for a snack and a spot of enlightenment, for Janet has special insights which are not given to others.

Michael Jayston, with terrific aplomb, teased Sam Spiegel about past movies: 'Was the scene with Rod Steiger and Brando in the taxi very difficult to achieve, Sam?' And Sam, falling for it and elaborating on it, 'Now you come to recall it, Michael, I must tell you that the taxi was my idea.' And Michael kicking me under the table. It was great. And as if that wasn't enough Jayston would swing the talk round to Greta Garbo and Sam would leap to the bait.

One day on the set of *Nicholas and Alexandra* during a difficult scene involving lots of elegantly dressed extras and two camera moves I managed, as Rasputin, to do my bit in one take. Everybody made a fuss of me and we finished for the day. As I was leaving the set surrounded by brand-new best friends, Sam Spiegel appeared and called out: 'Tom, come here while I speak.' Taking my arm and enveloping me in exquisite cigar smoke, he said mysteriously, 'I want you to know that I've just seen the rushes of yesterday's scene with you and Janet.' This was the scene when I first meet the Tsarina and the spell begins. Sam waited for me to speak. But I couldn't, I simply trembled. 'I would like you to know that I am pleased, very very pleased.' The relief was overpowering. Sam Spiegel was pleased with me! Never mind that I had betrayed God and slung my faith, never mind that I had cheated every good girl who had been willing to try and make me happy. Never mind that my two young children didn't know where I was and that I did nothing about it out of loathing for their mother, never mind that I had no idea who I was or how I was going to get through the night when there was no performance. Sam Spiegel was pleased. He was pleased with me! With me.

I looked at him and said, 'Sam, that makes me very happy.' I was already picking up the way he spoke.

He looked at me in surprise, no, with incredulity: 'It makes you happy?' he said, and went off shaking his head slightly as if to say, 'What odd balls these actors are.'

Of course he was right to be surprised. What had my happiness to do with anything? If the rushes had been bad I would have been on the plane home back to the all-night café in the Waterloo Road and the renewed search for an identity. But Sam was pleased and I was happy to feel unreal and to get away from myself.

The whirligig spun and I flew back and forth between London and Madrid first class with VIP on my ticket. I flirted with air hostesses and travelled with people like Alan Webb whose exquisite style of complaining about everything delighted me. He had no luggage to pick up at the carousel and therefore sailed through the airport with great panache. He told me that it was quite impossible to be mysterious when carrying luggage. At a distance, he said, 'even expensive luggage reduces one to refugee status.'

'Sam Spiegel may be common,' he added. 'But he never stoops so low as to carry his own luggage.' He said this with infinite malice, knowing perfectly well that I was lugging a large case in the manner of a refugee.

As the days passed I came to believe the publicity about my compelling, hypnotic eyes and powerful aura. What I couldn't know was that the aura came from the first-class ticket. That dawned on me later when the aura had vanished with the ticket and I was sleeping on Paul Angelis's floor in Holbein Place, Pimlico.

A publicity still from
'Robot', the very first of
my 178 episodes as
Doctor Who.

Above: A Daleks's meeting in
the rehearsal room at the BBC.

Left: Another problem fixed
with the string.

'Where are we?
In another quarry,
I suppose.' With
Lis Sladen, looking
ironical.

BBC special effects at
their best.

Davros, played with such
relish by Michael Wisher,
issues his threats.

Punting on the river at Cambridge
in the unfinished 'Shada' by
Douglas Adams.

John Leeson, voice of K9, and the unsung hero of all the rehearsals.

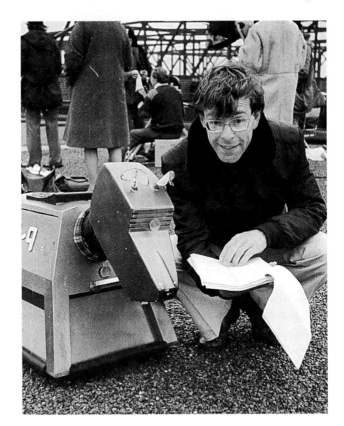

Me with K9: 'If it's a two shot, crouch down, Tom.'

Louise Jameson, my third assistant. Presumably this was a publicity still.

Ian Marter as Harry in 1974.

Lis Sladen, my first assistant.

During the filming of 'Destiny of the Daleks'. Far left: Peter Straker, a very good singer; with hands to face, Lalla Ward; peering over my right shoulder, June Hudson; with cigarette, director Ken Grieve.

Lalla Ward. We were married for a while.

Above: The Doctor Who company, 1976.
George Spenton-Foster is seated
centre-front in a white suit. To his left is
Graham Williams.

BBC all-purpose still.
I had plenty to smile about most
of the time in those days.

FIFTEEN

MY FILMING SCHEDULE was coming to an end and I was back at the Old Vic deliberately hanging about in the hope that John Dexter would send for me for his production of *A Woman Killed With Kindness*. I had heard a whisper from Aquinas Street that he had mentioned my name for a good part.

Within a day or so I saw him again in the pub but this time surrounded by a group of about six actors and some stage management. I ducked away out of his eyeline and got on with my pint. Suddenly there was a little messenger with a little message from the big man. 'John wants you,' and a tiny flick of the head due north towards Dexter's throne in case I had no sense of direction. I went over to his group. When you don't know who you are and don't even like what you suspect 'they' might think you are, you feel vulnerable and hopeful at the same time. It was within a director's gift at the National to recreate people like me. It was a bit like being in a fairy tale as a poor, wandering woodcutter who suddenly meets a hideous witch. Or in the case of John Dexter, a hideous wizard. He could call me into a new existence, much more interesting than my own. He could turn me from a poor strolling woodchopper into a court jester or even a prince. John knew it and he knew that I knew it, and received me with a smile like the glint of winter moonlight on a coffin lid.

There was no space made for me by the litter of six pups snuggled round the great wizard. John made as if he was assessing me. 'Well, if it isn't Mr Baker, the future movie star. Do you think, Mr Baker, that you can pretend with the help of a sword that you're dangerous

and would you like to be Joan Plowright's brother in my production?'
I looked at him as calmly as I could, dreading some awful put-
down. 'Don't try to look mysterious,' he beamed, 'the answer's yes,
isn't it?'

'Yes,' I said, and humbly, too, I'm afraid.

'Of course, it's yes,' repeated John, and the news is that you're
going to play Sir Francis Acton in *A Woman Killed with Kindness*.

When one receives a good bit of news in an alehouse, it is
customary to offer a drink to the bringer. 'Can I get you a drink,
John?' I asked him.

'No, you certainly can't,' he sneered. 'You can leave the pub and
start work on the script, we start in four weeks.' I stood before him
and his pups watched me with interest, they were seeing the great
bitch at work and they were liking it.

'Well? What are you waiting for?' cooed John. 'You've got something to do at last, off you go.' And I went, not daring to go back
to my unfinished pint in case Doctor Frankenstein changed his mind
and withdrew the offer of a new life from a poor monster who only
wanted to make people laugh.

I was still going back and forth to Spain when the rehearsals
for *A Woman Killed with Kindness* started. They took place in an
abandoned public library just across the road from the Old Vic. It
was a marvellous arrangement for Dexter. Once everyone was in,
there was no way out without passing him. A stage had been built
to raise the rehearsal area and beyond that was a study area with
lots of books about the period. There was a kettle for tea and coffee
and a lavatory and that was that. John stood guard like Cerberus.
There was no opportunity to talk. I was cast back to my religious
days in the novitiate in Jersey. I felt stifled and without ideas. What
was the point of making us into Trappists for six weeks? I had a
lovely part and a very severe problem with John. After his great
kindness to me in Spain I felt indebted to him and this made me
anxious. Because of the filming dates and my other commitments
at the Vic my schedule became frantic. I would be picked up at
5.30 a.m. at the theatre and driven by limousine to Heathrow, where

I was booked first class to Madrid. At Madrid I was met by the chief of security and rushed through customs and driven to the set where I filmed all day. So there I was involved in a big film, rehearsing a new production and also acting in two other plays all at the same time. I loved it all.

Once I missed the flight to London and had to be sent to Paris for the night. Next morning I was on the first flight out and driven at speed to the ghastly public library to face the sarcasm of the very man who'd helped me get the movie. John was very keen on discipline, he would have appreciated the training methods of the SAS, he could even have devised them. Every morning there were movement classes. During the first week no exceptions were tolerated, absolutely none. But by the end of the second week, John himself had to be elsewhere at meetings and I noticed that Joan Plowright and Anthony Hopkins were ducking the sessions. Dexter knew this and said nothing, but it depressed me. There were fight scenes to be prepared and bird-handling scenes too. The budget was big enough in those days to include six mighty hawks and their handlers. I was nervous of those great hawks. Derek Jacobi's bird seemed to dislike me intensely. I suspected Dexter had been on to him because I was suddenly allocated Derek's bird. I became terrified and John was delighted at my fear. The hawk would rise up and flutter like a bloody great eagle, all the while shitting over me as if he'd been on curry all night.

Perhaps I was tired and didn't quite realize it, but John seemed unable to stand the sight of me at work. I couldn't think what to do to heal his anger. He and Jacobi's hawk seemed to feel the same about me. It did not seem enough for John that the hawks were shitting all over me, he soon got used to that and was bored. Suddenly Dexter changed tack and found another way to get to me.

One morning he seemed particularly tense and I noticed that my understudy, Howard Southern, an excellent actor and a real threat to me, was standing by very obviously and looking towards Dexter as if waiting for the signal for the 'excuse me' cut in. Sword in belt and very lively, young Howard Southern was making me anxious. He was a much more fluid mover than I and a lot better looking and probably a better actor.

In the first scene of the play I had to enter to the sound of wedding bells and announce with great joy the marriage of my sister, Joan Plowright. After a long speech in a broad northern accent, the rest of the company would come pouring on and the play would race away. This particular morning I sailed on and gave the speech my all. But in my eyeline was handsome Howard, my understudy. Armed to the teeth, the complexion of a peach and a fine pair of legs, he looked very threatening.

I desperately recalled the days when I believed in God and was passionate to hug lepers. John Dexter was not impressed. As I finished and the rest of the company swept on he pulled us up and with the moan of St Sebastian as yet another arrow struck him and he ordered a restart of the scene. The rest of the actors took it well and got back to their marks. That morning they got used to those marks as time after time we did the scene because of John's dissatisfaction with me. My understudy was ready as we reached the sixteenth attempt, his legs seeming to get sturdier, his complexion more perfect and his sword shinier and sharper. I was in a terrible state and not getting any better as the words were, by now, meaningless. I looked towards the company for sympathy but they were exhausted and nobody said a word; it was between Dexter and me. On the nineteenth attempt he let us continue and the relief was palpable in the library. At lunch that day nobody said a word about the torment of the morning. People kept a reasonable distance from me, as though my fear and bad luck were contagious. But that day was a turning point. Dexter appeared to become resigned to me being in the cast and the gibes were less frequent. 'You are so boring, Baker that you might as well become a movie star,' he repeated.

The play was pretty well received and I got a few laughs during the fight scenes as I skidded about a bit in hawk shit. Anyway I survived it. Joan Plowright, playing a wonderful woman, had to do a very old-style death scene surrounded by her extended family. As her brother Sir Francis Acton I had to lead the grieving gang. Of course I couldn't do it as I had sobbed all those years ago in Liverpool at the gravesides of diphtheria victims – no, Acton was sterner than that. As I entered the chamber of death and we all gathered round, carefully grouped by Dexter, I was the first to speak. We all spoke in broad northern accents for no clear reason except that John felt we were Northerners. Anyhow, there we all were looking sad around Joan Plowright's bed and the company looked to me for the first sign of sympathy. And my line, in broad northern was: 'How do you feel yourself?' The rest of the cast were convulsed by this enquiry and so were a good number of the audience. I asked John if we could modify it but he pretended that the text was sacred and insisted I say it. And I did and the convulsions continued. That wasn't all. As we all knelt around the deathbed muttering the pat-ernoster, we began to vary the prayer to tease Anthony Hopkins. For some reason we started to say in guttural tones, 'Edward Woodward, Edward Woodward who art in Heaven'. This was all very silly but it amused those of us not playing very big parts and made life hard for Hopkins, because the dying Joan Plowright was supposed to be his wife. Hopkins grew to dread the scene and even begged me to use my influence on the others. I suppose our silliness was just a tiny bit of sabotage in revenge for what John Dexter had put us through in rehearsals.

The months fled by with established favourites remaining in the repertoire and new productions being announced and fought over. As Dexter's production ran its course we began rehearsing Pirand-ello's *Rules of the Game* during the day with Paul Scofield and Joan Plowright playing the leads. We toured this to great success, how could it fail with Paul on great form and Joan being deliciously operatic as Paul's wife? We came into London at the New Theatre and the play was set for a run. I was playing Paul Scofield's servant Luigi and I had the idea of playing him as neurotically possessive of Paul. It worked quite well and it amused Paul and the director Anthony Page tolerated my excesses.

Meanwhile Michael Halifax, our resident planner and diplomat, had told me that there was nothing for me in the next season. What a terrible job it was to tell people that as of August they would cease to exist. Only Michael with his great tact could have managed it. This crushed me a bit and I asked for early release which was granted with terrific speed. Joan Plowright gave a little party for me and Sir Laurence came and even Paul stayed for a few minutes after the play. What was to become of me?

Well, it so happened that the film of *Nicholas and Alexandra* was opening in America and I was invited to go over to help promote it, if I had time. Oh, I had time all right, and like Barkis, I was willin'. I was desperately willin'.

SIXTEEN

'CHRISTOPHER ISHERWOOD has written the script, Tom, and we'd like to think about you for the part of the monster.'

I was bowled over at the prospect.

'And who's going to direct it?' I asked, as if that mattered to me who was out of work; but actors ask that even though they know the film will probably not happen. It's probably part of the whole madness of movies. So they said 'Jack Smight,' and I said 'Ah,' as if that meant something to me. The film was *Frankenstein, the True Story* and it did get made.

For a few days everything went to plan, and I kept thinking about being a darling monster and how my performance might get me a Golden Globe award. And then, you've guessed it, the phone rang. It was Hunt Stromberg, the producer. The studio wanted a 'name' for the monster and also Christopher would prefer somebody who was er, well, handsome. There was nothing I could say to that, except that as far as I knew Dr Frankenstein was not a plastic surgeon and the monster had never been beautiful before. Hunt Stromberg is a prince of a man and he was sympathetic, very sympathetic, to my point but the studio was the studio, 'you know'. So that was that. I would not get to meet James Mason and Ralph Richardson after all.

Quickly I turned to the next non-event which was to learn to swim. Trying to stay ahead of the game, I thought that perhaps someone might want to do the life of Captain Webb and, as I smoked in those days, I'd noticed a certain resemblance to me in the picture of Captain Webb on the matchbox. I told my swimming coach about why I wanted to learn to swim and he was very encouraging as he struggled to teach me in the shallow end among the young mothers and babies – for I am nervous of water. My enthusiasm was high for about two lessons until I heard my chap telling one of his pals, a man with wispy hair and a very black mole on his very pale upper lip about my hopes of playing Captain Webb.

'But he only had one leg,' remarked black mole, obviously a man with a facility to down actors he didn't know. As soon as I heard that Webb was a one-legger I lost interest in him and in swimming and decided to learn to live with my fear of water.

Then somebody asked me if I'd ever taught English as a foreign language. No, I hadn't. Why? It turned out that there were schools all over the place who needed tutors in English. I was given the name of one and went along with the deep trepidation of the amateur conman. What did I know about teaching foreigners anything? I needn't have worried, the man at the desk, who seemed to be smoking two cigarettes at a time, was delighted to see me. He gave a very good impression of being my loving father and asked me if I could start right away as three tutors hadn't shown up for their classes.

'How many in a class?' I asked him.

'Oh, it can be as many as five or six,' he said. 'We have about thirty tutors in all and several levels of study.'

Five or six was a reassuring figure and I agreed to give it a go. He handed me a few textbooks, gave me the number of a room on the second floor and off I went to act the part of a tutor at a pound an hour. There were a handful of young people in room nine, all waiting to be taught to speak English. Four of them were Spanish, one French and a couple of Italians; they all worked in the catering industry as waiters or commis chefs. Not one of them spoke English that would have got him back to where he lived in London.

So there was my audience, only seven, but better than nothing. To begin with I found out their names and devised some games to play. I went home and worked out a few exercises using the same twenty-five verbs. I got some props from the lost property office at the school and we improvised situations and had fun. In the large room we had it was easy to move about and act out little plays. I got to play the dissatisfied customer, by turns sarcastic or loud or with a stammer. All our little games were about restaurants or shopping and progress was really good. This went on from Tuesday through to Friday, two hours a day with about the same time for me to prepare the lessons. Over Saturday and Sunday I worked out scripts with good lines for the students and I was looking forward to my Monday afternoon class. The students could only do afternoons as they all seemed to work split shifts. On Monday I strolled in ready for some fun and to my amazement found the room packed with young people, perhaps thirty of them. I sent for the secretary to ask why the sudden increase without warning and she explained to me that the word was out that my lessons were amusing and, as there were no rules about the movement of students between classes, they could go where they liked. I asked about the teachers in the classes from where my new students had come. 'Oh, they'll have an easy time until the students get tired of you,' she said, cheerfully. I tried to do what I could but the odds were against me. Some of the newcomers spoke better than my original seven and all of my seven were furious that they had to share me with the others. It was all too much and too sad to watch them trying to follow my desperate efforts to fascinate them. Within two weeks I was knackered and disheartened and I gave in my notice. 'Have you got any friends who might like to give it a go?' asked the jolly secretary. But I had no friends then and, come to think of it, I have none now.

During 1973 I felt very fragile. After the language school disappointment I was penniless and unwell and very sorry for myself. My girlfriend, Jo, had found a new love in Birmingham. *The Duchess of Malfi* often strains old love to breaking point. When you are in a terrific play in a terrific part in Birmingham, one's partner back home often ceases to be mysterious. This is especially noticeable if you have to share a bathroom. It's very hard to sustain any relationship with one bathroom, but if one of you is in *The Duchess of Malfi* as well, hell. The chances are you will cease to be an item before the run is over. And so it was with Jo and me. She called and said she had found 'great love with a man'. I put the phone down. The pain was exquisite. I resolved to be calm. But everywhere I looked I saw signs that wrenched at my heart; I kept passing Casa Pupa in Pimlico, where we'd shopped together, and seeing *Le Boucher* advertised at the Chelsea Classic. I took to popping in to the Church of the Holy Redeemer and gazing at the statue of the Sacred Heart, peering closely at the dripping blood. The Stations of the Cross became a great pleasure and consolation to me. I kept bursting into tears and once I deliberately cut myself deeply in my left breast. As the blood flowed all over me (I was naked as I struck the blow), I felt myself to be at one with the Sacred Heart of Jesus. I was alone, poor, bleeding and unwanted. I had never felt happier.

Just as I was fading away in self-pity at being abandoned for a new love from *The Duchess of Malfi*, a job came up. When depression sets in one longs for a contrast in one's work but fate, with marvellous casualness, invited Peter James to offer me Macbeth. It's an interesting part for someone in deep depression. Peter had just been appointed the artistic director of the Shaw Theatre in the Euston Road. The choice of play had nothing to do with him. It had been selected by the powers that be because it was a school text that term and therefore was sure to sell a lot of tickets. Peter had some good ideas for it, and one or two that were not so good. The really big mistake was to cast me as Macbeth. I just could not get a hold on it. During rehearsals I didn't get a single laugh. This is very unusual for any actor and should have rung alarm bells in Peter James's head. For all I know it did but Peter is a very loyal man and he decided to stick with me in spite of my lack of comic flair.

We had about four weeks to get the play together. About half-way through the rehearsal period Peter got a stiff dose of flu. He came in to work but was too unwell to be inspiring. So we struggled on knowing that things were not too good as regards the leading actor. We had an appalling first night when I suffered a terrific dry towards the end of the play. This caused havoc and took about fifteen minutes off the anticipated running time. The audience seemed quite pleased about it all and we hoped the rest of the run would be better.

But from then on the audience was made up of sceptical O-level students who were bussed in to the Shaw to watch a great play in which I took the lead. I was so shocked by my first-night dry and so sorry for myself at Jo's new-found happiness in Birmingham that my old desire for death came back. Suddenly I was convinced that I was going to die before the run of the play was completed. I think we were signed for about six weeks. At the time I was living in a room in Westbourne Terrace W2. I didn't have a great deal of property apart from some first-edition books and old play scripts that I'd gathered together. As the conviction grew that I was about to die, the problem of disposing of my bits and pieces worried me. I had grown fond of some actors who sympathized with my suffering. Every night before curtain-up I was violently sick. The actors in my dressing room used to run the water in the wash basins very loudly and talk at the tops of their voices to drown out the disgusting noises I was making. I was so grateful to them that each night when I came to the theatre I brought a few of my things in and gave them to any actor who fancied them. Most of them were quite pleased and thought I was a good chap to be dishing out books and little ornaments as presents.

And so the run of the play continued. I never dried again, of course, but I didn't get any better either. Several times I was booed at the curtain call and this helped to lower still further my already low self-esteem. During the matinees, the children drank beer and got quite rowdy; and when the play started they resented having to come in and watch me. I never blamed them. If I could have avoided it, I would not have come in myself.

Sometimes the children threw marshmallows on to the stage. I had cultivated, for the part, a special way of walking. I felt that Macbeth, feeling trapped, might express this in a rather jagged style of movement. The children in the audience may have hated my performance as mad Macbeth, but they adored my walk. Of course, because of the lights, I couldn't see where the marshmallows were on the stage but the audience could. Every time I stood on one a great yell of laughter went up from six-hundred sadistic teenagers. Several of my fellow actors advised me to modify my style of walking but it was too late. I thought I could hear the wings of the angel of death and in my despair I refused to accept their advice. I felt that if I couldn't hang on to my girlfriend then I could at least hold on to my walk.

In this way the evenings of agony passed slowly and, at the same pace, I fetched in my few remaining belongings to dispose of among the cast. By the last performance all I had left was an old Edwardian *chaise-longue*. It was about eight feet long and very heavy. Even in my strange state of mind I realized I could not get a *chaise-longue* on to a Northern Line Tube train. So it remained my last possession, everything else had been gratefully received by members of the cast.

The last performance arrived and passed and, dear God, I was still alive! I went home to W2 feeling cheated. Suddenly I felt that not only could I not trust life but death too was unreliable.

Some comfort was waiting for me in Passmore Street, SW1, where there is a warm little world called the Fox and Hounds, where the landlady is Diane. She is a wonderful woman with large eyes and a capacity to listen even to dull stories, so naturally lots of actors go there. She is known among bores as the Mother Teresa of the licensed victuallers. And it was in that snug little world that I was introduced to a man who was known as Derm the Worm. He was very handsome, a good talker and his girlfriend wanted to see him dead. It turned out he was an expert in Turkish carpets and *chaises-longues*, too. Without any trouble he took my last remaining possession off my hands and that was that. I wondered what would become of me.

One day in the Fox and Hounds, I was told that if I were to go to Ebury Street the following morning at 7.15 and stand outside number 182, where the young Mozart had written his first symphony, I would meet a man called Arthur Cordes who was in the way of needing a labourer. The work would be entirely menial, there would be no security and the wages were the legal minimum.

In a state of deep apprehension and joyous depression I loitered at the gate to Mozart's place at 7.05 and waited for Arthur Cordes. He came right on time in the shabbiest van imaginable, took me to the site, which was about three doors from Wolfgang's place, gave me a cup of tea and a piece of bread pudding the size of a half brick and I set to work as a builder's labourer. Arthur was my master and a good one, too. He was as jolly as Mr Fezziwig; though whether he could dance I never did find out. Fuelled by sweet tea and bread pudding I set to work, happy in the thought that nobody knew where I was or even cared, and that Jo was happy with the 'great love' she had found in *The Duchess of Malfi*. Arthur was intrigued to have an actor on the site and was amused at the way I used to come through the door in the morning. I've always found it difficult to come through a door sincerely and for that reason people often laugh. It's not as simple as it sounds. You just watch out the next time you're in the theatre. Or you could try it at home on your partner.

Tom Conti has a way of coming through a door that makes you gasp, and Jeremy Irons, even as Richard II, always excited great admiration as he entered – and there wasn't even a door in that production. The greatest of all is Donald Sinden. He is so astonishing at entering that you can sometimes tell he's coming two minutes before he arrives. He's my hero as an enterer, but somehow I've never been able to get the knack of it, as Arthur noticed during my time in Ebury Street, though he never held it against me as John Dexter had.

The work was so hard that it soothed me. I was shattered at the end of the day and that helped me to get through the nights. As it sank in to my poor nut that sheer bone-shaking activity was good for me I redoubled my efforts and always asked if I could do the Kango drill. To use a Kango drill without ear muffs three or four hours a day takes away all fear of death and memories of old loves finding new loves in Birmingham. I didn't entirely forget, of course, and sometimes that great Webster line came to me from *The White Devil*: 'He once bottled a fart that poisoned the whole of Dublin.' How I wished I was Doctor Julio and could rush away and poison all Birmingham.

Gradually, the Kango drill did its work and the pain eased. My desire to make people laugh came back and Arthur said I was coming through the door in the mornings with a bit more aplomb than when I had first started. This raised my spirits no end. The only side effect from the therapy of the Kango drill was that my arms and hands shook so much that I couldn't eat or drink properly. It was very bad for a few days and I began to feel dizzy. To keep my strength up I would wait till Arthur was gone to another site and then I'd put my bread pudding in a dish on the floor and get down on my hands and knees to it. After a while it's not as difficult as you might suspect. I noticed, though, that supping my tea from the same dish I made the same noise as my father had made all those years before in the days when he used to torture my mother at meal times. This bothered me a bit but not too much; anyway I was alone and only wanted to torture myself.

From time to time my agent called to encourage me. Now that I was getting a weekly wage, though being on an emergency tax code swallowed a good bit of it, I was able to go into the Fox and Hounds for a toasted sandwich and a glass of bitter and that made me feel even better.

Some years before this I had been in *The Millionairess* with Maggie Smith for the BBC's Play of the Month series. It was directed by Bill Slater and had been something of a success in spite of my not very good impression of Peter Sellers doing an Egyptian doctor. For a while the company of James Villiers and Charles Gray kept me amused and made me feel as if perhaps I was one of them. It was not to be. The production went to air and was reasonably well received and that was the end of it. So all those years later, sleeping on a mattress in Bourne Street, Pimlico, I remembered Bill Slater and wrote him a desperate letter. I pointed out to him that there had to be some sort of a part for me in the huge Series and Serials

188

Department of the BBC. I wrote the letter on a lonely Sunday night. Sunday has been a bad day for me for many years and often I've drafted a suicide note on a Sunday evening.

The letter was posted on Monday morning on my way past Mozart's house to pick up my bread pudding and start work for Arthur Cordes who was now my friend. It arrived at the BBC on the Tuesday morning and reached Bill Slater's office after he had left for a meeting with Barry Letts, a senior producer in the Serials Department. His responsibility was for *Doctor Who*. As chance would have it, Jon Pertwee had given up the part of Doctor Who and Barry Letts and other colleagues were having casting meetings to find a replacement. Jon Pertwee had been a huge success in the part and there was a good deal of talk required among the staff on who was to be the new Doctor Who.

That was the first coincidence. Now, how about this? The reason that Bill Slater was attending this meeting called by Barry Letts was that in the next week he was to become the head of the department. It was considered by Barry, who has exquisite manners, that Bill Slater, as the future boss, should be in on the discussions to recast Doctor Who. And so he was.

I heard later that an actor called Richard Hearn was being considered. Later somebody told me that Graham Crowden had been offered the part. I can't be sure of any of these points, and I don't really care. At the meeting, Bill Slater was asked if he had any strong views on who the new man should be; he had none, and went about the rest of his heavy schedule. Another meeting was fixed for the next day and Bill said he'd think about it.

Bill had a late meeting with other people that day and then, after some drinks with colleagues, he went to his office picked up my letter, and went home to Mary Webster, his wife. They had supper and got ready for bed and Bill told her about his day and about the casting session for Doctor Who. He told me he was actually getting into bed when he glanced at my poor begging letter. He read it to Mary Webster. The time was 11.15 p.m. in Great Titchfield Street where Bill and Mary did their conjugality. About three and a half miles away in Pimlico at exactly the same time I was tossing on my mattress in Bourne Street.

Bill and Mary thought I would be a good choice for Doctor Who and Mary said: 'Call him now,' and Bill did, and I answered. Bill was very nice and said he'd just read my letter and would I like to come and see him at the TV Centre the next evening at about 6.30 p.m.? He was not specific and I didn't care. All I wanted was to be seen by someone who could help me. Yes, I said, thanked him and fell back into my pit.

On the Wednesday morning Bill attended his second casting session for Doctor Who. Views were exchanged and names bandied about. Barry Letts again asked Bill if he had a view on the replacement and Bill said yes. He mentioned my name and added that I would be coming to see him at 6.30 that evening.

I was on time. Bill Slater was waiting for me and took me up to the office of the head of drama, Shaun Sutton. Barry Letts was there. So there I was with three very nice men who chatted and laughed at my jokes and seemed very pleased to see me. Someone fetched me a glass of beer but I couldn't drink it.

'We've got an idea, you see, Tom,' said Bill after nearly an hour. 'Do you think you could come back and see us tomorrow?'

I agreed to come back. I was quite willing to spend the night outside the office if they'd wanted it but I thought that would have betrayed anxiety; so I went home.

The next day I mentioned to Arthur that I'd been to the BBC and that they were thinking about me for some job. Arthur was delighted and began the teasing that actors get when between jobs. I was referred to as 'Sir Laurence' and generally had the piss taken something chronic. It didn't bother me at all. I fled the site at 5.15 and rushed to Bourne Street for a swill and a change of clothes, and then took the Circle Line to Notting Hill Gate, Central Line to Shepherd's Bush and a little gallop along Wood Lane to the TV Centre. I was a bit late but Bill said not to worry, and up we went to Shaun Sutton's office again. Like the night before Barry Letts was there. They sat me down, asked me how I was, and then fell into an interesting silence. By that I mean they were not speaking but it wasn't oppressive. They all looked at me and then at each other as if to say, 'Who's to speak?'

Shaun nodded to Bill who looked towards Barry who said: 'Tom, we'd like you to be the next Doctor Who. What do you think?'

I have to remind you that in those days, Doctor Who was a very big job in television. I have to remind you that I was living on the smell of an oil rag and bread pudding.

'Well?' said Barry, 'What do you say?'

The three of them looked at me and were smiling and all I could do was nod. You know how it is with pleasure, one nod led to another nod and soon I couldn't stop nodding and they laughed kindly. We all shook hands. I felt reborn in the good news.

Then Barry said, 'There's just one thing, Tom.' My heart skidded and my arse pouted in terror. What was this one thing? Did it mean that somehow I wasn't to be Doctor Who?

Barry saw my anxiety and said: 'It's just that we'd like to delay the announcement for a while, we think about ten days. Do you think you can sit on the news for ten days?' I nodded. And then they all started nodding and smiling and off I went into the darkness of Wood Lane heavy with the great news that had to be kept secret. On the tube I kept wanting to nudge somebody, anybody, and tell her the news. But I didn't dare.

I got back to the Fox and Hounds in Passmore Street, not any old Fox and Hounds, Diane's Fox and Hounds, the Fox and Hounds where I stood next to Fred Fellowes who worked on the London Underground and I couldn't tell him my news. He bought me a drink and remarked: 'Are you all right? You look as if you've just had some news.' I shrugged as if to say, 'well, you know how it is, Fred?' And I muttered about there being the possibility of a little job on the telly.

And so I stood there, bursting with my promotion from general labourer to Time Lord. The burden was too much and I went home to the mattress. No sleep came and when I got to work next morning the first thing Arthur wanted to know was how the interview at the

BBC had gone. It was an amazing few days. Dear Arthur who brought me bread pudding made by his Babs would have loved to hear what I had to say but I had promised Barry Letts and I was terrified that something might spoil my good fortune. To get through the time I went mad at the work. Naturally, the Beeb had got in touch with my agent who swiftly, very swiftly, tried to get in touch with me.

I deliberately did not return the calls for the first two days. I think I was possessive of the news and the jackpot I'd hit by my own effort. Eventually, though, I did call and went in and signed the contract. The first wages were not all that good, but I didn't know that. Later, Philip Hinchcliffe, my producer, was to assure me that he wanted me to have more money. And I accepted it and blew it as fast as I could. The odd thing was that as soon as I got some dosh the poor dodged me. The only people I met were those who were well fixed. I couldn't tell the difference and blew it.

Good or bad it's a terrible thing not to be able to tell someone. Anyway the day was fixed and I was able to say to Arthur that I needed a whole day off to go to the BBC about this little job I'd mentioned. I then went to my friend Ted Whitehead* and asked him if he'd like to come to the BBC for the enthronement of the new Doctor Who. Ted said he'd come and I was so proud to be seen with him. I kept hoping I'd have the chance to mention Ted's play *Alpha Beta*. And I did drop it out proudly to the script editor on *Doctor Who*, Terrance Dicks.

On the great morning Ted and I went to the centre of the universe in Wood Lane and were whisked – stars always get whisked – into the Bridge Lounge to await the presentation of the new Doctor to the waiting press. I wore a white suit and a Peruvian sweater and a tie painted by some poor exploited Atahualpa or other. Barry Letts led me forth for the presentation. Not since I'd faced the foreign press in Los Angeles for *Nicholas and Alexandra* had I felt so well. The press turn out was so great that we had to do the whole ceremony

* Author of *The Foursome*, *Alpha Beta* and *Old Flames*.

in the BBC bar. There was clapping, there was flashing of cameras and then more clapping; and I desperately hoped it would never stop and it didn't for quite a while. I whirled and posed and smiled and looked alien and the more they gasped the more I did it and so it went on. At last, I had ceased to exist and that was a great feeling. Ted Whitehead smiled to see me so happy and everyone wanted to touch me and I wanted them to touch me, too, and they did and it was just marvellous. Oh yes.

From all directions chaps wanted to discuss projects and girls looked at me in a meaningful way. Thousands of pictures were shot by snappers from all over the country. This gave me a lot of pleasure but when the man said he was from the *Evening Standard* my cup ran over. I knew that if I was lucky the men on the site and especially Arthur Cordes would see it that day and I wanted that so badly. But they wanted no more than the others and the moment passed. I was whisked – there I go again – into a special studio and was on air to the Midlands and the North. The man from the North asked me if I'd be doing the Doctor with a Liverpool accent and did I have a message for anyone. I was speechless. And when it was all over Ted and I went off and knocked out a few drinks in Shepherd's Bush. Then on to the whizzy West End. The second edition of the *Standard* carried a picture of me on the front page. Oh, bliss. Fuck off anonymity, hello everybody. Ted and I stumbled about and laughed. When I got back to the Fox and Hounds they roared with pleasure. I knew, of course, that Arthur and the chaps on the site would have got the paper and wouldn't be expecting to see me again.

Next morning I arrived on site as usual. The men were amazed. Arthur kept looking at me and laughing. And the day passed in a cloud of madness. I asked Arthur if I could leave a bit early and could we all have a drink at five thirty. Yes, he said, and off I rushed to the bank and then to Partridges in Sloane Street for little goodies to go with the booze. It was all too much. The men were so kind as well as totally incredulous. They kept shaking their heads and then shaking my hand. Somebody turned up from the *Daily Express* and asked if we could all be there the next morning for a picture, hods and shovels at the ready. And the joy increased as the fellows realized that they, too, were in on the madness and that people wanted to look at them and talk to them as well.

Never was there such keenness at a photo call the next day. We all stood in line with our tools at hand and obeyed the snapper's every whim. The *Daily Express*! It was difficult to work after our taste of stardom but somehow the day passed. The next morning we were all famous. A lovely picture and a very warm little article, too. That lunchtime I shook hands and swore eternal friendship with everyone and full of tears and good resolution I tottered off past Mozart's house. I never saw them again. I was Doctor Who now. I was an alien.

SEVENTEEN

AFTER I HAD SIGNED my contract and felt secure in a year's work, Bill Slater, Barry Letts, Bob Holmes, the script editor, and Philip Hinchcliffe, who was shadowing Barry before taking over the programme, took me out to lunch. It was at the Balzac Bistro on the corner of Wood Lane and Shepherd's Bush Green. After an hour's jolly chat and a few drinks Barry asked me how I might be playing the part of the Doctor. What a question! I had to tell him that I had no idea. Although I'd seen the programme a bit, I was not knowledgeable about it and I was so tense after my recent troubles that ideas just fled my head.

Barry was a little amused by my admission. He certainly didn't seem worried and for that I was grateful. Those four men at the lunch, who thought of me a couple of weeks earlier, are the ones who gave me the most important break of my life. At that lunch I had no idea that Doctor Who would be sold in seventy-four countries. The thought that I would be on more than two hundred stations in America alone would have flattened me. Even now, the thought that I am a star in Abu Dhabi tickles me. I often wonder how I can turn it to my advantage. So we just got on with the lunch and had a grand time. The changeover shot was done and I met the great Jon Pertwee at last. He was very nice and didn't wish me luck or anything like that.

And then things began to hot up for me. I was offered the part of the hero in a film called *The Author of Beltraffio*. Even at the time I thought the title was a bit naff. It sounded as if it had been lifted from a story by Henry James or some other out-of-copyright source. It was to be directed by a fellow called Tony Scott. Everybody even then used to say, 'Who?' And the answer was always, 'You know, Ridley Scott's brother.' And then they'd say, 'Oh, that Tony Scott.' You know the routine. Well, I didn't think he was a very good director, in fact I thought he was terrible. I believe he did try to be a car mechanic but he just couldn't get started though he certainly seemed to know a lot about cars. So he became a film director instead and probably did less harm that way. Anyway, I don't want to get trapped into saying anything too positive about Tony Scott in case he ever offers me a job.

But it was while I was doing this film and all dressed in late Victorian clothes that Peter (Lock up Your Daughters) Coe turned up on location and, seeing me all dressed up, offered me the part of Oscar Wilde at the Oxford Festival. But first we had to complete the Tony Scott job. Sometimes when we were shooting exteriors we had to wait for passing aeroplanes to go over. You can't have the sound of planes in a Victorian costume drama. We were also bothered by the bells of ice-cream vans. The tune of 'London Bridge is Falling Down' would irritate our director no end and that gave me a certain amount of pleasure. He was so impatient one day that he made a beautiful error of judgement. He sent one of the runners to pay the ice-cream man to go away. And the ice-cream man did go away. He went about three hundred yards in another direction, and rang his bell very loudly. Because it was from another direction Tony Scott assumed that it was a different ice-cream man. So he despatched another runner to pay off the van driver. The driver said, of course, that he would stop ringing his bell, took the tenner and drove off east by east, waited for ten minutes, and gave us the bell again. The first runner was sent this time and not having a terrific memory he failed to see that it was the same man. So the same man accepted another tenner and moved along. About £300 later Tony Scott's penny dropped. By which time the ice-cream man was planning a career in films, on the catering side.

But they were all very nice to work with and the time passed reasonably quickly. I met a girl on this picture called Marianne Ford.

She was marvellously amusing and very good to me. When the filming was finished I went straight into rehearsal for *The Trials of Oscar Wilde* and Marianne came with me. Thanks to her we were sometimes very happy over the next few years and the times we were not happy were all my fault.

We rehearsed *The Trials of Oscar Wilde* in an old hotel in Earls Court. It was terribly run down but very genteel. The permanent guests each had their own table in a very sad and neglected dining room which might once have been a ballroom. We worked there for about four weeks and discovered our characters. Aubrey Woods was Edward Carson, the prosecutor, and Nigel Stock was Sir Edward Clarke, counsel for the defence. I must say that Aubrey and Nigel were absolutely wonderful as lawyers. They fed me all the cues that provided me with the chance to fire off lots of witty answers.

EC: 'You were educated at Oxford, Mr Wilde?'
OW: 'I was educated at Trinity College, Dublin.'
And later from Aubrey as Carson, 'Is that beautiful, Mr Wilde?'
OW: 'Not the way you read it, Mr Carson.'

And so it went. It was a doddle really.

Anyway, we opened at the Playhouse, Beaumont Street, to very warm reviews. The boys playing Oscar's lads were simply amazing. They were irresistibly cocky and sly and very sexy. Lots of very heavy leather gays piled in to the play and followed us into the pub afterwards. I was always with the 'Boys', and this caused some jealousy in the bar and some pushing and shoving. It's always such a pleasure to be in a good piece of theatre and we whooped it up shamelessly. Gerald Cross, who played the judge who sent me down, gloried in his power to make the audience hate him. Being gay himself, this amused Gerald no end. So we were the hit of the festival, I think. Marianne organized witty parties in the green room for me and for the 'Boys', hampers from Partridges or Fortnums; they loved it and so did I and Marianne loved me. So before starting on *Doctor Who* in earnest, I managed a film and a play and a new love.

In those days I suffered from a very jumpy tummy and I was often, without warning, very sick. I hid this as much as I possibly could from the others in case the word got back to the BBC that I wasn't strong enough to cope with the heavy schedule of *Doctor Who*. One evening Marianne arranged for Barry Letts, Philip Hinchcliffe and others from the Beeb to see the play and have supper afterwards in a room at the Turf Tavern. They all said they liked the play, though it was a bit long, and the supper afterwards went brilliantly thanks to Marianne. So I drew a bit nearer to the chaps who were going to arrange my translation from 'who?' to '*Who!*'

The play ran to full houses and afterwards I went to live with Marianne in Notting Hill Gate and for a while we were happy. But the attention that came with the success of the programme brought temptation after temptation from curious girls whom were enthusiastic to lay a Time Lord. It had very little to do with me at all. How could it, they were strangers. But I didn't spot it. I thought that I was genuinely irresistible and I gave in to most of the time travellers. Marianne was very patient and I think she may have thought the madness would pass; but it didn't. And so I hurt the very person who was willing to protect me.

I remember I was asked to do a little piece in the *Sunday Times* called 'A Day in the Life of . . .'. I can't remember the details but when it came out and I read it early one Sunday morning I knew that Marianne wouldn't like it and so I tore it out of the magazine. What I hadn't noticed was that there was another reference to it elsewhere in the paper. So when Marianne turned it over and saw that I had ripped it out she suspected my motives. I was making myself utterly ridiculous and she saw it and couldn't help me. But I missed all the signs. I couldn't stop being ridiculous because I am ridiculous. The work at the BBC was very demanding but I loved it. I simply couldn't wait to get to North Acton rehearsal rooms and enjoy realizing the scripts. It was a pleasure to go to work in the mornings. And this whirligig of activity went on for all my time as Doctor Who.

Suddenly the crowd who'd found me boring found me fascinating. Like another Tony Lumpkin, I bought the drinks and sang out of tune and still got the applause. I also got the clap in return for my enthusiastic generosity. Ponces often do that: they take your drinks and food, share your cabs and give you crabs. But that's low life: 'Give me what you've got and I'll listen, and if you play your cards right, I'll infect you.' And like lots of victims I was grateful.

Life seemed to be one long party. Journalists were interested in talking to me, there were regular press calls at the BBC and endless personal appearances to promote the show or for charity. The faster it went the faster I wanted it to go. You know that wonderful feeling at a party when you never want it to stop? After rehearsals I was usually in Soho for some commentary or voice-over and after that went on to the Colony Room for champagne if Francis Bacon was there or very serious gins if he wasn't. It was an amazing period.

There was one break when I went to Italy for a few weeks to write a script with Ian Marter. We had an idea for a film (don't we all?), and somehow the director James Hill had become interested. The arrangement was that Ian and I would prepare the storyline for *Doctor Who Meets Scratchman* and write the dialogue and that James would shape it into a screenplay. It was basically a horror story about some scarecrows who came to life and began to terrorize a small community. We decided that if Ian and I went on a little holiday together we could finish the script and have a good time together somewhere nice. So Marianne and her daughter, Harriet, with a little friend called Sophie Maloney, the daughter of a *Doctor Who* director, David Maloney, went off to a house near Sienna.

We stayed in a large, interesting old family house, in reasonably good order, and heaving with fleas. For the first few days Ian and I worked hard at the script and tried to come up with some good stuff for James. But the fleas got to Ian, Marianne and the two children. They bled us every night and spoiled the fun of being somewhere pretty. We bought some Italian flea powder but it only seemed to make the buggers grow. Whenever we scattered the stuff on the beds it seemed to throw them into a frenzy of ecstasy – maybe it was speed.

There was a swimming pool in the garden which was the only pleasure for Sophie and Harriet, who refused to believe that I couldn't swim and was indeed very frightened of water. So did Ian Marter: 'Don't listen to Tom,' he told them, 'he's just being silly.' But the girls did believe me, and they gave me a swimming lesson and I made some progress. The children were delighted, but Ian was sceptical. 'I told you he could swim,' he said.

At first all went well and I began to feel a little less afraid. I was quite proud of my progress and off we went for a lovely lunch. About four o'clock, back to the pool we went for my second lesson. I did my ferocious doggie paddle and, with new confidence, I swam out of the shallow end. The girls shrieked with joy and yelled encouragement to me as they took the credit for my quick learning. It was then that I realized I was in the middle of a deep pool and didn't know what to do next. I lost all my new-found confidence and sank out of sight. In my panic, I touched the bottom. I remember trying to think clearly as I rose to the surface. I opened my mouth to breathe but couldn't take in any air. Fear took hold. I thrashed about bellowing and gasping like a buffalo. The girls on the side of the pool shouted to Ian who strolled over to see what the fuss was.

'Tom's drowning,' I heard Harriet scream. 'Tom's drowning.'

And then, to add to my terror, I heard Ian Marter laugh. 'No, he's not drowning,' called Ian, 'he's only acting drowning and very badly, too.' This harsh criticism wounded me deeply and, unable to breathe, my panic grew until, in despair, I sank again. Coming up, still I thrashed this way and that, trying in my agony to get a purchase on anything that might drag me back to the safety of life. And still Ian laughed and with his laugh condemned me to death.

But those wonderful little girls chose to believe me rather than Ian. Sophie jumped in and so did Harriet. They were both terrified by the noise I was making and the tumult in the water. Harriet held on to the side, and Sophie held on to Harriet's legs and tried to reach me. In utter despair, I suddenly caught hold of Sophie's leg and managed to heave myself to the side. At the same moment Ian at last believed in my performance and used his strength to pull me out. Oh, the terror as I spluttered and choked and felt I was going to suffocate. Ian was hitting me and shaking me and finally a breath got through. As I felt the life come back into me I remember resolving never to complain about anything ever again. I've never been near deep water since, and at home I only ever have showers.

The next morning we decided to cut short our holiday. I wanted to be back in Notting Hill Gate. I had had enough of abroad and fleas and scripts and new-fangled ideas like learning to swim. So we packed up and soon I was safely home in London. I forgot my new resolution and reverted quickly to ingratitude. We were back to normal.

The script was completed and briefly it flickered towards realization before being blown out for lack of interest. James Hill later had a huge success with *Worzel Gummidge* for Southern Television. Jon Pertwee was Worzel and very good he was. I never saw James again and didn't see much more of Ian Marter. He left the programme and died suddenly in a diabetic coma. Poor Ian. We might have became friends but, as usual, I let the chance slip. I'm afraid I have no gift for friendship. I quickly get tired of people and off they go. Only the other day I tried to think of a single friend I had made in my life and drew a blank. Odd, isn't it, not to have a friend. In particular, I have always admired people who can be friends with old loves. I can't do that. I find it painful even to think of them. I haven't even got a dog, though I'm acquainted with a man who has a border terrier. And yet during the run of a play or a film I'm able to be very concerned that people are well and fed. I also like to know about people's aunts. I have always loved tales of aunts.

Sometimes I wish that I had got *This is Your Life*, after Eamon Andrews died. It really would have thrilled me to have all those aunts about the place. After Eamon died, well, to tell the truth about half an hour after he died, I asked my then agent at London Management to ask the television people if I could take it over. I understood that for a moment they did consider me and then gave it to Michael Aspel. I haven't watched it much since then but when I have switched on I notice that they seem to have cut back on the aunts; so it all probably turned out for the best.

Playing Doctor Who came as a great surprise to me. I had no idea that I would enjoy it so much. All that was required of me was to be able to speak complete gobbledygook with conviction. Barry Letts and Philip Hinchcliffe seemed delighted with my efforts. It was easy because all my life I had been taught nonsense by priests and teachers on all sorts of subjects. It was no problem for me to say I came from another world and could go back and forth in time in my emphysemic old Tardis which was bigger on the inside than it was on the outside. Problem? For me who believed in Guardian Angels and was convinced that pigs were possessed by devils after their New Testament encounter with God's son. It was easy and I loved it.

I didn't see much of Barry Letts, who had given me the chance to play such a lovely part, as he was coming to the end of his period as producer when he decided to employ me. We got on very well for the little time left to him and I very much enjoyed being directed by him in 'The Android Invasion'.

The first story, still under his production, was about a giant robot played by Michael Killgariff, a very tall man with a big voice. He was splendid as the tin threat in the story but the office didn't seem to know anything about Michael apart from his tallness. Of course the rest of us in the cast knew how well Michael could perform as a music-hall artiste. He could play the piano and sing and spin all those lovely improbable Edwardian monologues that have lasted so well, and he had a marvellous natural authority as a chairman; he's great at being in charge.

Now it struck me very quickly that just being a solemn threat to the earth was not very surprising. I kept thinking to myself how it might be interesting if the Giant Robot had not been programmed perfectly. It occurred to me that if he suddenly went into some song like say 'The Galloping Major' or 'There's an Old Mill by the Stream,

Nellie Deane' then the earth people led by the Brigadier, Nick Courtney, would have something to react to. I did mention this to Patricia Maynard who tried to hide her natural glamour as she played the freezing Miss Winters. Patricia was amused by my notion so we got on very well together. Of course I didn't dare mention these thoughts to Barry Letts or Philip Hinchcliffe. I was still in the early moments of my deep gratitude to them for the chance to earn a living.

I did not allow my own thoughts to interfere with the fun of it all. Jim Acheson, our designer, told me I looked like his Auntie Wyn and I have never forgotten it. I wondered if it was the way I walked or wore my hat, but Jim just said that I had some indefinable air of an aunt. It was then I began to hope that one day I might play Lady Bracknell. Later on, as I got to know more and more people, I was often told that I looked like some favourite aunt. Never a nasty aunt, of course, but often a maiden aunt.

What struck me very deeply about *Doctor Who* was that the performers were often more fascinating than the characters in the script. You might ask, 'Who, for example?' And I might say, 'Well, everybody to be frank.' This is not meant as a slight on our writers; after all they didn't know anything about the people who were to realize their ideas; they had no control over the casting. If they had, then the results would have been very different.

Now we pressed on to the next tale, 'The Sontaran Experiment'. We filmed on location on Dartmoor, and while doing a fight scene out on the moor, I fell and broke my collar bone. This made me very anxious for a few hours. I needn't have lost any time worrying about it with Terry Walsh on the shoot. He was my stunt double and more. As I couldn't move without my bone clicking out of place and making me squeal, Terry did all the work and I just stood still for the close ups. I never ever overdid the fight scenes again, and I shall never stop being grateful to Terry Walsh.

'The Ark in Space' written by a deadly professional writer, Bob Holmes, who was also the script editor at that time, was something about a space station where the whole future population of earth was stored in deep freeze. The set was by Roger Murray Leach. It was marvellous, all curves and slopes. A bit hard on the camera crew but it worked out very well for all of us. The monster was called the Wirrn and was a hideous sort of giant bug that wanted to eat the sleeping humans. It was really grisly and very well done by Stuart Fell, I believe, despite the costume made out of green blister pack. Of course with the help of Lis Sladen and Ian Marter I overcame the Wirrn and returned to earth.

When Philip Hinchcliffe took over as producer we became very friendly and laughed a lot. He, Bob Holmes and I often met and discussed scripts. Philip pushed ahead with the Sword-and-Sorcery style of scripts, as he called those inspired by fairytale and King Arthur, and they were very successful. He and I were always at ease together and he certainly developed and consolidated the programme during his time in charge.

By now I was getting to know Lis Sladen and Ian Marter rather well and life became full of fun. When we were in hotels or pubs on location we usually had our meals together and discussed the day's filming and swopped ideas for the next day's work with our director. Lis sometimes talked about the Dalek stories she had done with Jon Pertwee and we all looked forward to Terry Nation's script in six parts called (wait for it) 'Genesis of the Daleks'. I was already meeting small numbers of fans who constantly wanted to talk about my attitude towards Daleks. Of all the monsters in all the stories, I have no doubt that the Daleks were the most successful. They could not go upstairs, of course, and they always screeched at the top of their voices about how they were about to destroy me but somehow, with the help of Lis Sladen and the writers, I always escaped them.

When we were rehearsing at BBC North Acton, the chaps playing the Daleks never wore their top bits. This meant that during the scenes when they were threatening me, they held out their right arms in place of the regular sink plungers. They took it all very seriously, of course, and this only added to the fun. Very often the cast of Z Cars would creep into the back of the rehearsal room and watch us with delight. They particularly liked my turn-of-the-century style of pretending to be frightened. Frank Windsor told me that I reminded him very much of his Great-aunt Mimi who never married because she was frightened of men, whom she saw as aliens from another planet. I was very flattered by this and I filed away the idea that perhaps, if they wouldn't let me play Lady Bracknell, I could do Miss Prism in the style of Frank Windsor's Aunt Mimi.

As the rehearsals went on it seemed to me that the BBC was missing an opportunity to make two programmes for the price of one. If they had recorded the rehearsals and the arguments that went on, they could have cut some excellent stuff for light entertainment. Our director, David Maloney, had just as much difficulty as the rest of us keeping a straight face. Michael Wisher, who can seriously be described as the creator of the character of Davros, used to work with a kilt on and paper bag over his head to maintain his feel for the part*. He took his work so seriously that he would not remove the bag even at coffee break. To see coffee and biscuits being pushed under the paper bag, followed by a cigarette, while the bag continued to express the most passionate views on how Davros felt about things was just bliss. He did allow us to make a hole in the top of his bag so that the smoke could escape.

If I wasn't in the scenes being rehearsed, I spent as much time as I could with Dennis Chinnery who was playing a small part in the Davros story and who was also the world's greatest authority on the Shakespearean actor-manager of the 1940s, Robert Atkins. As far as I know Dennis never did a one-man show on the subject of Atkins, but I wish he had. From what he told me, I think Robert Atkins would have approved of my style of doing things, and might well have given me a job.

Great discussions ensued during rehearsal when we examined the section of the script that dealt with the possible abortion of the Daleks. It really was a scream. I am trying to remember if it was

---

* Davros, for those who don't remember, wore a ugly mask (which Michael couldn't see through) and had no legs.

David Maloney who put in the line, 'Have I the right?' as I played with the Dalek umbilical cord. Of course, I didn't interfere with destiny and that must have been a great relief to Terry Nation who was really quite fond of his Daleks. Who could possibly blame him? To have created the creatures that terrified millions of children all over the world was an amazing achievement. And so I blew the chance of changing the whole history of the planet Earth. Looking back on it I can't say I regret it. Perhaps if the Daleks had been the inventors of tobacco the BBC would have asked me to cut the cord. Who knows?

It was not long after the Dalek story that I proposed that the Cybermen adventure should start with a clip from a Fred Astaire movie. The idea was that the Cybermen had got hold of an old film and liked the way Fred Astaire moved. Naturally they also liked Ginger Rogers who could do everything Fred did while travelling backwards in high-heeled shoes. You may recall that Cybermen moved as if their knickers were twisted, and not only twisted, but tightly twisted, too. Anyway, I said it would be funny if we started on a clip of Fred and Ginger dancing wonderfully. Then the camera should pan across and reveal Sarah-Jane and me tied to a post. And the first challenge from the Cybermen would be that we should teach them how to move as gracefully as Fred and Ginger. Bob Holmes, the script editor, did laugh and filled his pipe so that he could create a smoke screen between us while he turned the idea down. I didn't really mind. Most of my ideas were rejected and I got used to it. One can get fond of almost anything, even rejection.

So we did the script the way it was written. William Marlowe and Ronald Leigh-Hunt were the visiting stars and they played it really straight and were therefore hilarious. Just as Daleks could not go upstairs, Cybermen could not live if there was any gold dust in the air. Sadly, we never did devise a little gold-powder spray. As usual we blew them up. It used to get a bit monotonous solving things by explosion, it was so like the real world just outside the BBC. There was a character called Sheprah, played by a very funny actor named Brian Grellis. He had the idea of playing his robot as an asthmatic. This meant that when he tapped his chest to clear his throat he had a coughing fit. The whole cast thought it was very funny but it was cut at the recording, thus depriving children of a great deal of fun and Brian Grellis of the chance to further his career. Fortunately, he was a very good carpenter and this allowed him to earn a few jam butties when he was resting.

The really big drama on this tale was not the script but the disaster of nearly losing Lis Sladen while on location. We were filming at the underground lakes, all sinister black water at Wookey Hole. Elisabeth clambered into her little, paddle-less, craft and pushed out, and we rolled the cameras. About sixty feet away from her was a low arch, no more than three feet high, beyond which the black water ran and dropped into black nothingness. As the director called action, as if by magic, a current appeared in the treacly water and started to draw Elisabeth to her doom beyond the arch. Terry Walsh, our stunt arranger, was marvellously quick to spot the danger; he dived straight in like Superman and pushed the boat to safety and Elisabeth survived the fright. Even despite this episode, everybody found the long hours underground very oppressive and we were glad when we could finish and get on to our next adventure, 'Terror of the Zygons'.

Douglas Camfield was an excellent director. He ran the whole film unit like an army unit. His second-in-command was one of his favourite PAs, Edwina Craze. Douglas had plenty of bottle and wasn't at all anxious that the Zygon computers looked like abandoned pizzas. He also had the excellent idea of having the monsters whisper their threats. This made a change from shrieking Daleks. We filmed in Sussex, though we were meant to be in Scotland, but the Loch Ness monster connection got us a lot of publicity and, with a really astonishing performance from John Woodnutt as a duke and a monster, we were watched by more than eight-million people.

During the shooting of 'Planet of Evil' we filmed at Ealing Studios before going back to the BBC for the rehearsals of the interior shots at North Acton. Philip Hinchcliffe was not at the last day of filming and his absence led to a happy coincidence. There was a scene in which I had to seize some poor alien and threaten to kill him with a knife in order to persuade his comrades to reveal their leader to me. It was a very ordinary little scene; so ordinary that I hadn't really read it properly. When the knife was offered to me I felt suddenly impatient and then disgusted with the idea of using such a coarse threat in our lovely programme. The line I was to say ran, 'Take me to your leader or I'll kill him with this knife'. Yes, I think it was as plonking as that. So I refused to say it. We had very little time left on our final day of filming to get this scene in the can and my refusal caused a problem for David Maloney, the director. In Philip's absence he had to log the scene I was causing about my lines. I didn't really care. David and I were very friendly colleagues and he knew I was not just being difficult. But, without the producer there, who could take responsibility for a line change? Me, of course.

We rolled the cameras and, as written, I grabbed some pitiful little native of Zeta Minor, pulled him close, and said: 'Take me to your leader or I'll kill him with this deadly jelly baby.' When the other little Zetas agreed to comply, I bit the head off the jelly baby (orange was my favourite) and I think I offered the rest of it to the captured Zeta. That's the way I remember it. I don't think David Maloney was too thrilled with my effort and, reading this now, neither am I, but there you are, we did it, and that was the end of filming. We all went off to resume our lives and met up again a few days later at North Acton for the rehearsals. I asked David how the rushes were and he said they were fine (directors and producers always say that rushes are fine, sometimes they say they are fantastic and sometimes some actors believe them). But a few minutes after I had seen David in came Philip Hinchcliffe.

'How were the rushes?' I asked him.

'Oh, terrific,' said Philip, 'really fantastic. I loved that bit with the jelly baby.'

When at last the episode was aired, the children loved the scene and realized that I was bluffing the Zetas who wouldn't know a jelly baby from a kangaroo. It made just as much or as little sense as a knife.

It was really gratifying to have had that little bit of encouragement from Philip, since most of my ideas were thrown out very quickly. I hold no grudges against anyone for that reaction because most of my ideas were truly terrible.

All this happened in October 1975. A few weeks ago, in a bookshop in Manchester, a child of about ten offered me a jelly baby. He was so happy when I laughed, then he quoted my line, and it was my turn to be happy.

The viewing figures for 'Terror of the Zygons' were easily surpassed by David Maloney's production of 'The Talons of Weng-Chiang', written by Bob Holmes. He said the tale was based on *The Phantom of the Opera* and some of Sax Rohmer's tales of Fu Manchu and pretended to be amazed when I said that I had noticed the origins.

The locations – the moody sewers around St Catherine's Dock and the beautiful C. J. Phipps theatre in Northampton – were wonderful, and the characters ripe. London sewers in the late nineteenth century, giant rats, villainous Chinese Tongs and Christopher Benjamin and Trevor Baxter doing a great double act, like Naunton Wayne and Basil Radford in *The Lady Vanishes*. There were magic tricks arranged by Ali Bongo and Larry Barnes and a homunculus played by Deep Roy. I felt we were on to a winner, and we were.

These were the early days of the character of Leela, played by Louise Jameson. I can remember not liking the Leela character. I don't have much of a sense of humour so the ironies in Leela escaped me. Whenever she was threatened (her character that is) she simply slapped a Janus thorn into the nearest male buttocks. I didn't much like this – it made me very protective of the chaps and very mistrustful of Leela; I was afraid even to turn my back, let alone bend down. This meant that I felt a bit stifled at the rehearsals. I couldn't find any ideas to help us out. Fortunately David Maloney was in form and the visiting actors pulled it together brilliantly. John Bennett did a great turn as the sinister Li H'sen and I really think he enjoyed it. I know we did. My performance in this piece led to me being offered the part of Sherlock Holmes years later in *Hound of the Baskervilles*.

After a while, following three or four thousand fan letters, all expressing approval, I began to get into the part and then the part began to get into me and oh! I was the Doctor and the Doctor was me. From then on, we were one. I could do nothing else. In 1978, when we came to make the hundredth *Doctor Who* story, 'The Stones of Blood', I'd been playing the part for four years. By now, Graham Williams was the producer and he and I were not close. By this I mean that he often disagreed with me, though I have to admit that his casting was sometimes fun, and for that reason I have good memories of him. After one has been to a good dinner party the people who weren't there always ask about the people who were there. And if the people who were there were fun or dreadful or, better still, simply wonderful, then you have a captive audience at the office next morning. Well, at 'The Stones of Blood' party (host Darrol Blake) it was terrific.

The storyline was something to do with the Key to Time, a subject so serious that all we could do was howl with laughter. There were creatures called Ogri who were made of stone but fed on blood. They were crude symbols of big businessmen and just as dull. The real pleasure was when the Doctor met a girl called Vivien Fay who was four thousand years old. It was said that our producer had tried to get Molly Parkin for the part but that her agent, some ex-Cardinal or other, wanted so little money that the bookers at the BBC smelled a rat. I was never able to confirm that story so it may just have been malice on somebody's part. Anyway God was on our side and we got Susan Engel. She was obviously too young but never mind. That was the first bit of fun *chez* the Ogri, blood-suppers that they were. No matter what was going on in rehearsals, I couldn't wait to leave the floor to get back to Susie Engel and her tales of her aunts in Vienna's patisseries: 'Go on Sadie, put some jam on it and make it really nice.'

The second bit of amazement for us guests was Professor

Rumford, played by Beatrix Lehmann. Now Beatrix had a powerful line in heavenly hypnotism. To be with her was to feel grateful for life. So many theatricals make one long for death – and occasionally they fit in with one's mood – but Beatrix was just wonderful.

The third magic strand to this little BBC do was a girl by the name of Elaine Ives-Cameron. Why she has never become a great star I cannot even guess. She was a tall, slightly built, dark and beautiful girl, an exquisite spider-like creature who could walk through a door, say hello, and turn your blood to quicksilver. She was dangerous just to look at. I won't ask you to imagine what it was like to have a hot, toasted teacake with Elaine; you wouldn't believe me anyway. But I can tell you this, I've never had a teacake like it. No canteen is the same without Elaine Ives-Cameron. And why she isn't a world-famous actress baffles me. All I can offer by way of an explanation is that there is no truth, no justice and no God in this industry; apart from Bill Kenwright* and Elaine would dilute his tan, which perhaps is why he has never employed her.

Evenings at the hotel were such fun during this bit of tosh. Bea Lehmann took a real shine to John Leeson, the voice of the insufferable K9 (Canine). During the run of the series I had to be a bit tactful on the subject of K9. Graham Williams knew that I didn't like it but we glossed over our hatreds by simply ignoring them. It was a bit like the days of my religious mania. If we didn't mention a problem then it didn't exist. It was no use trying to tell our producer that John Leeson's performance in rehearsal was sublime, poor Graham couldn't see things like that, he was hopelessly earthbound. I have read that people say he crawled about the floor with enthusiasm – John Leeson, that is, not the producer – but that is not true. The mischievous quality and the affection in John's voice was reflected in his performance at the North Acton rehearsal rooms. Only the actors can know that. When I gave K9 an order or praised him for being clever we used to cut to this boring, expressionless, little robot

* Now the most famous producer in the world and a close associate of Sir Peter Hall.

and nothing could nourish the viewers. Some people said that the creation of it was to do with the commercial arm of the BBC looking for something to exploit. I can't believe that. But in my opinion the dog was a disaster compared to what John Leeson could have done. The wonderful thing about John Leeson's performance was that he helped the scenes to move swiftly and often very wittily. He would scamper about, stand on his back legs and smile and was just so expressive that we were captivated. But our producer was already committed to the tin dog that I disliked so much.

Every shot was the same because the dog was on the floor. Two shots had to be realized by me kneeling down. If there happened to be a matchstick on the ground K9 stopped abruptly. John used to scamper about and be terribly concerned with the tensions of the tale. Sometimes we could hardly contain our love for him. I wanted to do scenes where I gave him biscuits for being clever and which allowed the viewer to see that K9 used to put the biscuits back for me to have later. This meant that if he thought that I had been clever then he could give me a biscuit.

I hope I'm not making too much of this. It's just that I feel that the series could have had another astonishing character which would have appealed to the children among our audience and to the parents, too. Adults are always pleased by what makes their children happy. I remember being pinched in Harrods by some delirious granny who adored *Doctor Who*. And why? Because when the children were frightened they would bury their faces in her bosom. Every Saturday she would hope the story would be terrifying so that her little ones would cling to her like sticky buds. And they did, and I got pinched by the grateful grannies and I was grateful in my turn.

Back at the hotel with Beatrix Lehmann, John Leeson and I just lapped up her stories. She was so taken with John that she gave him a lovely Leica camera. She was so taken with me that she allowed me to buy her a drink and three times she winked at me. She knew that John was a keen photographer but she rightly sensed that I preferred winks to cameras.

Over a few evenings she told us things from her past. How she had known Ralph Richardson as a young man and washed his shirts. She told us he was very bossy and wanted to give her notes on her performance all the time. And it became clear that she had admired him very much and considered him a friend. Anyway, as time passed he elbowed her and she was deeply wounded.

About a year after this snub she was at some smart party or other and who else should be there but himself. She spotted him across the room and detecting his shiftiness made certain that he couldn't escape her by remaining between him and the door. As the party went on there was a movement of people and suddenly Ralph was alone and Beatrix pounced.

'Hello, Ralph.'

Ralph looked at her amazed.

'Good God! Didn't I once meet you at a party at the French Embassy?'

Beatrix looked at him sadly. 'Ralph, Ralph.'

He said: 'Yes, it was at the French Embassy and I think, no, I'm sure, Herr von Ribbentrop was there. I think.'

Bea said: 'Ralph, Ralph, it's Bea. Why are you pretending? Why do you do this, Ralph?'

She said that he looked hunted and haunted and, glancing about, he said:

'Bea, the thing is you see, I have absolutely no personality of my own.' And as somebody else approached them he reverted to his opening dottiness:

'Yes, the French Embassy, that was it and you were wearing a thing, long and full of silk. Nice to see you again.'

And he was off to seek another scene.

And there we were, John Leeson and I, hearing the little tale from fifty-one years ago. And it was just good to be with her and the whole encounter was so much more interesting than the script we were doing. It was Beatrix's last performance. We watched her riding a bicycle and we shivered with fear. And so, although I can't recall the script, I still feel grateful to those three women and to

John Leeson, who if he'd been allowed to be a dog could have been immortal.

In the meantime, I worked hard at raising the audience figures. There were BBC exhibitions around the country at places like Longleat and in towns such as Blackpool. These shows were run by Terry Samson, the head of exhibitions at the BBC, and his assistant Lorne Martin. They realized I was enthusiastic to help and so they took care of all the travel schedules and the accommodation. At the *Doctor Who* exhibition in Blackpool the children always signed their names, gave their dates of birth and wrote in their addresses. Children like doing that sort of thing. This meant that through the year I could send out birthday cards all over the country. Wherever we were, I was writing messages to children I'd never met. That didn't matter as they used to meet me every Saturday during the season on the telly.

The effect of these cards was dramatic. Sometimes we would send them to schools but usually they'd go to the children's own homes. We heard that these cards caused little explosions of interest in any street and this led to a large increase in viewers. I knew all this from the letters that came back to the office. It was also great fun to do. Terry Samson organized visits to schools all over the country. I was taken to visit dying children in the hope that my presence might help the poor things. I cannot say what anguish this was, as distraught parents watched while I repeated what they told me might rouse their child. It never did but they insisted I try and were so sweet even in my constant failure. They would thank me for trying. Thank me!

I did long signing sessions, too. On one occasion at Longleat, the Marquis of Bath's place, it needed an army platoon to get me to the signing desk. They had perhaps twenty thousand visitors. I smiled and signed for seven hours. The cramp was so bad I had to be helped away from the table and into some tea tent. As Terry supported me along the way we passed two fat harpies who jeered at me: 'Pissed already? They could not imagine my murderous thoughts. Of course they couldn't, they couldn't imagine anything at all. All this activity became an extension of the show. It meant that I never stopped being the Doctor. The endless enthusiasm of the children and parents fuelled us all.

Sometimes the events left the staff with the problem of having to calm down the children for a long time afterwards, but they never complained. Once when I was in a closed ward for children, an eleven-year-old boy who hadn't spoken for nearly a year came out of his secret world and embraced me very cheerfully. The doctors and nurses were so pleased. And I was able to avoid myself during all these activities and pursue the fantasy life of the benevolent alien. It suited me very well. I've never liked myself much and being able to escape the despised self kept me in good spirits.

The welcomes and the smiles came from all levels of the audience. There was no hostility anywhere, I think because the character I played didn't threaten anyone. It was all rather dotty and the tumultuous welcome from children gave me the imprimatur of approval. If they approved then so did the rest of their families. The days all mixed, and rehearsals and recordings and appearances for charities all mixed. I became used to being called Doctor by real doctors and nurses and the pleasure the children derived from all this was enough to make me happy. It was no great sacrifice, I can tell you.

By the time we reached 'The Deadly Assassin' in 1976 I was completely immersed in the part of the Doctor. The character was a wonderful cover for my smallness of mind and my lack of real courage. The children all assumed I was the Doctor and they responded accordingly. I tried so hard never to disappoint them but being a charlatan is exhausting work. Never once was I challenged by anyone to 'come outside and let's see how hard you really are.' I went to any lengths to avoid unpleasant scenes. I carried dramatic pictures and jelly babies by the hundred and little cards of all descriptions to give out to anybody who smiled or scowled.

In 'The Deadly Assassin' there was a scene where I was being held under water and where I had to appear genuinely afraid of death. It wasn't too hard for me to do this because I really am very afraid of water and I suppose this fear made me overdo the terror. David Maloney said it was very powerful and this made me faintly ill at ease. I didn't see the editing, and the broadcast came as I happened to be going through Preston on the way back from the Doctor Who exhibition in Blackpool. I was with Terry Samson and talking to him about this episode and my anxiety about the water sequence. Terry suggested we watch it in the window of a TV shop. We tried to but all that time ago in Preston the shop was either closing or the sets were tuned to the other channel. So the driver took us disappointedly off through some suburb or other and, as he slowed down on a corner, I saw a couple of kids' bikes in a garden and wondered if I dared invite myself into the house to see *Doctor Who*. Terry encouraged me and stayed tactfully with the driver while I went to the back door of this house and knocked.

The programme was due at any moment and I felt a bit self-conscious about barging in on some innocent family at sacred tea time. I need not have feared. A young man of about thirty opened the door to me and I asked, 'Do you watch *Doctor Who* in this house by any chance?' For a split second the young man looked puzzled and then he smiled, opened the door wide, and simply said, 'Come in, Doctor.' And in I went.

As he ushered me into the sitting room I heard the title music and I quietly sat in the chair the man pointed to. As I took my seat, he pointed towards two little boys sitting on the sofa, eyes glued to the screen as I appeared. They watched with terrific intensity as a bit of the drama unrolled and then, as someone else took up the plot, they lost interest slightly and glanced up at their dad and then at me. Just as they did so, I reappeared on the screen and they looked at me there. Their amazement was simply amazing! They were utterly gobsmacked as the two images jostled in their heads. They could not grasp how I could be in two places at once and then, to the delight of their dad, they couldn't believe Doctor Who was in their house. What a wonderful hour or so that was.

After the episode ended the two little boys became anxious that nobody at school would believe them when they said that Doctor

Who had just dropped in at tea time on Saturday. For the first time ever I had no souvenirs with me: not a picture or jelly baby. Everything had been used up at the Blackpool event, I suppose. Terry Samson joined me and his presence and the promise of proofs through the post eased the children's anxiety. Terry was as good as his word and better. Pictures were sent from the BBC and Terry called their local paper. A reporter was sent round to the house and the children became famous and were believed. It had to be true, it had been in the newspaper. Oh boy, those were the days. I was a hero in Preston and all over the world. And now what? Now I get mistaken for Shirley Williams and scowled at for closing the grammar schools.

Nowadays I escape into the world of Charles Dickens. What a Pecksniff I might have been! But any of the great hypocrites would do me. There is a serene quality in a fine hypocrite that I greatly admire. I don't think it's possible to be a frenzied hypocrite. That wouldn't do at all. There is nearly always a sublime self-assurance to a good hypocrite, don't you think? Hypocrites are not prone to self-doubt. I always imagine that great hypocrites have no interior life at all. What you see is what they are. All good actors have a touch of the hypocrite. I think I was born to be a hypocrite, all exterior and hollow, but wanting to amuse. Hypocrites can be very generous; as long as the world is watching. I'd like to specialize in them: Bounderby, Sapsea, Fosco and Chadband. Oh, and Turvey-drop that master of deportment, he'd be another good one. I'll get my agent on to it. Perhaps I could do a one-man show of hypocrites? And I could call it *Hypocrites* with Tom Baker.

Once in Chicago, a PhD student who was doing his thesis on 'The Improbability of TV Heroes' remarked to me in front of about a thousand people that he thought I was a unique actor. As I lowered my head to hide my pleasure he cited as evidence of his claim my manner of coming through doors. This brought me up with a jolt and the blood fled from my cheeks. Was he taking the piss, I wondered? Doors? Doors are my *bêtes noires*. I heard John Dexter's voice echoing in the horror vault of my memory: 'You can't walk through a door sincerely, Baker.' But my PhD man was not taking the piss.

'When I perceive the delicate way you cross the threshold of the Tardis, Mr Baker, and you close the door with such precision, and you never lean back against the door the way that most actors do. Why, I just marvel.'

I thanked him with shameless humility and decided not to explain that it was often impossible to enter into our sets and close the door 'naturally' without the whole set shaking. Not that I objected to the sets shaking; it was the producers who called for retakes. I could never persuade them that on other planets the architecture was a bit different. This led to bickering between us all in the rehearsal room, the bar or the canteen. I used to see Graham Williams struggling to control himself as I developed my notions about how it all should be. But he never did lose his rag with me. And I never stopped insisting that if the Tardis was bigger on the inside than it was on the outside then it could be very big. I could not understand why my potting shed should not be the interior of Wells Cathedral or, indeed, why I should not sometimes get lost there. I suspected that Graham Williams was longing for me just to get lost anywhere. But I kept at him. Sometimes I felt that the entire production office was staffed by people from another world, a world that was preventing the Tardis world from being wonderful. This was because my judgement was a bit wonky. As the part took hold of me I began to think that the entire BBC was colonized with hostile aliens who were slyly spreading a hideous and incurable virus of ordinariness. This could not have been the case but it was the way I was seeing things.

At one time I toyed with the idea of suggesting that Doctor Who and K9, with John Leeson in vision, should take over the Open University. I'd seen some Open University stuff and thought it was so turgid we could do it better. It even flashed through my mind that perhaps we could take over the whole National Education programme in Whitehall. But I stayed schtum in case they locked me up.

The response of the children gave me these delusions. I felt I could do anything if only the stories were good. My lack of identity was so complete and the vacuum so deep that I found myself wanting to run Save the Children or the United Nations from North Acton rehearsal rooms. But it didn't happen as you probably know. And I have never mentioned all this until now.

Madame Tussaud's called the office and wanted to make me into an effigy, or whatever they call it, in Marylebone Road. Yes, I said, and went along to be operated on. It was probably rather uncomfortable but I was so far removed from such a trite consideration as discomfort that it passed without notice. I do remember that nearby was an undressed figure in wax of Barbara Cartland and when my sculptress turned her back I jabbed old Cartland with a sharp tool I was holding; how silly that was.

To be in the waxworks and from a hiding place see the children gather about my effigy and take photographs gave me great pleasure. It was rather a good likeness, too. Years later when I turned down the chance to be in a special programme called *The Five Doctors*, they simply used my wax effigy. Nobody noticed any difference. So much for my acting.

EIGHTEEN

ONCE IN A TAXI in London about 1976 I asked the driver to take me to Chepstow Gardens, Notting Hill Gate. The pick up took place in Soho and we were facing the wrong way in the rush hour. As most people are, I was glad to find a cab and suitably humble once I was inside. For two or three minutes the driver ignored me and I thought I was going to get a little rest on the way home; I was slightly plastered from a couple of hours in the Colony Room. Then the sliding window was pushed along at the next red light and he bawled above the noise: 'It's a pleasure to have you in the cab, Mr Pertwee.'

'It's a pleasure to be in the cab,' I replied, being patient in my gin and tonic.

'You know, Mr Pertwee, my wife thinks you're the business.'

'Really?' I smiled, wondering if I'd ever get the chance to pass this compliment on to Mr Pertwee, whoever he was.

'Oh, yes,' relished the cabbie, warming to a celebrity on board, 'my wife . . . whoops, bloody idiot', as some innocent soul without a creature from outer space to share her car came a bit close to us, 'my wife thinks that you, get this Mr Pertwee, she thinks that you are sexy.'

He glanced in his mirror to see how Mr Pertwee was taking this promotion to sex symbol. 'What do you think of that, then?' he asked triumphantly, as though he was the man from Littlewoods with the Big News and Joanna Lumley on his arm. I tried to look incredulous, but because of the gin and being slumped in the corner of the cab my shrug of amazement was probably a trifle less than convincing.

'Are you all right, Mr Pertwee?' asked my interrogator.

'Oh, fine,' I bellowed, longing for us to be crushed under a passing juggernaut, anything to shut him up. Death itself would have been a relief from him.

'Well? What does it feel like to be desired by my wife, then?' he asked, looking at me with his head cocked on one side like a lecherous old panda.

'Very flattering,' I screamed, as a juggernaut with the chance to put me out of my misery turned me down and roared past.

'What did you say?' shouted Torquemada. 'What did you say?'

Leaning forward, I yelled clearly and with articulation, 'I'm very flattered.'

It suddenly went quiet as we came to a juggernaut-free zone. The cab driver roared with laughter and over his shoulder he said, 'You wouldn't be flattered if you saw my wife, she's a right pig.' And then, turning right round as if he was going to try and get into the back of the cab with me, he said, 'Are you Jewish by any chance?' The loud hooting from a passing vehicle made my man change his mind about trying to get into the back of his own cab through the passenger window and gave me the respite I needed to wonder what I should answer to the Jewish question.

'Why do you ask if I'm Jewish?' I enquired of my torturer.

'Well, Mr Pertwee, if you've ever had a bacon sandwich you'd know what my wife was like, and if you've never had a bacon sandwich . . .' he continued. Swinging into Moscow Road, and pausing by the pub on the corner, he said, 'Do you ever use that pub, Mr Pertwee?' By now I was beaten. He had mastered me. All I wanted was to die. And for a few moments it seemed like I was to have a little convalescence. Then: 'Were those frilly shirts yours, Mr Pertwee? Or borrowed from the BBC?' I must have looked as gobsmacked as I felt. 'You know, the fancy shirts you wore when you was being so sarcastic to the monsters.' And then, with the most wonderful casualness he asked: 'Who was it came after you, Mr Pertwee?'

It was a chance for me to try and be myself. Quick as a flash I said: 'You mean that tall, curly-headed fellow, Tom Baker?'

'That's the one,' agreed the driver. I waited for a tiny glimmer of a word of praise, anything not to be Mr Pertwee for a moment. 'That's the one,' exclaimed my master. 'What a piss artist he was, do you know he was always drunk, used to throw up all over the place. What happened to him then, Mr Pertwee, I never see him on the box these days?' Desperate for some reassurance, maddened by this crisis of who I wasn't, I pushed out my plea for a small gesture of affection from a cab driver.

'Didn't you hear?' I said, perched only on my coccyx as I leaned forward to catch a crumb of kindness. 'Didn't you hear, he died in a basement flat in Clapham, not a pot to piss in.' And I added, to guarantee some humane response: 'He's buried over that way at Saint Michael and All the Holy Angels, Elm Road.' This invention of a parish and a road I thought was a stroke of eloquence. No answer.

And then from Charon, 'What a tosspot.'

Distraught for a kind obituary from him, I added, out of God knows what wastepaper basket of my mind, 'If you go to the grave, you can actually smell the fumes of Carlsberg Special.' And in despair, I gilded it with, 'Sometimes, you can see some skint old alkie lying on the grave having a sniff.' I watched and hoped, like a dog that's been kicked nineteen times hopes that the kicking is over and the kicker for a change might become St Francis of Assisi and fondle him.

But, 'Well here we are Mr Pertwee.'

As I got out of the cab he said, producing a little red book, 'Would you just do the business for the grandchildren before you go, Mr Pertwee?' And then, and this is a sign of how reduced I was, I gave him a two-pound tip and signed his autograph book, 'Happy Days, from who on earth is Tom Baker?' I handed him the book and, without glancing at it, he slung it on to the dashboard.

As I turned away, some happy piss artist weaved by us clutching his can of lager. 'Possibly the Greatest Lager in the World', intoned the driver with a quite good impression of a TV voice-over. This was twenty-one years ago, and I still tremble when I have to use a cab.

On charity trips to Belfast I was carted about by the British Army. I took great care to hug my long scarf close to me. The blades of the helicopter filled me with thoughts of Isadora Duncan. As my scarf was twenty feet long it went through my mind that should it get entangled in the blades of a chopper it would swing me clean out of the Province. But the same thought had gone through the pilot's head and we were all very careful. To guard against charges of partiality, I went to Protestant and Catholic schools. It was an amazing sensation to receive the same wildly affectionate reception.

'The Doctor's here,' they shrieked. Coming from another place – Gallifrey, in the constellation of Casterborous – allowed me to be very casual with everybody. They didn't expect me to have a bias and I didn't disappoint them. All prejudice was forgotten. All the children wanted to know was if I was afraid of monsters. I was constantly invited to listen to whispers on how to solve the Dalek problem.

'Just run up the stairs, Doctor, and they'll be foxed,' whispered seven-year-old children. And their pleasure at my amazed reaction is a precious memory. But the same reaction came from the tense young soldiers. The appearance of the Doctor reminded them of tea times past, of Basil Brush and meals of baked beans served by 'Me Mam', at home where they were loved and didn't have to walk backwards in fear for their lives. So the healing power of popular drama was clear. *Doctor Who* fans don't fight. Why should they? They are all agreed that he's the tops. I often feel the same about rock and roll. Rockers don't fight much either. Rock bonds them together. Rock music has been a vitally important influence for peace among the young. It is the universal language of youth. I have occasionally been to rock concerts and the friendliness of the fans always amazed me.

Football, too, can be a help in cultivating friendship. But it has to be the football of the past, mellowed with age and the memories of when we were all young. If you're in Hungary, and they discover that you're from Liverpool, out come ejaculations of joy and amazement. 'Bill Shankley!' says someone and everyone nods and murmurs approval. And you come back with, 'Pushkas,' and they all roar and embrace you. Now, of course, the magic name is Ooh Ah Cantona. The supreme Eric of our times*. When the name of a great god is mentioned, it often defeats words. Shoulders shrug and heads nod; hands wave and lips are curled down to express the simple phrase: 'What a man!'

For a few years it was like that for me. To be a children's hero was my supreme pleasure and pride. 'Don't talk to strange men,' did not apply to me. In any family where there were children I was welcome. In the park I could buy the ice cream and goodies and they would sit by me on the park bench and laugh, and when an anxious mother came rushing up to find out who this man was in the Burberry coat and fright wig, as they thought of my hair, the children would be embarrassed and mutter, 'Go away, Mum, it's Doctor Who.'

There were no exceptions as long there was telly. A small Arab boy was introduced to me in the Fulham Road. 'Look, Ahmed, it's Doctor Who, say hello to him.' And the little fellow held my hands tightly and said, 'I think I am about to faint.'

Fortunately I always had jolly pictures and badges with me. Never trust an actor who doesn't carry at least a hundred pictures of himself. Show me such an actor and I'll show you someone with a sense of identity; or, worse, a man with a private life. For more than six years I left myself and floated about as a hero. Nobody was allowed to smoke or swear near me. I always sat down if I could for the children were always a bit alarmed at my height.

Once, walking along Westbourne Grove I was surrounded by a group of ecstatic children and for ten minutes or so I entertained them and their teacher. As they went off, chortling with pleasure and waving affectionately to me, I noticed a young Greek shopkeeper watching me. As I turned to go on my way he said, 'Everybody knows

* Not to be confused with *Eric, or Little by Little* by Dan Farrar.

224

you, Doctor, and I was thinking as I watched you with those children, who knows me? Who knows Dimitri? When I walk down the street nobody knows Dimitri, no children hold out their arms to me.' And he was right and I shall never forget it. Once I was a hero.

The students of St Andrew's University wanted me to put my name forward as Rector. The ultimate expression of student power was to appoint a fiction to the governing body. But I turned them down when I discovered that I was not the first choice. By universal acclamation Basil Brush was announced as their first selection. He was my hero, too.

While we were on our little tours about the country to promote the programme, I was often pulled by women who were keen fantasists. The *Star Trek* women seemed to be very libidinous and extremely forward. But, of course, there were *Who* fans and Dracula fans and ex-nuns, too, who were all keen to have a slice of me. I had never been so sought after in my life before.

George Simenon, the creator of Maigret once remarked that the world is divided into two groups, the Spankers and the Spankees. Simenon was very sure of himself but when I noticed that remark I was inclined to disagree with him. I don't want to suggest that I'm an authority on this harmless little hobby, but I certainly came across a good few of them while on the road as Doctor Who. Simenon didn't mention that a Spanker, if the conditions are right, can become a Spankee and vice versa.

Once when I was out on a promotion for the Doctor, I accepted an invitation for coffee in someone's hotel room. She seemed so proper and serious when she asked me up. Several large gins later I entered her room for a coffee which became a green Chartreuse! After a couple of those holy sips and with a few clothes left on I suddenly noticed that there was a Bible on the bedside table and that laid across the Bible was a whip. I must admit that these scenes scared me a bit. I didn't like the whip to be too fierce and I cheated on the bondage. By that I mean I always made sure I wasn't too tightly bound and I never allowed myself to be noosed or hooded.

Personally I prefer tickling to the whip but there's a price for everything and one has to take the rough with the smooth. A good few of these women wanted to whip or cane me. For most of them it was probably as a punishment for my performance, so I couldn't complain too much. But when it was my turn to be the spanker my passion would fade a bit. Sometimes the screams and moans provoked knocking on the wall from some poor rep trying to get some sleep in the room next door. And at the cries, 'Harder! Harder!' I frequently got softer and softer. But that's life, I suppose.

One young university don asked me if I had my costume with me. I said no, but that I had three hundred pictures of myself and would one do? She looked at me and then looked towards the open wardrobe behind me.

'Isn't that your scarf hanging out of that suitcase on the shelf?'

'Scarf?' I said. 'Scarf? What scarf, where?'

'This scarf here,' she said brazenly flicking open the lid of my BBC costume case.

'Oh, that costume?' I said. 'I thought you meant my swimming costume, and the reason I said no is because I can't swim, you see . . .'

'Can I just look at it?' she asked with the sort of smile that suggested she was perhaps a superior secondhand clothes dealer.

'Oh, certainly, certainly,' I said, thinking, Christ, she's going to ask me to wear my costume while we do the deed. But no, she didn't want me to put the costume on – oh no, she wanted to put it on herself. And she did and she looked terrific and as she threw herself wantonly on to the wide Holiday Inn bed she growled: 'Come on, Doctor, let's travel through space.' She really did say that. She did. I nearly laughed in her face at the line. But then we were not in our right minds at the time and we had been drinking champagne. I managed to travel as far as the bed and then I fell aboard. As we grappled like demented stoats and her in my gear I kept thinking I was shagging myself. At least she didn't want to whip me, which made a change. But for a long time after, the questions, 'Are you a swinger?' or worse, 'Do you swing?' used to make me fear the end might be nigh.

By late 1978 we had Douglas Adams as our script editor and he was full of energy. He had just written the first part of *The Hitchhiker's Guide to the Galaxy*, and his first story for *Doctor Who*, 'The Pirate Planet'. It was something to do with a planet that could hop about the Universe and suck out the energy of other planets. The earth was threatened and that's where I came in. It is too long ago for me to remember the storyline but I can vividly remember the performance of Bruce Purchase as the rogue captain of Zanek. He was half-robot and had a mechanical parrot fastened to his left shoulder. It was a very funny performance. Years later when I was invited to be in *Treasure Island* as Long John Silver, I remembered Bruce's performance and applied some of his extravagance to my own.

By now I had done more than 120 episodes and felt so proprietorial about the part of the Doctor that I found it hard to take direction or notes from the directors. I don't mean there was any great hostility between us; it would be truer to say that the directors sensed my difficulty and were very sympathetic. Part of the problem was the fact that I was so familiar with the formula. I knew where all the shots were in the Tardis and often had to remind directors that we had filmed a sequence in such or such a way only the week before. And then I became too sensitive to the dialogue I was given. Of course, I usually did my job which was to act the lines provided by the office. But after a time I felt that I could write my part better than the writers. I was wrong, but I think that Graham Williams found me tiresome.

Under June Hudson's influence my costume became more and more operatic. This pleased me very much. Some people said that my performance became more and more operatic, too, and they were probably right. Anyway June Hudson was very influential and she and I became friendly. We still are. She also designed lovely things for Lalla Ward, who had now taken over the part of my 'assistant'. Lalla was marvellously witty and so good to be with that

I fell in love with her. Later we got married and were happy for a little while. Our wedding made the national news. How we laughed.

Douglas Adams's next piece was 'Shada', a story in six parts, filmed on location in Cambridge. It is one of the most talked about stories among the fans because it was never shown because of a strike at the BBC. We went off to lovely Cambridge and had a wonderful time. I was staying just opposite St John's College where the music scholars go. Every night a group of undergraduates would come into the pub and sing for us. I persuaded Pennant Roberts, our director, to put this group of about ten young singers into the story. As I cycled madly past some college or other, there they all were,

'Pardon me boy, is that the Chattanooga Choo-Choo?'

If it had not been for that strike, those boys might have become the Who Singers. But it was not to be.

One bit of the script required me to punt along the river and, at a certain spot, to get my pole stuck in the mud and leave the punt drifting on out of control. The camera may have been in another punt, I can't remember. Anyway, it took an awful lot of takes. My bit was easy enough as I had an eyeline for when to lose my pole; but the camera crew had a harder time of it because of the movement in the water. What made it hard to bear was that about a thousand students were gathered on the riverbank to watch us. Because they didn't know the script, they assumed that I kept getting my pole stuck in the mud through incompetence. On each take a great roar of derision would go up as my pole stuck in the mud. They were all probably very good at punting and seemed to enjoy my mistake. After perhaps fifteen rounds of jeering I was fed up. I have always found filming in public very difficult. But when finally we got the shot, the students were convinced that we had given up on the sequence because I was a bad punter.

So we had all the filming done and then the strike came. For years the footage lay at the BBC and seemed to be of no possible use. That was all changed about fifteen years later when ex-producer

John Nathan-Turner devised a way of making a video for the BBC. On various locations at the Museum of the Moving Image, I faced a camera and told the audience what we would have done if the strike had not happened. The fans all seemed interested and the video sold well, I believe.

There had been four producers during my time as the Doctor: Barry Letts, who had made the decision to employ me in the first place, followed by Philip Hinchcliffe, followed by Graham Williams and then, finally, John Nathan-Turner. It would be impossible to have a nicer man than Graham Williams as a producer, and indeed for a lot of the time we got on very well. But there was something about me that made Graham insecure. As time went by there was increasing tension between us and I'm sorry to say I was probably at fault. He was younger than I was and yet I thought of him as older. I grated on his nerves a bit and some of my notions just exhausted him. They exhausted me. By the time he finished as producer things were very cool between us.

I had known John as the production unit manager for Graham Williams. He was very friendly and very knowledgeable about the programme and was naturally keen to influence it, and he did, and that was fine: for him. I was now finding the work a little arduous and the new characters who had been brought into the series didn't stimulate me at all. It was time to go.

It had been an amazing period for me. After seven years I had come to think of it as my programme. How silly I was. The thought of leaving it after 178 episodes, the equivalent of forty-five feature films, filled me with apprehension. I pretended to be philosophical about it and I really did think that I could beat the problem of being typecast. But I couldn't.

NINETEEN

I REMEMBER GOING INTO a hairdresser's shop in Chelsea to have some of my hair cut off. As I went in the staff were delighted to see me and asked for my autograph. I sent out for a bottle of vodka and some peach juice and we all had a slug of it before the selected cutter got to work. He was very chatty and it took about forty-five minutes altogether. I told him to take off quite a lot. He did so and as I strolled out nobody recognized me. It was a great shock. I felt as if I was invisible, as if I were dead. But I tried to make the best of it and hoped that new work would come in to distract me from the death of the Doctor.

There was no quick coming back from the dead. The very success of the programme and my efforts to promote it were now factors that worked against me. I think it is very common for actors to feel that they have died when a job comes to an end, and sometimes they lose confidence, too, as they are forced back to real life and lines that have not been written for them.

In my case, real life was something I was only very tenuously connected to. The hardest thing of all was to be aware that I was no longer a hero to children. I had become used to being greeted ecstatically by children and their parents everywhere. I suffered dreadful withdrawal symptoms, I was bereaved of my fictional existence which was so much more important to me than a real one. During this visit into my past I realize that the reason I was so obsessed with religion and going to church was that I wanted to get away from me and find a fantasy that I could immerse myself in. As a boy, the idea of being a martyr, of suffering for some cause,

God's cause, filled me with hope and happiness. I was delighted to lose my name, to be changed, to be directed by someone wise, to have a good part.

Now, after seven years of adulation, my future seemed bleak. Nobody wanted an old Doctor Who. 'I suppose you've retired now,' people would say. Retired? Retired? Go back to the only identity that one has been struggling to escape from all one's life? What kind of a fate is that?

In the old days of the Music Hall the leading comic turns would perform in perhaps three or four theatres a night. They would rush from one to the other, polishing and refining the act. The distance between the theatres was not large and could easily be managed on foot or by cab.

In the West End the busy drinkers would also move between their theatres, which were the pubs, in the way that George Robey had done so long ago. The alehouse run was a cabaret circuit, too. You could test your new lies in the French Pub and if they didn't go well there was always the possibility of more applause in front of another house like the Swiss Tavern or the Coach and Horses, or the Helvetia in Old Compton Street if you were feeling particularly insecure. This is true of all pub crawling. But the movement between alehouses was less to do with the quality of the beer than the quality, the star quality, of the top turns.

In the square mile of Soho there were probably a couple of dozen circuits. If fruit and veg was your living then the Blue Posts in Berwick Street was probably a decent meeting place for you, or the King of Corsica. If you were an off-duty policeman, an opera singer or an actor then the Kismet Club in Great Newport Street was a good meeting place. Down a curved flight of stairs, and with a choice of two bars, the Kismet Club was the place where the lunatic mixture of anxiety and hope filled the fetid air and Bing Crosby sang 'I'm Dreaming of a White Christmas' all the year round.

The licensee was Maltese Mary, the *nom de plume* of Mary Dowsie, a disciplinarian of the old school. Everything that went on there did so on Mary's terms. 'I'll have no fuckin' swearing in my club' she would scream, without the faintest trace of irony. And the Law and the actors and certain chaps who could always supply a watch and wore camel coats drank side by side and spun yarns while demented members of the Opera House chorus sang from *Nabucco*.

Mary Dowsie's sole indulgence was henna; her head gleamed like a horse chestnut in October. Of course, lots of actors and opera singers have a tendency to go coppery as the times roll by; so Mary's use of henna was not criticized, it was merely noticed and its intensity was frequently the cause of deep sighs from other conker heads. Her favourite song was 'The First Time Ever I saw your Face', sung by Roberta Flack. If you wanted to cash a cheque it was wise to spend sixpence in the jukebox before edging up to Mary at the counter and smiling uncertainly towards her right eye while gently waving your folded cheque in your left hand.

The other bar was dominated by another Mary, an Irish girl called Mary Parperis, married to a Greek chap who wore silver-grey suits and was charming. Mary Parperis's bar often seemed a bit quieter than Mary Dowsie's bar. A rather less noisy group talked horoscopes in a cloud of Paco Raban and Senior Service ciggies. Actors' agents sometimes used this bar and, in the jolly madness of the atmosphere, tales were told of the lives of great drinkers from the past. The favourite supper of all was, without any doubt, Wilfred Lawson. Everybody thought he could do a good impression of the legendary Wilfred. We were all consoled to think that no matter how much we were lowering down our throats Wilfred Lawson had lowered more.

I remember Richard Ainley told me he used to drink with Wilfred in the Two Brewers in Upper St Martin's Lane where there is a wonderful large picture of Buster Keaton. One evening talking about acting – what else would they talk about as they kept dull domesticity and ageing at bay – Wilfred remarked that he had always wanted to play Anthony if only he could think of a satisfactory Cleopatra.

'But, Wilfred, Wilfred,' Richard said. 'You did play Anthony, you played him twice.'

232

Wilfred looked astonished and said: 'Did I?' And as Richard nodded reassuringly, Wilfred asked, 'Was I any good?'

Richard replied 'Wilfred, you were marvellous, old cock, absolutely marvellous.'

Lawson looked at Richard with tears in his eyes and said, 'I say Richard, what a marvellous memory you've got, did I get my laughs?'

Anyway, in the right-hand corner of the left-hand bar as you went down into the Kismet, John Bay, an American actor, sat drinking Guinness. He knew an awful lot about films and the tragic private lives of many actors and he would very much have liked to be Groucho Marx. In those days I had a lot of curly hair and was very shy. At the sight of me John Bay would interrupt any conversation he was having and cry out: 'Why, Harpo! When Chico gets here we'll start rehearsing.' And he would jump off his stool and walk like Groucho through into the next bar shouting: 'Harpo's here, Harpo's here, we'll start rehearsing in about ten minutes or whenever Chico arrives.' This always got a laugh and somebody would buy us a drink. And I would stand near to John and smile and smile and play his brother, Harpo the Trappist.

As long as I said nothing the drinks kept coming. Of course within an hour I was incapable of speech of any kind and so my transformation into Harpo was complete. We loved John Bay and longed for him to love us but he was, for so gregarious a fellow, just slightly remote. Years later to the amazement of everyone, he married Elaine Stritch and lived happily with her at the Savoy until his sudden death from a brain tumour. With his marriage he ceased to be Groucho and I lost the part of Harpo and all the free drinks that went with it. For years after his marriage I was pretty sober and pretty sad, too.

My cabaret performances in various pubs were sometimes interrupted by work in the theatre. I didn't get important parts, of course. In a production of *Richard II* at the Oxford Playhouse I played Scroop and the Marshall to the astonishment of the audience, who up until then did not know they were the same man. A bit later in *A Winter's Tale* I was the Bear, and also Rogero, a gentleman, and two dancing rustics in masks. I also covered the part of Autolycus for Jim Dale unofficially. I actually played it in the West End one matinee when Jim was filming at Pinewood. The director did not stay in the theatre to see my performance and it did me no good at all.

But apart from my sad performances as Harpo Marx in the Kismet Club, most of the acting I did was in the Swiss Tavern, artistic director Charlie Stevens; the French Pub, where Gaston Berlemont was the creative man; the Colony Room, where the presence of Muriel Belcher was supreme even when she was no longer there; and the Coach and Horses, where Norman Balon practised his rudeness and was secretly kind to several stars and to bit-part players like me. A certain amount of time was also used up in Gerry's Club, Shaftsbury Avenue. And it was in these places that I got to know other performers on the circuit.

In Gerry's Club Peter Crouch introduced me to Jeffrey Bernard. Jeff then introduced me to Frank Norman, Francis Bacon and Ian Board at the Colony. Gaston, in the French, was particularly good to me and would always cash a cheque. The way of life in these places meant that we didn't have to use banks or post offices at all. There was always someone around who would run off and post a letter or put on a bet while the sender carried on talking and drinking.

Once, in the Colony a fellow came over to me with the racing page open and asked me if I'd like to have a bet as he was just off to the betting shop. I was with Jeff Bernard and, wanting to impress him, I looked casually at the runners for the next race and had a £5 win double on Wedded Bliss and On a Promise. I think I'd just got married at the time and so was full of sentimental hopes. I hadn't mentioned it much in Soho in case they left me. Anyway, Hassan, the runner, came back within the hour clutching a handful of fivers and the news that my two choices had done the business. Hassan got his cut, Jeff Bernard laughed approvingly and I was happy. My winnings swiftly made the short journey from my pocket to the Colony Room till and my moment of triumph was forgotten.

These new companions became important to me over the next

few years. It didn't matter where I was working or what I was working at, I always wanted to get down to Soho and be with Jeff Bernard and perhaps Francis Bacon and Dan Farson, too, when he was in town. Dan Farson, like Francis Bacon, would often disappear from the club scene as he withdrew to do some work. I didn't know how Francis worked but I was aware of how hard Dan Farson kept at it. He interviewed me a few times for the *Sunday Telegraph* and maybe did me some good. Dan also like to drink gin and tonic which was my favourite number in those days, and that was a tiny little bond between us.

It was Jeff Bernard's company that I enjoyed the most. He was a born cabaret artist who was tragically shy and virulently misanthropic but, among the small groups in Soho and the very select groups in the racing world where he was very well known and greatly loved, he was a star. He still is a star, a one-legged star, but still glittering in Soho. He was sometimes short of money and this would make him uneasy and irascible, but he bore his poverty with great fortitude.

Jeffrey Bernard compels affection from those he meets, and his wry and sometimes savage sense of humour is very nourishing for his friends. There were people who mocked him for his lack of seriousness, whatever that means, but the more they sneered, the more we cared for him. Sometimes he would mention one of us in his *Spectator* column and it would be the imprimatur of existence. People would often speak to me after a little mention in Jeff's piece.

He could talk brilliantly on Lord Nelson and could not bear to be gainsaid. He has a slightly irrational regard for admirals, come to think of it, but Nelson is his favourite by a long sea mile. Jeffrey was Nelson's Hardy in Soho. Nor would he tolerate an argument on the merits of Sir Thomas Browne or Lord Byron. He seemed to have read all Byron's letters to his agent, Hobhouse, especially those that were on the subject of money, and most of Byron's letters seemed to be about money. Jeff would allow us some leeway on the subject of greed or revenge. He knew *Treasure Island* better than I did and I had played Long John Silver. But when we got on to the subject of revenge, Jeff was the very John Chrysostom of the Coach and Horses; and when he started on about *The Count of Monte Cristo*, the company would fall silent.

In some ways I would describe Jeff as a saint. I never ever heard him say an unkind thing about the rich. No matter how viciously others might bad mouth the wealthy, Jeff would leap to their defence. Poverty simply disgusted him and he didn't care who heard him say so.

He was often in the company of Graham Lord, then the literary editor on the *Sunday Express*, and a very cutting girl called Eva Johanssen. She was Jeff's big fan and was, I think, in love with him, though as far as I knew there was no biblical connection there. Another daily contact was Conan Nicholas who worked for Cassell as an editor. Nobody could tell a story with such passionate conviction as Conan. Jeffrey would shake his head in astonishment and would often say he didn't believe him, but it didn't deter Conan. And when he wasn't with us in the Coach and Horses, we were often talking about him.

Conan, who originally came from Yorkshire, was so poor as a child that his father had great difficulty affording the fare for the little family holiday to London he liked to organize every year. One year he discovered that it was cheaper to catch a cargo boat from Hull and sail with the entire family to Norway. They would then disembark at Oslo, catch another boat sailing to Tilbury, London, where they would catch a tram to Camden Town and have a few days' excitement in town. They say that it is still cheaper to do the same trip nowadays.

Eva Johanssen, who sometimes seemed to think that the Coach and Horses was the Algonquin, had a friend called Gilly Conyers. Now Gilly sometimes thought she should take care of people like Jeff Bernard and even Tom Baker. Usually solicitous females would have enraged us. We were on the run from deeply caring girls nearly all the time. But Gilly Conyers was not only generous and glamorous, she was fun to be with. If she decided that Jeff should have a beautiful blazer, then she got it organized. Jeff loved beautiful things and was always very elegantly dressed. He particularly liked things from Jermyn Street: lisle socks and silk ties and marvellous shirts. I shall always remember Gilly Conyers arriving in the French Pub to give Jeff a fitting for his new blazer.

I realize now that we were competing for Jeff's affection. Actually I realized it then but I'm admitting it late. We tried to outdo each other in little ways to please him. I did not know of anyone else in Soho who had quite that effect on so many people. Francis Bacon and Norman Balon felt the same and so did many of the racing people from around Lambourne. Whenever Jeff fell ill and seemed about to die – and he did so quite often – a shiver ran through us all. What would we do if he died? So Norman Balon would secretly arrange smoked salmon and other goodies, Eva would hold her head like Greta Garbo in *Queen Christina*, Conan Nicholas would rise up and down on the balls of his feet and shake his head in a way that suggested that this time Jeff was to be called home, and very glamorous ladies would arrive from Oxfordshire bearing gifts of vodka disguised in Perrier bottles.

In the hospital, the medical staff would rise to the occasion and try to prise Jeffrey free from the vice-like grip of jealous death who also wanted to get in on the act and steal Jeff away from us. Once when I went to see him in the Middlesex Hospital, I was shocked and frightened to see how weak he looked. He was suffering from an attack of pancreatitis, I think. It must be an agonizing ailment to have reduced Jeff so quickly. There was a youngish doctor there who wondered if perhaps Jeff could knock off the vodka. Bravely, Jeff shook his head and the doctor sighed in admiration.

'Perhaps you could cut down on it, Jeff?' he suggested.

But Jeff was not to be dissuaded, 'I've been with Sally Smirnoff too long to leave her now.'

The doctor understood perfectly.

'OK, Jeff,' he said, 'we'll just hope for a miracle, then.' And off went the wise doctor. And the miracle happened and we all sighed with relief and admitted that there was probably a power somewhere that was not entirely malevolent. And within a short while the show was back on the short road that ran between our day centres.

Everyone, except perhaps Tony Harrison* who was said to run a book on the next one of us to die in the French Pub and had Jeff as the next to go, was pleased. And we went on laughing and doing anything to avoid going home to those who loved us. It is a common anxiety among drinkers that they find it hard to go home. We don't like to leave each other. I have often noticed that when someone from home enters the pub scene, then the personality of the drinker dies. It's a fearful sight to see a man diminished by the appearance of a loving partner who has only turned up to please.

I think what we liked was the sense of seeming to be free from the nightmare of domesticity and all desperately together: the desperation was the feeling. I never met anyone who was, say, a Buddhist, or who talked about Transcendental Meditation. The talk was of Derby winners and heroic jockeys, of tragedies at the Grand National and the state of Ian Board's nose at the Colony Room.

One day Billy Connors took a group of us out for lunch. It was Wheeler's Fish Restaurant, I think. Jeff was there and so was Francis Bacon and maybe John Edwards who was to be Francis's heir, and Michael Nelson and, perhaps, Conan Nicholas. We had a marvellous time. Billy Connors was as generous a host as Francis Bacon was. It was Billy who would take a whole double-decker busload of his friends to the Derby every year. And so there we were in Wheelers, laughing and feeling secure in the knowledge that when the ecstasy of Billy's lunch was over we could all go on to the Colony Room and the next level of our heaven.

Wheeler's Restaurant was one of Francis Bacon's favourite places. The staff adored him there because they knew that they were in for a good time and great tips just waiting on Bacon's table.

Not everybody was as besotted by Francis as we were. Sometimes other people in the restaurant were made uneasy by our noise and chat. Jeffrey told that once he was in Wheeler's with Francis and a few friends for lunch after a few starters at the Coach and Horses.

* The well-known Soho spoofer, now dead. Alas.

There were several rather solemn Americans in there, too. Everything about Francis Bacon was unusual. I suppose his paintings were unique, I don't know. Francis certainly had a very penetrating voice. People say it was a sort of posh cockney: it was just his way of speaking, that's all. But there is no doubt at all that Francis had a tremendous presence. He was, above all, very funny. He had such a droll way of saying things that the company would crack up. He had a way of saying something very suddenly and directly without any preamble that seemed very funny to me. He said to Jeffrey one day in Wheeler's: 'Tell me, Jeffrey, what are you going to do for a living now that you've lost your looks?'

This caused a couple of the solemn Americans to glance at each other and then to glance at Jeff. Even dull Americans could see in Jeffrey's face the ruins of a certain delinquent beauty. He had been very handsome as a young man. Anyway, the conversation ran along the lines of the sadness of fading looks and the cruelty of time passing, that sort of thing. During these odd conversations Francis was quite likely suddenly to whip out his comb and do his hair without the slightest self-consciousness. And the talk ran over former loves and fantasies; which are perhaps the same thing.

Francis said, 'Tell me, Jeffrey, who do you admire?' And Jeffrey, quick as a flasher, said, 'Cyd Charisse'. The American listeners sincerely approved of that choice but then frowned in irritation when Francis said: 'Cyd Charisse? Never heard of him.' Jeff explained that Cyd Charisse was an American film star and that her legs were amazing and lots of men dreamed about her. To change the direction a bit and irked by the Americans, Jeff asked Francis to name someone he admired.

'Well,' said Francis, instantly breathing in dramatically and showing his profile, 'I've always rather fancied Colonel Gadaffi.'

There was a certain clicking of old tongues and expensive top dentures among the Americans. The waiters were delighted. And when one of the other lunchers asked a waiter in a sharp whisper: 'Who is that man?' The waiter smiled and smiled and with the same feeling he might have used for His Holiness the Pope, said: 'He's

Mr Bacon, very famous artist. Very rich. A very very nice man.' This reassured the Americans and they got on with their lunch in a respectful quietness that was not to be allowed to last.

Just as suddenly as he had launched the subject of the decline of Jeffrey's beauty, Francis said: 'I was in Paris the other day, Jeffrey, and waiting for the aeroplane I got rather bored. So I thought, why not treat yourself, Francis? And I did.'

The Americans paused to hear the details of the treat, and even the waiters were still and didn't interrupt with 'Is everything all right, sir?' Francis sailed on with marvellous casualness: 'So I bought myself a little watch to pass the time. A Piaget, it was. Yes, a very pretty little Piaget that told the time.'

And then the waiter came over and said: 'Everything fine, Mr Bacon?' and being told it was all fine the waiter disappeared to everyone's relief while Francis carried on with his tale.

'Well, the next night I met a sailor without a ship to his name and I picked him up and took him home. He seemed very grateful, now that I come to think of it. Anyhow, there I am lying on the bed like a vestal virgin while my rescued matelot is in the bathroom doing his ablutions or whatever seafarers do when they're alone. And suddenly I thought, "He 's not having my Piaget." So I took it off the bedside table and slipped it under the bedside mat.'

The silence in Wheelers was sacred, holy even, as the blessed congregation waited for the climax.

'Yes, I slipped it under the mat out of sight. And at that moment the bathroom door opened and out sprang the bos'n who reached the bed in three strides. Down came his heel as he leapt aboard and I heard a dreadful squelch as he crushed my pretty little Piaget to purée.'

At the other tables, mouths gaped and gestures remained incomplete. One man stroked his Rolex in the utter silence that often falls after the climax of a great tragedy is revealed. And out of this silence and with perfect timing, Francis, disdaining self-pity remarked: 'I suppose it was the most expensive fuck I've ever had.'

For a while the Americans seemed to have died where they were lunching. And then gradually the spark of life reasserted itself and like a group of Lazaruses they began to talk quietly among themselves. Francis paid the bill and something towards the waiter's mortgage and he and Jeffrey strolled along to the Colony Room for another drink and a glance at Ian's nose.

Some time later Keith Waterhouse adapted Jeff's weekly column in the *Spectator* into a play called *Jeffrey Bernard is Unwell*. As I remember John Hurt was considered for the part but the idea was dropped and the mighty Peter O'Toole decided he would do it. Ned Sherrin agreed to direct it and a copy of the Coach and Horses was built as the one and only set. Peter O'Toole was simply brilliant playing Jeff and the play was a big success in London and later in Australia. I saw it twice and marvelled at O'Toole's capacity to make the character he was playing so lovable. The success of the play made Jeff very happy and gave him some financial security at last. The success of a close friend is always wounding especially if he has been poor for so long.

I've always found the marriage of drinking partners deeply distressing. When my agent Peter Crouch got married I felt I had to leave. The marvellous thing about Crouch was that he understood perfectly and wished he could do the same. We remained friendly.

Somebody once remarked that the Kismet had a strong smell of failure. I didn't detect that sort of smell. It is true that Eugene O'Neill was often the subject of conversation, especially *The Ice Man Cometh*. But in the Kismet, a Hickey was always arriving in the shape of Ronnie Fraser or James Villiers or Peter Crouch. And unlike those in Harry Hope's bar, we always managed to leave as the regular pubs reopened. Sometimes as I walk through Great Newport Street nowadays, I find myself pausing where I think the door to the Kismet Club was. I am no longer certain of exactly where it was. I glance over my shoulder to see where Max River's rehearsal studio was and that too has gone, and the Pickwick Club. And then I remember the Cranbourne pub next to the Arts Theatre, which later became The Frigate and had tapes of seagulls screaming and ropes creaking, and I wonder how Sandy Fawkes* and Tom Hawk-yard† are getting along.

Gerry's Club in Shaftsbury Avenue was the favourite late-night roost for actors who were in work. There is a natural impulse in actors to move around a bit when they're in work and make it clear to their drowning comrades that they, at least, are in the lifeboat and that so far it is so good. The ones who are full of hope and loud laughter are surrounded by the ones who were in work until just recently and who would like to suggest by the way they buy drinks that they expect to be in work again in the near future.

And then there were the ones who were not in work but, mysteriously, were in the funds. This was a potent group. 'How do they do it?' we would ask ourselves. 'How do they hold on to their dosh?' We never found the answer to this question. For while people are willing to give one advice on how to play some great comic role like Coriolanus or Laertes, they will never explain the secret of how to hold on to the dosh.

But there was fun to be had in Gerry's. The regular pilgrims were to do with acting or actors; agents were very common in Gerry's bar, extremely common. And there were casting people. If the word got out that somebody in the bar was casting a film or a big telly series then she had no need to buy a drink that night. Casting agents seemed to us to be the people who were dishing out the secret of life. 'I've got a part,' a friend might whisper.

'Does it speak?' one would ask.

'No, but it moves,' might come the response, and the tiny smile would be very wry.

'Does it move a lot, though?' would be the next wounding question.

'Not a great deal,' the victim would murmur. 'But I do have to wave to a taxi driver. Twice.'

---

* The fashion editor on the *Daily Express*.
† The picture editor on the *Telegraph*.

'My advice would be to do it,' would be the counsel offered. 'And by the way what's that smell you're wearing, French Fern?'

And in another corner a voice would be heard to cry out incredulously: 'Michael Denison? Playing Macbeth?'

I once met a young actor down in Gerry's who was showing his old English master a bit of low life. He came from Banbury. The old teacher was a very nice man and I gladly got him a drink and asked him how he was enjoying his visit to Soho. He told me he was having the time of his life and then fell to the floor unconscious. I didn't take this too personally, although he was not the first person to collapse while talking to me; to tell the truth it has happened quite often. And I think that it is why whenever I offer to buy a drink for someone he usually chooses brandy. There just happened to be a nurse in the club at the moment of the fall of the teacher. She was having a pre-theatre snack and she seemed very fed up at this collapse. 'What terrible timing,' she growled at me as she jumped on the teacher's chest.

'Well, you see he's not an actor.' I explained to her. 'He's a teacher. He comes from Banbury.'

The nurse got on with the business but to no avail. The spark appeared to have been extinguished. But she kept at it, pressing with her right forearm on the teacher's chest and holding her bacon, lettuce and tomato sandwich in her left hand. Somebody had called an ambulance and the few people there were very tense; especially the old pupil who was looking at me as if I were responsible.

'Look,' said the nurse, finishing pushing for the vital spark and popping the last bit of her BLT in her mouth, 'I've got a ticket for *The Norman Conquests* and the curtain goes up at eight, I've just got to go. Sorry.' And she smiled swiftly at the distraught young actor. He understood perfectly.

'Of course, of course,' he said to the departing nurse, 'the show must go on. I'm sure he would understand,' he added as he glanced down at the crumpled heap on the floor. And so the nurse went to see Michael Gambon as the vet in *The Norman Conquests* while the remaining eleven of us wondered how long the ambulance might be. The drinking now was very furtive and the conversation muted. The tension was palpable. And as if to break it and go for the miracle, the young actor fell to his knees beside the unconscious form of his old master and began to pray. It was an amazing sight. I've seen actors on their knees to their agents, desperately seeking an advance, and I'm sure lots of actors believe in gods, but to show it and do it in Gerry's bar!

'Hail Mary, full of grace, the Lord is with thee, blessed art thou among women and blessed is the fruit of thy womb,' that was as far as he got before the management stepped in. The barman was appalled at this introduction of the divine element into the club without permission. He leaned over the bar and bawled at the young actor who was by now well into his pleading for the life of his beloved old teacher.

'Oi, Oi,' roared the barman. 'Knock it off, knock it off. No prayers in here.'

Just then a couple more punters came down the stairs, both actors, and took in at a glance the figure of the kneeling actor at the side of his dying friend. Realizing that a Hail Mary was of no help at all, the grieving actor, bowing as well as kneeling to the will of God, went straight into the *De Profundis*. 'Out of the depths I have cried unto Thee, O, Lord, Lord, hear my voice.'

The barmen was now frantic with anger and then nearly collapsed himself when he realized that the two newly arrived actors thought that a rehearsal of *Romeo and Juliet* was in progress.

'Hear my voice, you deaf bugger,' he screeched. 'You're barred, do you hear me, you're barred. No more prayers, this a drinking club not a fucking chapel of ease.'

'Dear God!' the actor moaned, unaware that the Holy Spirit had suddenly entered into him. 'Dear God, how long is that bloody ambulance going to be?'

And raising his eyes towards the ceiling the sceptical, mocking, sneering barman said: 'Dear Christ, let it be soon.' And as the words passed his lips three ambulancemen, three of them, came down the stairs and relieved us all of our misery. Some people might call that a miracle.

The terrors of 'real' life had been eased for a while by my new marriage. I was comforted in my anxiety by the steadiness and wonderful wit of Lalla Ward. But Lalla is more intelligent and serious then I am, she didn't need the low life of Soho at all. After a while I realized that I preferred the smoky comfort of the Colony Room in Soho to the domestic certainties of Hereford Square with Lalla. Our relationship was not moving in any direction at all. I knew that and if I had spotted it then so had Lalla. I wasn't going anywhere except Soho, and the Colony Room was the terminus.

It was such a tiny little world – one room, that's all. But it was a refuge for a lot of desperate people. Not everyone there was desperate, of course; some simply used it as a place for an afternoon drink after the pubs had shut. But for me it was a place of comfort, a place where we could laugh at the world on the other side of the green curtains of the Colony.

To arrive at the club in the company of Francis Bacon, Jeff and Conan Nicholas after a lunch at Wheeler's in Old Compton Street was such pleasure. Francis would have paid for the lunch, of course; with the exception of Billy Connors I never knew anybody who was able or allowed to pick up the lunch bill. Francis would pick it up and pay with terrific style, always in cash; and then off to the Colony. Once there Francis would order champagne. And the whole place would be revitalized by his presence.

Of course there were always some who just wanted to drink for nothing, and Francis didn't seem to care. He was quite able to look after himself. Once I was in the Colony with Micky Nelson, who had been the PR man for the Bookmakers' Association and who adored low life in Soho. It was really lively in there and Micky and I were well on the way. I can't remember if it was Micky who was attacking Francis or some totally plastered guest we'd signed in but somebody was having a go at him.

'Those fucking disgusting paintings of yours, Bacon. Fucking screaming Popes and butcher's shop scenes; bloody disgusting I call them; fucking bloody disgusting.' And the same fellow was actually drinking Francis's champagne. 'You should be ashamed of them. People are just so much pork to you, Bacon, that's all, just so much bleedin' pork, aren't they?'

And Francis, listening carefully and even smiling as he considered the insane outburst, waited till the gap came. And then, as if he had really pondered on the points made, he said, with an air of calculated insouciance: 'Oh, I don't know, I think they're really rather pretty.'

There was a pause.

'Anyhow, what about another drop of champagne?' Francis said.

These mad little incidents amused us and passed the afternoons away before the disintegration of the evening arrived – for many of us feared to leave the Colony. If it had been large enough to let rooms as the Groucho is I would at one time have lived there. All this was in spite of the endless petty rows that broke out all the time. No group of people is so utterly treacherous as drinkers are. We often bitched about each other's drinking and behaviour. Alcoholic amnesia was regularly invoked as the excuse for some small act of betrayal or unreliability. Even some landlords who depend on piss artists for their living will backbite the drinkers.

It was a mad and dangerous time for me. I knew it could not continue at that pace but I didn't care. I was just waiting for something to happen. Several of the group I was with died in falls. It was not at all unusual, especially for those who lived in basement flats. The smokers were even more at risk. A last cigarette at three in the morning after a thirteen-hour drinking session could really turn out to be the last cigarette prior to an unscheduled appearance before God. Several witty but reckless drinkers burst into flames and were seen no more, including Eva Johannsen who had become our very own Dorothy Parker after Muriel Belcher fell off her stool in the Colony Room.

And one evening after a gentle, kind and quite short conversation with Lalla, we parted. She had swiftly realized that domestic life did not nourish me at all and she very kindly made it easy for me to escape it. We decided in a very gentle discussion that it was time to go our different ways and see what happened. We never saw each other again.

So something did happen to me. But it had no deterrent effect. A broken marriage was obviously not the event I was waiting for. Life went on as usual. And if I wasn't working I'd head for town to have the first one with Jeff Bernard or Frank Norman. Frank didn't often come out early as he was happily married and quite enjoyed seeing something of his wife, Geraldine. Frank had once had a stupendous success with *Fings Aint What They Used to Be*. He would often talk about it and I liked to hear the tale. Barnardo's boy writes West End smash hit is my idea of a good story. And in Frank's case it was a true story. So if I was in Soho early, I would go to the Swiss Tavern, now called Comptons.

One morning, Charley, the governor, called me over.

'Sorry you can't have an early one, Tom, but the police are here.'

I said, 'Oh, yes, what do they want at this time of the day?'

'You know little Julian, the Maltese ponce?' Charley said.

'You mean the little fellow who sleeps here sometimes?'

'Yes,' said Charley, 'he slept here last night, and when I came down to make the tea this morning he was lying just there.' Charley pointed to a spot between us and where the electric kettle point was. 'Anyway,' he said, 'I gave him a little kick and said, get up you drunken Maltese ponce, it's tea time.' Charley looked at me, waiting for his cue. So I said, 'What happened then?' As I did so, two policemen came through the bar on their way to West End Central, I suppose.

'We'll be in touch a bit later, Charley,' one of them said. The other one looked at me, recognized me and nudged his mate knowingly.

And Charley, savouring the added importance the two passing bobbies gave his story, continued.

'So I put the kettle on and the wireless and little Julian was just lying there. So I went over and kicked him again.' And Charley

247

looked at me again before he gave me the news I'd already guessed.

'So I turned him over with me foot, and there he was – dead. Do you fancy one now that the Law's gone?'

I was quite shocked at this piece of news but the death of a tiny little Maltese ponce was not what I was waiting for either. We had a whip round to bury him, for piss artists dread a pauper's grave, and several of us who didn't like him but had sod all else to do went along to the disposal ceremony. It kept us together and was the excuse for yet another session. The thing about piss pots is that although they often can't bear each other, they can't bear to be apart either. Some marriages are like that, too.

I was working on *Hedda Gabler* at this time, playing Judge Brack. Tom Bell, Ralph Bates and Irene Handl provided the fun and Susannah York provided the gloom. It was directed by Donald McWinnie and designed by Voytek. Although Donald was very nice and had done wonderful work before, this was not one of his best productions.

One day there was a demonstration in Parliament Square and Susannah York persuaded several members of the cast to go and show willing, including Irene Handl. Donald gave his permission for them to have a couple of hours off rehearsal. He and I stayed back at the rehearsal room and talked. Irene Handl was rather elderly to be in among thousands of people but the demonstrating members of our cast promised to look after her. After about two and a half hours back they came but minus Irene. It really was very funny that each one thought someone else was looking after her. So it turned out that they had left Irene Handl on her little stool outside the Houses of Parliament.

We rehearsed for about three weeks, minus costume fittings and political demos. Somehow we could not raise the play off the page. Paula Wilcox was very funny as Mrs Elfstead, much funnier than Hedda Gabler. This caused a slight imbalance as you may guess and not a little tension. While we were at the Cambridge Theatre playing to poor houses, Tom Bell looked after us all and saw to it that we were well fed. Tom makes wonderful summer pudding.

Irene Handl summed up our feelings one evening as she came slowly off stage. There is a reference in the play to a dead aunt called Aunt Julie and as Irene passed me in the wings she said:'I'd rather be with Aunt Julie.'

Well, Aunt Julie died first and one by one we all died until finally the blessed release of The Notice put us all out of pain. But I would not have missed the experience for anything. Now I remember that Donald McWinnie is dead and so is Irene Handl and so is darling Ralph Bates.

Immediately after *Hedda Gabler* I joined the Royal Shakespeare Company for *Educating Rita* and had one of the few successes of my life thanks to Mike Ockrent and Kate Fitzgerald. We toured for about sixteen weeks and did terrific business everywhere. We filled the opera houses of Glasgow and Belfast. During the tour we used to meet wonderful people who had managed to get a degree at the Open University. The most amazing ones were the housewives who had succeeded in spite of having children and husbands to take care of. Most of them confessed that it had changed their lives. Willy Russell's play certainly worked for such people and they roared their approval as they watched Kate Fitzgerald and me act out their journey to success.

The tour was to go on for another three months, but I had an option to leave. Due to a mix-up over a film that was supposed to happen but didn't, I left the cast of a great success and took the train to Soho via Euston. What a prat I was. What a prat I am. For the sake of some poxy old movie that wasn't a patch on Willy's play I threw away the chance to be happy in a good piece of theatre with lovely people to support and comfort me. I never saw Kate Fitzgerald again as I never saw anyone from *Hedda Gabler* again. Come to think of it I have never seen anybody* again after the end of any production of any kind, marriage, play or television.

Barry Letts who had changed my life so long ago by offering me Doctor Who now called up and offered me Sherlock Holmes. The

---

* Apart from June Hudson.

BBC was to do *The Hound of the Baskervilles*. As you know, it is a story that gives Doctor Watson the star part for a change. Terry Rigby was to play Watson. My two favourite performances of Holmes have been by Douglas Wilmer and Jeremy Brett. Both suggested that Holmes lived in a secret world that remained secret. Well, then I had my chance. I so enjoyed working with Terry Rigby and he was terrific as Watson, but as in my *Hedda Gabler* experience, I couldn't lift the character into that special world that makes Holmes so funny and so fascinating.

The only relief for me was during the shooting of the dog scenes on Dartmoor. The dog who had been engaged by the BBC to play the hound was gentler than Mother Teresa. He didn't want to threaten Nicholas Woodeson who was playing Sir Henry Baskerville. In fact I can tell you after all this time that the bloody dog had fallen in love with Nicholas. He just adored him, and it was obvious in spite of its SAS make-up. After hours and hours of trying, with the dog becoming more and more infatuated with Sir Henry, somebody had the notion of hiding chipolata sausages under the lapels of Nick's dinner jacket. It was all of no use. The dog actually appeared to be blowing kisses at Nick. And then a member of the camera crew suggested that, as Nick was not a giant, why didn't we throw him at the dog and then run the film backwards? Nick Woodeson was not amused but I was. I laughed so much I was hoping that the joke was what I had been waiting for all these years before I died. I never saw Nicholas Woodeson again and later on the BBC apologised in the *Daily Telegraph* for my performance as Holmes.

Then there came a phone call from Hunt Stromberg who had once wanted me to play the monster in *Frankenstein, the True Story*.

'What's the part,' I asked him.

'Oh, it's not too terrific,' Hunt told me. 'It's the part of Raymond Burr's servant in a motion picture, *The Curse of Tutankhamun*.'

Peter Crouch, my former agent, advised me to go to Africa just for the hell of it. So, as usual, having nothing much to do, I accepted.

'You never know what might happen when you're there,' Peter said. He was such a lovely man he could get away with paralysing observations like that.

So I said yes. They also offered a first-class ticket and promised me billing. It sounded mad to me so I couldn't resist it. At London airport somebody met me and, true enough, the ticket was first class and I was reassured; the part might be paltry but the ticket was great, and that's important to a fellow who isn't sure of himself. People may say it's a first-class script, but what I want to know is, is it a first-class ticket? I always read the ticket before the script and, usually, the ticket is more dramatic. Sometimes I have done scripts that are less dramatic than ironing a shirt.

Somehow I was nearly last to board the plane so I hadn't got to meet anyone from the production. So there I was in an aisle seat BA first-class to Cairo. I was having a quiet but immense gin and tonic when it dawned on me that the two fellows across the aisle and a bit ahead of me were well tanked up, not to say bladdered. They were bickering away very charmingly and I was intrigued to know who they might be, as they were both very well dressed and obviously very confident; though that might have been the champagne. It turned out that it was the champagne. I looked questioningly at the air hostess and, as she delivered me another blinding gin, she whispered: 'They're your producers, VIPs.' It's a small world, in the first class. Further up front and across from me I could see Harry Andrews being very distinguished and charming to a lady I guessed must be Eva Marie Saint. The cocktails having been served, orders were being taken for dinner. One of the VIPs across from me said he didn't want any dinner but his companion ordered quite happily and charmingly for himself.

As the place was being got ready for the meal I recognized the voice of our producer, Hunt Stromberg, saying to his pal: 'Time for a wee wee, Joe.'

And Joe said: 'Well if you feel like a wee wee go take a wee wee.'

But Hunt said, 'Not me, Joe, I don't want to take a wee wee,

251

I was thinking about you taking a wee wee; take a wee wee, Joe.'

This suggestion seemed to puzzle Joe a bit and he was silent for a moment. Then: 'Anyway, what makes you think I need to take a wee wee? If you don't want to take a wee wee why should I want to take a wee wee, I mean we're partners, aren't we?'

I noticed Harry Andrews glance towards the producers and clear his throat before resuming his conversation with Eva Marie Saint. Harry's voice became more resonant as though to drown out the wee-wee boys. But they could not be drowned out.

'Joe,' said Hunt as if he was talking to a beloved old aunt, 'Joe, Joe Joe! It's dinner time, Joe, and just before dinner you always want a wee wee. Sometimes you wait till I'm pouring out the white wine and then, no matter who's there, you suddenly want a wee wee, now don't you?'

Joe said, 'Well, it's not my fault that you pour the wine like someone was taking a leak, no wonder it makes me want a wee wee. It would make a horse want a wee wee.'

Hunt said: 'So you're sure you don't want a wee wee now?'

'Absolutely,' said Joe. 'If you don't pour the wine I don't want a wee wee.'

At that moment the trolley arrived and the stewardess put a bottle of Pouilly Fumé on the eating desk in front of Hunt who immediately poured some into his glass.

'That's it,' said Joe, 'I'll take a wee wee.'

The girl who was in charge of the trolley looked thoughtfully at her carving knife as she backed up to let Joe go the wee-wee house. Hunt apologized for his pal and the girl smiled at his obvious affection for his friend. As she was serving Hunt with his beef Wellington or whatever he had chosen, Joe suddenly reappeared on the scene apparently rather annoyed about something.

'Hunt,' he said. 'I told you I didn't want to take a wee wee and then you pour out the wine like that and suddenly I thought, oh Christ, I've gotta take a wee wee and off I go and then nothing happens. No wee wee, Hunt, no wee wee.' The plane pitched slightly and Joe was dumped into his seat without hurt. 'Anyway, where's my dinner ?' he asked the stewardess as she turned away from serving Hunt.

'You said you didn't want any dinner, sir,' she said quietly.

'I didn't hear me say that,' said Joe. And then rather ominously and with great politeness he said: 'May I please have something to eat, young lady?' She went off and Joe slumped back in his seat and wearily lit a cigarette and mumbled something to Hunt who seemed very cheery and was eating happily. The stewardess appeared with a portion of foie gras and rather frostily offered it to the now dozing Joe. He looked up at her with incomprehension, saw the round of foie gras on the plate, and thinking it was an ashtray, he muttered, 'Why thank you,' and stubbed his out his cigarette in the foie gras. I shall never forget the look on that girl's face. And later, when I got to know Joe, I just adored him.

TWENTY

AFTER LALLA AND I PARTED and in between bouts of madness in Soho I began to see Sue Jerrard again. I had met her first when she was an assistant editor on *Doctor Who*, and for a while things went very well with us. Then, as they usually did with me, things went very badly, which was all my fault. I went off and got married to Lalla and that was the end of Sue Jerrard, I thought. But it wasn't the end at all.

After Lalla there were times when the cracking pace in Soho was too much for me and I looked for some peace and comfort elsewhere. I called Sue and we met and laughed and began to have a good time again.

And the result of this good time was that the itch to get to Soho every day began to fade. I noticed that after some voice-over or commentary I found myself walking past the Colony Room door and going back to Sue. This was a very peculiar feeling which made me uneasy for a time. But for the rest of the time, I began to feel better and the uneasiness faded a bit, apart from missing Jeff Bernard. At around this period, I began to drink more often with Michael Nelson who seemed to have ditched the 'whizzy West End' as he called it. We started to go to the Phene Arms in Chelsea and to the Man in the Moon on the corner of Park Walk and the King's Road and to the Cross Keys. Francis Bacon, Ian Board and their crowd came down on some Sundays and we would all go to a Chinese for a pissy lunch at about four o'clock.

Life was a bit less feverish and just as enjoyable. Sue used sometimes to come over to Chelsea from Kensington where she had a place and spend time with Ted Whitehead and his wife, Gwenda, who were regular pals of mine. It was all very agreeable to me. I thought it would go on like that indefinitely and saw no reason why it should not. But there was a reason and when it came I could not at first believe what I was feeling. Is it possible I wondered that I could be ready to leave London and go to the country?

Over a period of several months this urge to ditch London became much stronger. And then I was offered a job in Dublin in a new play called *The Mask of Moriarty* by a fine writer called Hugh Leonard. The play was about Sherlock Holmes and one of his adventures against the devilish, Moriarty. What attracted me towards this piece was that I could play Holmes and Moriarty. This had never been done before as far as I knew. Anyhow, whether it had been done or not didn't matter as I thought the play excellent. So off to Dublin I went, putting aside thoughts of the country for the moment.

The Gate Theatre management in Dublin were marvellously kind to me. They found me a flat that I liked and made sure that, since I like ironing, that I had an ironing table and a good steam iron. The rest of the cast were very nice to me and the director confessed he'd never directed a play before. Apart from that small detail everything appeared fine. We worked very hard at the piece and several times the author came to watch rehearsals. He seemed happy, the rest of the cast seemed reasonably happy, and the designer, Poppy Mitchell, had done us a fine set. But somehow nothing much happened. The play opened and was received politely and took a fair amount at the box office. But it was not an exciting time for me as I realized that I was making theatre history in two ways: I was the first to play Holmes and Moriarty in the same play and the first to fail at both parts. This conviction sent me to my bed. And for nearly the entire run I only got out of bed to go to the theatre for the performance. Sue came over for a few days and consoled me but I could not shake off the despair at failing in both parts.

As the run in Dublin came to an end, Sue who at that time was working at TVS near Maidstone was passing though a little Kent hamlet and she saw an old school for sale. She told me about it just as I finished in Ireland and I came back rushing to see the house she thought she could be happy in. Her intuition was right. I adored the school. There was a bell tower to be restored. There was a sitting room that was fifty feet long. There were two graveyards around the place – heaven. We could have cats, lots of cats, I thought; we could be happy there.

So in 1986 we bought the place and moved in. Sue already had two cats, Willow and Magic. We got two more, two Burmese called Garbo and Horace. It wasn't for a week or two that I could ask myself if this was what I really wanted. When I asked myself this question the answer was yes. I wanted to be with Sue in the country and be quiet and have lots of cats.

We do have lots of cats, eight of them. The bell tower had been restored and Sue has a firm grip on the garden. I help out here and there but only as a second man in the kitchen and at rough work in the garden. Ten years ago on 1 April we got married in Maidstone. During the ceremony the registrar recognized me and asked for my autograph. Sue was slightly irritated by this but I was amused. We are still here together with no complaints and really very happy. We are.

It is part of my duty as a decent member of my local hamlet to mow the grass in front of the church. It's a pleasant little task and mowing is a favourite activity of mine; it gives me a lot of pleasure to make the churchyard look tidy. I sometimes pause at the grave of someone or other and speculate what he might have been like when he was alive; but gravestones don't tell much.

Sometimes I pause at my own stone, which is very beautiful and already engraved for the moment of the great escape. It, too, doesn't tell very much, but I have inside information. I haven't put the closing date on yet as I suspect that would expose me to comment among the members of the Parish Council. One wouldn't want to be ostentatious. But sometimes I stand there by my gravestone and think about all the convictions that I might have had in the past.

Right now I'm thinking about a letter I received this morning. The writing suggests tension. In the top left-hand corner there is an illegible place and then Iran. Iran? The programme doesn't show in Iran as far as I know. Abu Dhabi, yes. They tell me at the BBC that I'm still a big star in Abu Dhabi. Never mind that, what can this morning's letter mean? It was postmarked West London. That bodes ill to me. I was never happy in West London. Here is the letter.

Prince of the Air

Dear Tom,

It seems I am to be murdered.
If I am, note to be made of my passing.
Please raise a subscription for a set of Apache Arrows I promised to Princess Margaret.
May we meet at the Pillars in happier climes.

Ultra regards
J.

Apache arrows for the Princess Margaret? I don't care for these mysterious instructions. I don't care for any instructions.

I resumed my mowing and tried to forget the letter. After a quarter of an hour or so, as I bent to dump a load of clippings to the sheep, I noticed a strange figure standing at my gravestone. I could feel a little snag of quick in the corner of my left thumbnail; so it obviously isn't me standing by my gravestone.

Its head is bowed. So? Any fool can bow his head. Yes, it is probably a he. There's no evidence at this distance of where he comes from. You can't tell that a man comes from West London at a glance. Anyway, the letter was only postmarked West London. Perhaps he comes from Pimlico?

I find I can mow away for hours, gradually becoming deaf to the noise of passing tractors and cess-pit lorries. This simple pleasure is only surpassed by my love of ironing. I do nearly all the ironing in our house, in fact it would be very true to say that I'm rarely far from my Rowenta.

He's still there. What can he want? Anyway, I don't know Princess Margaret.

When I'm in London and have an hour to spare I often go into John Lewis and stand for an hour or so in the household goods department. I particularly enjoy the ironing-board section. I find I can pass an hour or more admiring the various ironing boards. The Brabantia is my great favourite. I have a very good model with a flowered cover, pretty though fading slightly. It folds so smoothly that all fear flees. It's the folding action of good modern boards that has removed the terror that so many men used to feel at the prospect of opening or closing the old, temperamental type of ironing board when naked. Now a naked man can iron with confidence and take unimaginable pleasure in pressing a shirt. The old, wobbly, sudden-collapsing type of board caused many a man of strong will to tremble and feel adrenaline in the pelvic area. All these fears are in the past.

The man at my gravestone is now looking about the place. He's tired, then, of the respectful attitude and is now just curious.

Forget him.

To stand in the ironing-board department of John Lewis with other chaps who have overcome their fears is deeply satisfying. Quite often I get invited home for tea but, so far, I have never accepted. Some people go too quickly for their own good.

As I mow and sometimes read the graves I feel comforted by the quietness of the old churchyard and the unchanging thoughts on the old stones. 'Not Dead, only sleeping' makes me smile wryly as I rev my powerful Honda in the ear of a deceased. As far as I can see, they are all dead and not sleeping at all. And as I go about my little task, people sometimes toot their horns or shout from their car windows as they roar past. Usually they cry out: 'Aye-aye, Doctor,' or something like that. And I bawl back, 'Aye-aye, there,' and wave my right hand. But sometimes people stop and get out of their cars and loiter nearby and watch me in a funny way.

Like the fellow who is near my gravestone right this minute.

Christ, he's sucking his thumb now and looking at me in a funny way.

Not everybody knows that looking at people in 'a funny way' is the commonest cause of sudden murder. I happen to know that because I read a Home Office brochure once.

I feel very edgy. My watcher seems to be wearing a sort of mahogany-coloured coat and – is his hair mahogany, too? After about forty minutes I can bear it no longer and I say rather tartly, 'Good afternoon.'

No answer, and as I empty a load of clippings I'm suddenly aware of Mahogany standing close to me. We look at each other and he says: 'I'm a fan,' looking past me as if he saw something to my disadvantage over my shoulder.

'I've just been standing by your grave paying my respects.'

This fetches me round to face him again. (If I'd been able to see myself, I'd probably have said that my eyes narrowed.) Not being able to see myself, I say nothing. Then he says: 'You see, I'm a great fan, and I just thought I'd put some flowers on your grave.'

Suddenly I want to say: 'Why do you want to put flowers on my grave when I'm standing in front of you? Can't you see that I'm alive?' Too obvious.

He looks rather foolish and I feel sorry for him. A car goes by and he says, 'You've got a lovely Honda.' His voice is rather thick.

'No,' I said, 'I've got a Peugeot, a French job, an estate. I like it.'

He looks at me sadly.

'I mean your mower; I'm so sorry to hear about Mr Pertwee.'

This swift jump from Honda mower to dead Time Lord makes me feel uneasy. Who does he think I am? Come to think of it who am I? It's very true that I'm often mistaken for other people so I avoid leaping to conclusions when people talk to me. Recently I was in Berwick Street, Soho, where I often work, when a man said to me outside a studio: 'I'll never forgive you for what you did to our grammar schools.' The man looked extremely respectable and sane too.

259

I said to him: 'What did you say?'

And he said: 'I'll never forgive you for what you did to our grammar schools, and neither will my wife.'

I was suddenly very irritated with him: 'What are you talking about, you silly bugger, what have I done to grammar schools?'

My aggression obviously startled him, for he looked at me rather more carefully, cleared his throat and said, 'I do beg your pardon, I thought you were Shirley Williams,' and he went off muttering.

Quite baffled, I went into the studio reception and sat down. What did he mean? Shirley Williams? I glanced at my reflection in the window of Silk Sound and suddenly I felt I was turning into Shirley Williams. I felt a bit regretful. I am used to being mistaken for Miriam Margolyes; *Private Eye* noticed that, and once I was even taken for Gertrude Stein. But that was at Chelsea Flower Show where uncertainty of identity is in the air. But Shirley Williams?

When I was younger I used to be mistaken for Jonathan Miller, and I remember that once during the interval at a matinee of *The Three Sisters* I shook hands with about thirty-five Americans who thought I was Dr Miller.

'What a great pleasure to meet a true polymath, Dr Miller,' they said. I didn't like to embarrass them by saying I wasn't Dr Miller so I went along with their mistake and chatted on about the sadness of ambition not being realized and the humiliation of varicose veins. The generous Americans took it well, probably thinking that they'd caught Jonathan on a bad day. Anyway I didn't feel at all threatened with so many people there.

But now, standing in the churchyard with someone who has come to pay his respects, and who seems not to be sure if I am alive or dead while he's talking to me makes me feel uneasy. Some *Doctor Who* fans tell me they believe in reincarnation and maybe this mahogany fellow is confused about something, you never can tell. Christ, I'm thinking in play titles now. Just because he is feeling something strongly doesn't mean he is right. We are all quite capable of believing in anything as long as it's improbable.

Last year I had to be at the British Film Academy in Piccadilly for some little function or other and in the crush at the bar I heard a woman's voice say:

'Well, hello there, dear, dear, Tom.' This was said with that challenging inflection which means: 'Well, isn't this a surprise, and you'll never guess who I am.'

I turned to face the inflection who was forty-something and very pleasant to look at apart from the way she held her head on one side as though one side of her head was heavier than the other.

'Oh, hello there,' I said, wondering who on earth it could be. 'How are you?'

She looked at me steadily and said with a tiny but superior edge, 'You don't remember me, do you?'

Trying to bluff it out, I said with terrific confidence: 'Of course I do, it was the National Theatre, wasn't it?'

She shook her head triumphantly:'I knew you'd forgotten. Oh, how could you, Tom?'

Her confidence unnerved me a bit and I found myself guessing wildly. 'Play for Today?' She shook her head and smiled on. 'The Royal Shakespeare Company?' Surely that was it, everybody's worked at the RSC. She went on with the enigma and suddenly I knew the impulse to strangle someone. 'Doctor Who! Yes, it was Doctor Who, wasn't it?' Again she shook her head unhelpfully. I was now caught up in this little mystery and was curious to find out where I had known this head-on-the-one-side tease. Smiling in as friendly a way as I could I said: 'It was a play though, wasn't it?'

She looked at me rather sadly, still shaking her head and said: 'No, we used to be married.'

I spun round towards the bar to find my pale ale and when I turned back she was talking calmly to someone else.

I was disturbed. In the same way I am by this chap in the churchyard who seems to think I am dead even though he is talking to me.

'Yes,' he said, 'I'm very sorry to hear about Mr Pertwee, that's why I came.'

I said to him, 'Yes, these things happen. Anyway nice to talk to you but I must be away now.'

And as I pushed off, with my Honda in front of me, the fan added: 'Do you realize that you are now the senior Doctor Who?'

The tone of voice in which he said this made me feel cold.

At one o'clock the following morning two balaclava-wearing thieves reversed a flat-backed pick-up against my garage and attempted to pull the doors off. I woke in time and lit up the house to distract them. They went away without any sign of panic.

The sight of balaclavas at one o'clock on a Sunday morning struck terror into my wife and me. When the police arrived and investigated the attempted theft, they deduced that the villains were probably after my Honda mower.

Is that why Mahogany said I had a lovely mower?

The Law had no comfort to offer and tacitly conceded that they are a beaten lot, a spent force. The fear we felt was terrific. All this terror for a mower! Even though it is a Honda. There was no sleep to be had as the police warned us that the balaclavas might come back. When it got light at 4.10 a.m. I wandered out to the churchyard to look at my stone. There it was leaning in its usual place against the porch of the church, waiting for its last resting place on my head.

TOM BAKER

1934 –

I can't of course be sure of the second date. But scrawled in chalk across those simple lines was the word WANKER. I felt quite desecrated. With a clump of grass clippings and a lump of sheep shit I rubbed out the insult and went indoors feeling defeated and defaced.

Now I keep the Honda by my bed and it's not easy to go for a pee in the middle of the night. Life is not so comfortable. On the bedside table, for fear of more balaclavas, I keep an axe. My intention is to chop off my head before they can get to me.

Before who can get to me? As for the Apache Arrows for Princess Margaret, let her go to Lillywhites and get her own arrows.

INDEX